T0330126

The Decline of the South African Economy

The Decline of the South African Economy

Edited by

Stuart Jones

Professor, Department of Economics, University of South Africa

In association with UNISA, University of South Africa

Edward Elgar

Cheltenham, UK • Northampton MA, USA

© Stuart Jones 2002

All rights reserved. No part of this publication may be reproduced, stored in a retrieval system or transmitted in any form or by any means, electronic, mechanical or photocopying, recording, or otherwise without the prior permission of the publisher.

Published by
Edward Elgar Publishing Limited
Glensanda House
Montpellier Parade
Cheltenham
Glos GL50 1UA
UK

Edward Elgar Publishing, Inc.
136 West Street
Suite 202
Northampton
Massachusetts 01060
USA

A catalogue record for this book
is available from the British Library

ISBN 1 84064 392 7

Printed and bound in Great Britain by Biddles Ltd, *www.biddles.co.uk*

Contents

Figures

Tables

Contributors

Roger Baxter, Chief Economist of the Chamber of Mines, Johannesburg, South Africa.

Trevor Bell, Professor Emeritus, Rhodes University and Senior Researcher at the National Institute for Economic Policy, Johannesburg.

Stuart Jones, former Head of the Division of Economic History at the University of the Witwatersrand and Professor in the Department of Economics of the University of South Africa, Unisa Pretoria.

Trevor Jones, Professor of Economics, University of Natal, Durban.

Gavin Maasdorp, Professor Emeritus, University of Natal, Durban.

Nkosi Madula, Researcher at the National Institute for Economic Policy, Johannesburg.

Philip Mohr, Professor of Economics, University of South Africa, Pretoria.

Stefan Schirmer, Senior Lecturer in the Department of Economics, University of the Witwatersrand, Johannesburg.

P.D.F. Strydom, Professor of Economics, Rand Afrikaans University, Johannesburg and former Chief Economist of Sankorp.

Nick Vink, Professor of Agricultural Economics, University of Stellenbosch.

Acknowledgements

The editor would like to acknowledge the constant support he has received over a long period of time from Jean Richards, the invaluable computer assistance from Jon Inggs, the last-minute typing assistance from Elna Van Rensburg, the friendliness and stimulation of colleagues in the Economics Department of the University of South Africa and, last but not least, the financial assistance of the University of South Africa, without which this book could not have been published.

1. Introduction

Stuart Jones

By 1970 the South African economy had experienced two decades of vigorous growth. The mining sector had declined in relative importance, notwithstanding the development of new gold mines in the Free State and the Far West Rand, as manufacturing industry set the pace, protected by tariffs and import controls. South Africa's manufacturing base widened and deepened considerably in the two decades prior to 1970. Agriculture, too, had experienced far-reaching changes, as grain growing was modernized with the introduction of tractors, combine harvesters, chemical fertilizers, irrigation and the building of huge grain silos. Pig and poultry production was also mechanized at this time. In the financial sector the beginnings of a local money market took shape with the founding of the country's first merchant banks and discount houses, supported by an expansion of instalment finance houses, new insurance companies and a new American-type bank. Transport stood out as the laggard in 1970.

Admittedly there was some cause for alarm on the political front. However, in 1970, this did not appear to be insuperable, despite the arrival of large numbers of new African states at the United Nations. In other words, in 1970, there was cause for optimism on the part of both business and the authorities – an optimism that reflected the economic successes of the two previous decades and which had been underlined by the arrival of two new London-based merchant banks in 1969.

What happened after 1970 did not live up to the expectations of that year and the title of the book has accordingly been adopted to reflect these realities and to counter the 'media-hype' about an African renaissance. The harsh fact is that in real terms per capita GDP in 2000 was lower than it was in 1970. After experiencing vigorous growth in the third quarter of the twentieth century, the South African economy went into a decline in the fourth quarter. This decline was halted in 1994, but recommenced in 1998 and, despite the ending of sanctions and an inflow of aid, the economy has not been able to recover to the level of 1970. Economic well-being is measured by per capita incomes, not aggregates. China and India have large aggregate incomes, but low per capita incomes, which are the driving force behind market growth and diversification.

This economic failure was revealed in the collapsing value of the rand. In 1970 the rand had already begun its long depreciation against the dollar, but this was concealed in the 1970s by the rise in the gold price. This insulated the rand from the full effects of developments in the domestic economy and led to the rand being overvalued throughout the 1970s. When the gold price began to decline in 1980, this artificial prop was removed and the currency began to reflect more accurately developments taking place within the South African economy. By the end of 2000 the rand, which had been worth £0.58 in 1970 was worth a mere £0.09 in 2000. The market had picked up the economic decline taking place in South Africa long before the media and politicians were aware of it.

The failure of the South African economy in the last quarter of the twentieth century does not mean that dramatic changes did not occur in some sectors of the economy. They did, in mining, finance and transport, but together the growth in these sectors was not sufficient to counterbalance the growth in population and the failure of manufacturing to act as the engine of growth. Traditional agriculture, with its communal ownership of the land and private ownership of animals, continued to pose a threat to the environment.

The triggering mechanism and immediate cause of this economic failure were sanctions combined with increased military expenditure, but the real long-term causes were the population explosion and the failure of the manufacturing sector to maintain its growth after 1970. Between 1970 and 2000 the population more than doubled from just over 19 million to just over 44 million. With limited water resources and a small tax base, population growth of this magnitude presents a time-bomb ticking away that will, one day, result in disaster, if it is not halted. This of course is an African phenomenon. No African government has had the courage to acknowledge the gravity of the problem, let alone adopt a population policy, or encourage birth control. Indeed, leading figures continue to beget large families and present themselves as role models to their followers. Admittedly the rate of growth of the population is slowing down, but it is still too high. Meanwhile the media gives vent to worries about an AIDS-induced population decline, at a time when the real problem is unemployment as a result of population growth. Over half the population is below 17, so that the number of entrants to the labour market is going to increase for many years to come, even if the birth rate should drop significantly in the new century. It is this extraordinary increase in population growth that is the driving force behind the growing poverty in Africa. Not only has this development been ignored by African politicians, but they have compounded the disaster by trying to impose 'First World' social policies on to a 'Third World' economic base. These social factors, together with aggressive trade unions, made it difficult for South Africa in the 1990s to experience secondary sector-led growth along the lines of South Korea,

Taiwan or China, but the roots of the decline in manufacturing, as Trevor Bell and Nkosi Madula show, go back to the decade from 1965 to 1975, when the annual growth rate of manufactured value added fell rapidly at a time when the foreign exchange value of the rand was appreciating. High minimum wages (compared with Asian competitors), combined with low productivity, has led to all three sectors of the economy shedding labour in the 1990s. Moreover, in the case of manufacturing the 'First World' labour legislation was imposed on a sector that had for generations been sheltered from the full force of international competition – the price paid for industrializing behind tariff barriers via the import-substitution route. India and Australia have followed similar paths and they, too, have had difficulty in developing internationally competitive manufacturing industries.

High taxation in South Africa has exacerbated the difficulties facing entrepreneurs. In 1970, South Africa was a low-tax country, but the demands of military and homeland expenditure, coming on top of the massive infrastructure spending in the 1970s, quickly led to double-digit inflation that brought an end to the era of low prices and low taxes. It is easy to forget that South Africa still had a penny post in 1970! High taxation had the effect of shrinking the domestic market and retarding capital accumulation in the hands of companies at a time when public sector borrowing was raising the price of capital. The cosy monopolies that dominated the South African economy had little incentive to raise productivity and fight for export markets, when the rand price of both primary products for export and manufactured imports kept increasing, which the government ensured by depreciating the rand.

Bell and Madula's chapter on manufacturing provides the key to understanding the economic failure that occurred in the last three decades of the century. Moreover, despite the fact that mining, in Rostovian terms, experienced three consecutive leading sectors, gold in the 1970s, coal in the 1980s and platinum in the 1990s, declining gold exports, together with the failure of manufacturing industry to raise productivity significantly, made the goal of trade-led growth unattainable. Deteriorating terms of trade made the task of primary producers more difficult, but they were not the major cause of the difficulties of the developing economies in the last quarter of the twentieth century any more than they were in the last quarter of the nineteenth century – a period of rapid growth of the international economy. While the tiger nations of East Asia were experiencing export-led growth, in South Africa, between 1970 and 1999, GDP grew faster than external trade. While there is no single cause for the failure of manufacturing to lead South Africa into sustained economic growth, it is likely that government politicians were primarily responsible for it.

Macroeconomic monetary and fiscal policies, discussed by P.D.F. Strydom, were often contradictory and harmful. Other policies were more directly damaging at the microeconomic level. Influx control policies and job reservation pushed up wages in the urban areas and decentralization policies, together with the railway monopoly of long-distance transport further added to manufacturers' costs and, as Nick Vink and Stefan Schirmer show, the government's policies towards agriculture were costly, discriminating and harmful. It is, though, debatable whether the future of grain growing lies in small family farms. The recent experience of both North America and the European Union would suggest the opposite. In transport, too, when the costly and inefficient railway monopoly ended in the 1980s, it was replaced, as Trevor Jones has explained, by an almost *laissez-faire* attitude towards road transport, that led to the taxpayer subsidizing commercial road transport users and the neglect of minor roads. In manufacturing, despite the lip-service paid to globalization and official support for the World Trade Organization, protectionist feelings were never far from the surface. Outright support for autarky was presented in the guise of 'Buy South Africa' campaigns. Misguided policies were behind the failure to invest in primary and secondary education, which reduced the flow of skilled workers and raised labour costs. Import controls, determined by bureaucrats and supported by tariffs, reduced competition at home and further added to costs. Throughout these years too, exchange controls were exerting their baleful influence upon the economy. It is no exaggeration to say that the South African economy grew despite the government policies and not because of them in the last three decades of the twentieth century.

The reason for beginning this study in 1970 rather than in 1975, the date after which real per capita incomes declined, is that 1970 was the peak year of gold output. Although the value of gold output increased with the rise in price, giving the appearance of prosperity, the long-term decline had begun, which has diminished South Africa's role in the international economy.

Gold mining was no longer the country's major engine of growth in 1970 – it had been overtaken by manufacturing many years earlier – but it underpinned the balance of payments and provided South Africa with a readily acceptable trading commodity. Gold provided South Africa with influence in world economic affairs greater than warranted by the country's size. The beginning of the long decline in output, therefore, marked a watershed in the country's economic and political fortunes, though this was not apparent until the 1980s, when the gold price rise reversed and began its long decline.

Double-digit inflation also featured in this period. While, in 1973–74, this was primarily exogenous, initiated by the unparalleled rise in the price of oil, it very quickly became endogenous. In other words the chronic inflation, from which South Africa suffered for over 20 years, was the result of developments within South Africa. Government policies were primarily to blame, but they were exacerbated by the existence of local monopolies and relatively uncompetitive conglomerates. As Philip Mohr observed at a University of South Africa Economics Seminar, the oil price rise hit Japan harder than South Africa and led to a rapid increase in prices that lasted for one year, during which the Japanese economy adapted and absorbed the cost increases, thereby bringing inflation to an end. This kind of adaptation never occurred in South Africa, despite the presence of plentiful supplies of coal and the capability of producing oil from coal. In the 1970s the authorities in Pretoria embarked on a number of ambitious and costly infrastructure projects that were reinforced by massive military expenditures. Heavy government borrowing followed and budget overruns became normal. The depreciation of the currency was a consequence of these policies. When the military expenditures declined in the mid-1990s with the change in government, inflation also began to decline, but by then enormous damage had been done to the economy. Saving of all kinds had been discouraged. Saving was not a rational economic practice when prices were rising faster than interest rates. Not surprisingly gross savings as a proportion of GDP fell rapidly and the savings ratio to disposable income collapsed to a mere 0.8 per cent in 1999. Most of the collapse came after 1993. By 2000 the economy was more dependent than ever on foreign direct investment to finance its development, while consumers were increasingly dependent on credit to sustain their lifestyles.

Finally, a word of caution about South African statistics. The figures for the population are controversial and it has been argued that both distant rural areas, such as Kwa Zulu and the Transkei, have been undercounted, as well as densely crowded areas such as Soweto and Alexandria in Johannesburg. In the last census the writer does not know a single person who received a census form that was collected! Statistical adjustments were made to take account of omissions, but it does raise questions about the accuracy of per capita statistics. Doubts have also been cast about the accuracy of the inflation statistics, with critics arguing that they too have been understated. In 1999 the consumer price index fell markedly, but much of this was the result of mortgage rates coming down from the previously extraordinarily high levels. A very high weighting is given to mortgage interest in the index. Yet most South Africans are not buying houses on bonds so that such weightings skew the index. The owner of a large confectionary and bakery business told the writer that the cost of his inputs in 2000 had risen by 16 per cent. Economists have to rely on the published statistics, but these need to be read with caution.

Between 1970 and 2000 very considerable changes took place in the South African economy. The mining sector was transformed by the decline in gold and the rise in platinum and coal. Transport, too, was changed out of all recognition by the arrival of motorways, container ships and the decline of the railways. In finance, ownership changed among the banks, as the foreign banks disinvested, and consolidation took place among the insurance companies. In the 1990s globalization appeared to embrace South Africa, with the turnover on the Johannesburg Stock Market rising astronomically supported by a boom in unit trusts and asset managers. Yet manufacturing had failed to lead the economy into sustained economic growth and, by 1970, South Africa had become a country of high prices, high taxes and low incomes – a very different situation from that in 1970.

2. Economic survey, 1970–2000

Gavin Maasdorp

2.1 INTRODUCTION

At the beginning of 1970, the last year of the seventh decade of the twentieth century, South Africa's economy appeared on the surface to be in reasonable shape. There had been a high rate of growth since the end of the Second World War, the major export – gold – sold at a fixed (albeit low) price, political stability appeared to prevail, and foreign investment was flowing into the expanding manufacturing sector. Yet, all this masked a number of disturbing features: a race-based economy (highly regulated with state socialism to advance the interests of Afrikaners) was causing structural problems (including a lack of skills), the opportunity costs of social engineering to separate the races were high, and there was seething black resentment.

In the last three decades (1971–2000) of the century, the country's economic policy and performance would be significantly shaped by political developments both domestic and external – by the interaction of growing internal unrest, the response of the government, the response of the international community, increasing isolation, growing influence of trade unions and other radical groups, the change from minority to majority rule, globalization and transformation. This chapter is an eclectic account of how the economy responded to these forces.

2.2 ECONOMIC GROWTH

Population growth peaked in the 1960s at about 3 per cent per annum. The two most accurate population counts pertaining to the last three decades of the century were those of 1970 and 1996. Censuses of 1980, 1985 and 1991 were rendered difficult by the existence of four 'independent' homelands, each of which had its own independent count. After 1994 the population series was reconstructed, and showed that the population grew by about 2.4 per cent per annum between 1980 and 1996. The population increased from 21.8 million in 1970 to 40.6 million in 1996, and then to an estimated 43.3–43.7 million in 2000. The lower figure made allowance for AIDS (aquired immune deficiency

syndrome), and indicated that the population growth rate was down to about
0.6 per cent per annum.

Table 2.1 shows real GDP growth rates for the 1946–2000 period. After the
Second World War, South Africa experienced high rates of real economic
growth until 1974. The mean annual rate exceeded that of population growth,
implying an improvement in the overall standard of living. This situation
changed abruptly in 1975, and the last quarter of the century was a period of
dismal economic performance with falling standards of living as real
economic growth lagged behind population growth, punctuated only by mini-
booms between 1979 and 1981 (based on record gold prices) and in 1984
(based on reckless government consumption expenditure).

The 30 years of sustained economic growth in fact destroyed any possibility
of economic apartheid, led to breaches in social apartheid, and made a
different political dispensation inevitable. This is a theme that will be returned
to in this chapter.

Nowhere was this better illustrated than in the employment field. The 'job
reservation' laws which reserved certain categories of skilled work for Whites
were a cornerstone of apartheid. Until the mid-1960s the White population
was sufficiently large to meet the demand for skilled workers, but from about
1966 onwards the pace and extent of economic growth led to the country
running out of Whites: a shortage of labour developed both at the skilled and
unskilled levels, and from then on economic growth would depend
increasingly on Black skills (Williams 1990: 100–106). The next ten years saw
significant vertical job mobility of all races: as shortages of White skills
occurred, Whites moved up the occupational ladder, the jobs they vacated
being filled by Indians (especially in Natal), Coloureds (especially in the Cape
Province) and Africans. The corporate sector began to pay serious attention to
the training and promotion of Blacks, although it would be many years before
this was translated into promotion to executive positions.

The informal economic sector grew from the 1970s and absorbed increased
numbers of Africans for the remainder of the century as employment creation
in the formal sector lagged hopelessly behind the number of new entrants onto
the labour market each year. The labour absorption capacity of the economy
fell drastically between 1970 and 2000: whereas in the 1960s 97 per cent of
school leavers could expect to find employment, this fell to 72 per cent in the
1970s and then to 7 per cent in the late 1980s and less than 5 per cent in the
1990s (Hofmeyr 1996: 2). The official unemployment rate in 2000 was 22.5
per cent, or 36.2 per cent under the expanded definition (SAIRR 2001).

Table 2.2 shows that both total non-agricultural and total manufacturing
employment fell significantly. In the case of manufacturing employment, the
level in 2000 was almost the same as that in 1974–75. This poor performance
was attributable not only to the low real economic growth rate but also to a skills

Table 2.1   Level of GDP at market prices (constant 1995 prices) and growth rates (%), 1946-2000

Year	Rm	%	Year	Rm	%	Year	Rm	%	Year	Rm	%	Year	Rm	%
1946*	102 043	n/a	1951	12 5554	4.8	1961	193 332	3.8	1971	338 349	4.3	1981	476 213	5.4
1947	103 995	1.9	1952	129 355	3.0	1962	205 276	6.2	1972	343 948	1.7	1982	474 387	-0.4
1948	111 647	7.4	1953	135 158	4.5	1963	220 412	7.4	1973	359 674	4.6	1983	465 627	-1.8
1949	114 168	2.3	1954	143 993	6.5	1964	237 912	7.9	1974	381 653	6.1	1984	489 370	5.1
1950	119 857	5.0	1955	152 183	5.7	1965	252 479	6.1	1975	388 124	1.7	1985	483 441	-1.2
			1956	160 711	5.6	1966	263 685	4.4	1976	396 956	2.2	1986	483 528	0.0
			1957	168 018	4.5	1967	282 661	7.2	1977	396 483	-0.1	1987	493 685	2.1
			1958	172 769	2.8	1968	294 401	4.2	1978	408 435	3.0	1988	514 421	4.2
			1959	180 767	4.6	1969	308 285	4.7	1979	423 917	3.8	1989	526 740	2.4
			1960	186 174	3.0	1970	324 466	5.2	1980	451 983	6.6	1990	525 066	-0.3

Year	Rm	%
1991	519 720	-1.0
1992	508 613	-2.1
1993	514887	1.2
1994	531539	3.2
1995	548100	3.1
1996	570 855	4.2
1997	585 102	2.5
1998	589 120	0.7
1999	600162	1.9
2000	618 666	3.1

Mean annual	%		%		%		%		%
1946-50	4.2	1951-60	4.2	1961-70	4.5	1971-80	5.7	1981-90	3.4	1991-2000	1.7
		1951-55	4.9	1961-65	4.9	1971-75	6.3	1981-85	3.7	1991-95	1.2
		1956-60	4.1	1966-70	4.1	1976-1980	5.1	1986-90	3.1	1996-2000	1.7

Mean annual, 1991-2000 column: 1991-2000 1.7; 1991-95 0.9; 1996-2000 2.5.

Note: There is no reliable figure for 1945, and therefore no growth rate for 1946 has been calculated by the South African Reserve Bank.

Source: South African Reserve Bank.

9

mismatch (a rising demand for skilled labour whereas unskilled labour was the abundant type) exacerbated by a net emigration of skilled persons; the rise of trade unions and their role in labour unrest; average wage increases exceeding the inflation rate; and labour legislation leading to rigidities in the market.

REASONS FOR ECONOMIC DECLINE FROM 1975

2.3.1 Structural Problems

Economic growth between 1946 and 1974 took place under growing government intervention in the economy. The extent to which South Africa had diverged from *laissez faire* was clearly demonstrated by Horwood and Burrows (1963) and later by Williams (1990).

The structural problems in the economy may be traced to the policy of import-substituting industrialization behind high tariff barriers. Although this policy had exhausted its economic opportunities by the 1970s, and the industries which had been built up under protection were not export orientated, it was continued by the National Party government in order to avert any shortages of strategic imported materials which might arise should trade sanctions (threatened from the 1960s onwards) be imposed on the country. In the 1970s the interventionist tendency was compounded by the oil crisis and the Soweto riots, followed in the early 1980s by a slowdown in the economies of major trading partners and the growing sanctions and disinvestment campaigns. The government protected the economy by adopting strict controls on capital movements. Surplus corporate funds were invested not in new production but in takeovers and mergers giving rise to conglomerates, usually with some degree of monopoly power. Continued protection gave them little incentive to train their workforces in order to improve productivity and become internationally competitive.

The government's Bantustan policy – the cornerstone of political apartheid – was designed largely in the 1950s, implemented tardily in the 1960s, and moved up several ratchets in the 1970s. From the point of view of producing economically viable entities, the policy had been shown to be unworkable (Maasdorp 1975) but the government nevertheless persisted and persuaded four Bantustans – Transkei (1976), Bophuthatswana (1978), Venda (1979) and Ciskei (1981) – to accept 'independence'. They were provided with the trappings of full nationhood – state presidents and cabinet, parliaments and new government buildings, embassies and so on – at considerable expense. Even non-independent Bantustans were provided with new capitals, specially designed and in remote locations, in the process absorbing considerable amounts of public funds.

Table 2.2   *Indices of total non-agricultural and total manufacturing employ-*
ment, 1970–2000 (1995 = 100)

Year	Non-agricultural	Manufacturing
1970	72.1	73 7
1971	74.3	75.2
1972	75.4	76.3
1973	79.7	78.9
1974	83.3	83.4
1975	88.6	86.6
1976	90.3	88.9
1977	89.3	86.8
1978	89.5	87.1
1979	91.4	89.6
1980	96.5	95.5
1981	100.9	101.3
1982	102.4	102.2
1983	101.9	98.9
1984	103.8	99.2
1985	103.5	97.0
1986	105.0	98.5
1987	106.3	101.6
1988	108.4	105.3
1989	108.8	105.4
1990	108.1	105.7
1991	105.9	103.3
1992	103.8	100.7
1993	101.5	98.6
1994	101.1	99.4
1995	100.0	100.0
1996	99.3	96.3
1997	97.6	92.3
1998	94.0	88.6
1999	92.2	86.4
2000	89.9	85.4
Mean annual percentage change		
1971–1980	2.9	2.7
1981–1990	0.8	1.1
1991–2000	–1.8	–2.0

Source: Data provided by Research Department, South African Reserve Bank.

In order to prop up the Bantustan economies the government had, in 1960, designed an industrial decentralization policy around 'growth points'. These were in White areas but close to Bantustan borders, hence they were known as 'border areas'. This was another manifestation of the high opportunity costs of apartheid: industrial estates were developed at these growth points, and firms were granted various incentives to locate there. Eventually the government, in 1972, recognized that industry ought to be established inside the homelands if they were to be developed into viable entities. This led to the designation of growth points at numerous locations which were unfavourably situated for industry. The estates were developed there at great expense and, although some of these locations did attract numbers of factories, much of the investment was of a fly-by-night nature, relocating after the incentive period (usually seven years) expired.

The government was forced periodically to scale up the incentives and review its policy, for example, at the Good Hope Conference in 1982 (Maasdorp 1985; McCarthy 1985), and eventually it appointed a committee in 1988 to investigate the policy. This committee reported (DBSA 1989) that the policy was theoretically flawed and had been implemented at great cost to the fiscus. A new policy was introduced in 1992, taking some of the committee's recommendations into account, but the whole scheme petered out with political change, many of the growth points being abandoned by industries.

As discussed earlier, the labour market underwent a substantial change between the late 1960s and the early 1970s (Hofmeyr 1996). Firms increasingly turned a blind eye to job reservation by training Blacks, and the government ultimately acknowledged the need to train Blacks and to expand education rapidly. African workers moved into skilled positions from the early 1970s with a concomitant increase in their wages – at higher rates than White wage increases – and legislated apartheid in the labour market had largely disappeared by the early 1980s. By the end of the 1970s unemployment was rising, especially among Africans. The labour market required liberalization but instead the government extended conventional collective bargaining and other rights to unskilled workers, thus exacerbating distortions. However, once Black trade unions were able to influence wages, the earnings gap within the African population widened at the same time that income inequalities between racial groups narrowed. The new conglomerates in particular were ready to meet wage demands of the unions rather than to confront them. The gap thenceforth was essentially between those with formal-sector jobs in the major industrial sectors and those without such jobs, especially the unemployed.

2.3.2 Domestic and Foreign Pressures, and Government Responses

Although the period since 1962 had been politically quiet, tensions were again beginning to show by the early 1970s. In 1973, a wave of strikes broke out in the clothing industry in Durban – the first industrial unrest for years. There was a resurgence of Black trade union activity, much of it illegal in terms of the prevailing legislation and encouraged by a remarkably rapid growth (in keeping with the trends abroad) of Marxist teaching at the liberal English-medium universities. A considerable cleavage emerged among economists at these universities with the liberal and Marxist schools jockeying for position and influence, and Marxist influence filtered into the trade unions as graduates took up positions as union organizers. The political situation suddenly exploded in 1976 when the Soweto riots ended 15 years of containment, and from then on the government was faced with regular displays of Black political militancy.

In 1975 the British government released guidelines on employment and wage policies for British companies operating in South Africa, and American companies began to implement equal-opportunity employment programmes. In 1977 the Sullivan Principles were endorsed by 12 of the biggest US firms in South Africa, pledging to end segregation and job discrimination. In the next few years other American companies also subscribed to these principles. The resurgence of unions led other governments to follow the British example while, domestically, the Urban Foundation introduced its code of employment practice to eliminate colour discrimination.

All these developments drew responses from the government. One response was increased militarism. In 1977 a Defence White Paper referred to a 'total national strategy': the country was virtually at war and national service was increased to two years. The government admitted to having built up a reserve stockpile of fuel, and stated that the South African weapons industry was self-sufficient in the production of armaments to combat terrorism. The armed forces, already involved in the Angolan conflict and in containment activities in South West Africa/Namibia, consumed a growing slice of the budget. President P.W. Botha's vision of a 'total onslaught' undercut some indications of greater pragmatism under his predecessor, John Vorster, who had been forced out by the 'Muldergate' scandal of 1977–78 which involved the misuse of public funds.

The other response of government was one of mild reforms. By the second half of the 1970s it was becoming clear to some government-supporting intellectuals (especially economists) that the realization of the grand design of apartheid was not possible. In 1976 the Nationalist press stated that the electorate was ready to accept much faster change, and this was consistently borne out by opinion surveys. Even in National Party (NP) ranks alternative constitutional models were being suggested, and a spate of conferences were organized around the subject with economic implications as one of the concerns. 'Little apartheid' was regarded as expendable, and a new constitutional plan for separate parliaments for Coloureds and Indians was raised in 1977. The Botha regime recognized the economic, social and political problems facing the government, and took steps to address these by, for example, organizing a national conference on job creation in 1980, and establishing a dialogue with the private sector. In 1984 central business districts were desegregated as trading areas, and in 1986 urban freehold rights were granted to Africans and influx control was abolished. The regime introduced a Tricameral Parliament in 1983 which, although seriously flawed and overwhelmingly rejected by Coloureds and Indians, nevertheless once and for all buried the idea of Whites-only rule – so much so that it led to a significant split in Afrikaner politics.

However, the real opposition to the NP from the early 1980s onwards came not from parliamentary parties but from the unions which brilliantly exploited the opportunities they were presented with when the government legalized African trade unions in 1979. With African political parties outside the Bantustans having been banned since 1960, it was only to be expected that the new unions would build on their militancy of the 1970s to fill the void in African (especially urban) politics. The unions, by mobilizing civil Black society into a mass movement, easily outsmarted the Bantustan leaders, and the mass movement set out to make the country 'ungovernable' by fomenting township unrest, rent and school boycotts, and so on.

2.3.3   Sanctions and Disinvestment

The government's cautious reforms met with some response from the new US administration in 1981 when the Assistant Secretary of State for African Affairs, Chester Crocker, stated that the US government supported a policy of constructive engagement as long as the South African government pursued its anti-apartheid efforts. However, the strong-arm tactics employed by the government in trying to contain the mass movement then provided an opening for renewed moves for economic sanctions against South Africa. This opening was opportunistically exploited by black Americans supported by religious leaders and social democrats (usually but incorrectly described as 'liberals') following the second successive defeat of a Democratic Presidential candidate in November 1984. Within weeks these groups were out on the streets calling not only for sanctions but also for disinvestment by American companies operating in South Africa. This campaign induced some but not all US fims to disinvest, while many city and state governments imposed sanctions and even a Republican president felt obliged to sign appropriate legislation. These measures were copied in several other western countries.

Afrikaner economic progress had followed from 30 years of rapid economic growth. As mentioned above, economic growth had killed economic apartheid and led to gradual social integration. After that political integration was inevitable, but it was a question of how to go about it. From the mid-1970s the government had accepted the need to reform but wanted to control the pace and process. This was not acceptable to the banned parties or to trade unions. Nevertheless, by the 1980s the situation was one of continued White rule but now with a significant reduction of race barriers, the government ruling by force (Giliomee 1997). The outside world had a choice of how to influence this situation: continued rapid economic growth would have been a major force for further change, but the West instead decided to apply sanctions and disinvestment, that is, to support a process with the certain, predictable, long-term consequence of a stunted economy.

That the West needed to keep the pressure on the Botha government was indisputable. That sanctions were the appropriate tool was disputed. More creative ways were possible, one of which – the constructive engagement policy – was derailed by the US sanctions lobby. The economic result of sanctions and disinvestment were always clear to profesional economists, and the long-term destructive effects were still being felt as the twentieth century ended. However, the South African economy had become a pawn in the internal political dynamics of the West as well as of the Cold War. Many foreign interests were concerned with their own short-term political or economic gain, not with short- or long-term economic welfare in South Africa.

2.3.4 Effect on the Economy

Sanctions and disinvestments were essentially short term with one aim in mind, namely, to expedite the demise of a political system which was an outright embarrassment to the West. However, their long-term consequences were lucidly pointed out by local opponents of apartheid such as Mrs Helen Suzman and Chief M.G Buthelezi as well as by business leaders, and the point was taken by conservative groups abroad. These consequences were predictable: sanctions would not stop South Africa from trading inter-nationally but they would impose greater costs of trading, erode foreign confidence, lose markets which would not be easily regained, impose great hardship on the poor who would bear the brunt of job losses and economic downswing, not necessarily lead to a return of foreign investors once political changes had been made to the satisfaction of foreign powers, but ensure that the successor to the apartheid regime would inherit an economy that would be badly run down and difficult to reinvigorate. All these things came to pass.

Jenkins correctly points out (1995: 120) that sanctions did not cause the country's structural economic problems, but they certainly did not help to overcome them. The government did not liberalize the economy soon enough: in 1960 South Africa's per capita GDP was similar to Korea's, but in 2000 it was only one-third the size, and this can be attributed to open policies in Korea as opposed to interventionist policies followed only by late liberalization in South Africa. As Jenkins (1995: 98) and Mohr (1999: 339) point out, South Africa's economic problems had emerged by the mid-1970s, but they were exacerbated by isolation. By the time widespread sanctions were introduced in 1985–86 the economy had been on a slowing growth path for ten years caused by both endogenous and exogenous factors. The financial sanctions were particularly felt, and worsened the weak economy by forcing the country to run a current account surplus. As a consequence, domestic saving was partly used for net repayments of foreign debt and was not available for domestic investment. As Jenkins (1995: 117) puts it: 'domestic savings were absorbed by expensive capital-intensive projects, reducing investment in sectors which might have generated higher growth of output and employment. Despite successes the country's dependence on foreign technology remained one of its most important areas of vulnerability'. Although firms circumvented trade sanctions by finding new markets or new ways into existing markets, this was at a cost as trade (both export and import) now involved middlemen. Coal exports were achieved at a 10 per cent discount on the price (Jenkins 1995: 113) while imports such as stockpiles of crude were obtained at a premium. All this was at a high cost which could not be calculated, given the secrecy surrounding the issues (Jenkins 1995: 116).

Mohr (1999: 309) points out that 'the pace of economic activity and direction of economic policy in South Africa have frequently been governed by the state of the balance of payments'. The fact that, after 1976, the country could not depend on net inflows of foreign capital (especially direct long-term foreign investment in the private sector) led to 'a binding balance of payments constraint on economic activity and policy which was to reappear in the 1980s and become an almost permanent feature of the South African economic scene after the foreign debt crisis of 1985' (Mohr 1999: 340) when the government imposed repayment restrictions on US$14 billion in foreign debt after foreign banks had refused to roll over short-term loans.

Of the two types of sanctions – financial and trade – imposed against South Africa in the 1980s, it is now generally agreed that it was the former which had the greater adverse impact on the economy. Financial sanctions did not cause the foreign debt crisis of 1985 (Mohr et al. 1994: 139), but after the foreign debt standstill of August 1985, financial sanctions were introduced and intensified, and South Africa was forced to become a capital-exporting country. A repayment schedule was agreed with foreign bankers, and monetary and trade policies were shaped by the foreign debt problem. In addition to debt repayments, South Africa experienced capital flight. Whereas average net *inflows* of capital amounting to 2.5 per cent of GDP were recorded between 1946 and 1974, there was a total net *outflow* between 1985 and 1989 of 3.3 per cent of GDP (Mohr et al. 1994: 139). Disinvestment generated substantial outflows of long-term capital, while inflows of such capital were cut off completely 'by a combination of perceptions of growing risk in lending to South Africa and successful political pressures on banks to stop lending' (Jenkins 1995: 109). Considerable amounts of short-term capital also left the country and these outflows, together with regular repayments on short-term debt and the cessation of inflows of foreign direct investment (FDI) and long-term loans, led to a substantial, sustained deficit on the capital account. Reserves were greatly reduced to very weak import coverage levels. The monetary authorities, therefore, were forced to turn the historical current account deficit into a substantial surplus to fund the net capital outflow, but the repayment schedule, together with the US Comprehensive Anti-Apartheid Act of 1986, placed serious obstacles in the way of achieving such a surplus (Goedhuys 1994: 161). The outflows of capital 'reduced the availability of savings for investment, limited the flexibility of economic policy, and made recovery extremely difficult' (Jenkins 1995: 119).

The balance of payments reflects domestic and international economic developments and determines domestic economic variables. From 1985 onwards, balance of payments considerations (especially foreign debt commitments) often dictated macroeconomic policy. Deflationary policies were introduced to reduce domestic expenditure in order to maintain surpluses on the current account. The country could not afford to increase imports because of the strain which would be placed on the balance of payments. Thus, strict monetary policy measures to curb domestic spending remained until well into the 1990s. South Africa had to generate trade surpluses through export growth and import restraint, and this situation also obtained until 1993. The capital

Table 2.3   Gross saving and gross capital formation as a proportion of GDP, 1961-2000 (%)

Period	Gross saving	Gross capital formation
1961–65	24.0	23.0
1966–70	23.0	25.8
1971–75	24.5	28.5
1976–80	28.7	27.3
1981–85	23.8	25.6
1986–90	21.8	19.2
1991–95	16.9	16.3
1996–2000	14.9	15.9

Source: Data provided by Research Department, South African Reserve Bank.

account and low foreign reserves restricted the country's 'capacity to import and therefore also the scope to stimulate the economy' (Mohr et al. 1994: 143).

As a result of financial sanctions, limited access to international capital markets and scheduled repayments of debt, South Africa ended the century with a relatively low foreign debt exposure. During the financial sanctions period of 1985–93, outflows of capital exceeded the current account surplus of the balance of payments by R1.7 billion, that is, net reserves declined by that amount. Between 1994 and 1997 net reserves began to climb, increasing by R19 billion. After 1994, net capital inflows reappeared, the volume of trade increased and trade surpluses shrank. From 1995 the current account of the balance of payments was again in deficit, peaking in 1998 at R12.87 billion and then falling to R3.05 billion in 2000 when it was the equivalent of 0.3 per cent of GDP.

The exchange rate weakened consistently from 1984 onwards. In 1970, R0.71 purchased one US dollar; in 2000 the rate hit R7.82:US$1 at one point. The initial decline of the rand was due to poor economic fundamentals, but subsequently political considerations exerted a significant influence until 1994.

Trade sanctions and boycotts of South African products abroad reduced the sales of products such as sugar, wine and fruit, and again had long-term effects. South African producers fell behind in technology and market information, and the wine and deciduous fruit industries, for example, were in 2000 still making efforts to regain lost ground in these areas. Fruit, in particular, had not moved with changing consumer tastes for new varieties abroad.

Disinvestment led to the intensification of the concentration of ownership in the economy, as foreign multinationals were bought out by large South African conglomerates. The effect of sanctions and disinvestment on employment was indirect rather than direct: by restricting economic growth and damaging investor confidence, fewer jobs were created than might otherwise have been the case.

Sanctions and disinvestment contributed to falling real incomes, especially for Whites whose real wages fell throughout the 1980s. By contrast, Black wages in the formal sector rose rapidly, partly because of the influence of the new African unions but partly also because of continued company policies to eliminate discrimination.

POLITICAL CHANGE AND THE ECONOMY

2.4.1 A Problematic Legacy

The ninth decade of the century was a turbulent one, both politically and economically, for South Africa. By the time the National Party (NP) celebrated 40 years in office in 1988, it was racked by increasing complacency, inefficiency and corruption. Only in the late 1990s, however, would a fuller picture be drawn of the extent of government misspending and corruption, especially in the security and military establishments. The NP government, bereft of ideas, began to drift.

Simultaneously, communism in the Soviet Union and its Eastern European satellites was beginning to implode. This was a fortunate juxtaposition of events for South Africa. With the end of the Cold War in sight, the NP government could no longer use the threat of international communism to justify its policies. From 1986 onwards there was a proliferation of post-apartheid economy conferences at which economists, political scientists, business leaders and politicians from across the spectrum in South Africa were brought together with political exiles, trade unionists and representatives of the mass movement. After the release of Nelson Mandela in 1990 international big business, in which the World Economic Forum played a prominent role, also brought pressure to bear on the African National Congress (ANC) to modify its tendency towards a planned economy. These conferences and meetings did much to break the ice and bring an element of realism into the ANC's economic policies, which moved rapidly to a market - or perhaps social market - orientation.

It was clear, however, that the new government in 1994 would have a difficult time in restoring rapid economic growth. It inherited a number of problems: the structural defects of apartheid, the effects of sanctions and disinvestment, and the products of 'struggle politics' (militant trade unions, a 'lost generation' with an ungovernability ethic, and the need to reward supporters through patronage, notably through an alliance with trade unions and the South African Communist Party). All these were unpromising elements. Added to this was the climate of globalization: its open economy meant that South Africa had no choice but to embrace globalization in order to retain existing markets, regain lost markets and develop new markets. This would involve liberalization with the short-term problems of structural adjustment (such as retrenchments), adopting new technologies and improving productivity.

2.4.2 The Paradox

What was needed in 1994 was to continue economic liberalization; to go for growth; to put the country to work through large-scale public works programmes (UF 1994); to take advantage of centres of excellence in education and health; and to combat crime. Whatever efforts the government made in these directions, however, were hampered by trade union opposition and, particularly significant in a country with a shortage of skills, considerations of Black empowerment and transformation which inevitably led to a loss of experienced personnel, and to focus and energy being diverted away from economic growth. The net result was a paradox of sound macro-economic policies combined with disastrous labour legislation; increased inefficiency, cronyism and corruption at all levels of government; and declining ability to deliver to the poor. Emigration of skilled persons rose in a climate of globalization and affirmative action as well as of a weakening exchange rate. In this climate, investors stood off, a new elite developed, the poor became poorer, the radicals became angrier, and economic growth was kept at levels below what it could otherwise have reached.

Macroeconomic policy
The NP government had come late to a market-based policy of deregulation and non-intervention. From the early 1980s onwards it had sought to enhance the role of the private sector in policy making. These were moves in the right direction, and there was continuity after 1994. The ANC, once in power, elaborated on this economic liberalization, adopting macroeconomic policies which could scarcely be faulted. These policies rapidly led to the containment of the fiscal deficit – allaying fears of a populist stance (Mohr 1993) – single-digit inflation and lower interest rates. Macroeconomic policy was welcomed by the private sector both locally and abroad as well as by international institutions such as the International Monetary Fund and the World Bank, but not by unions. The economic growth rate picked up from 1994 although in 1998 it suffered from international financial shocks (Table 2.1).

The government in 1996 launched a macroeconomic plan (called 'Growth, Employment and Redistribution', or GEAR) which projected a GDP growth rate of 6.1 per cent by 2000 and adopted ambitious job creation goals. GEAR saw job creation as the way to beat poverty, and also stressed export-orientated growth and recovery in investment as the engines of growth. An evaluation of GEAR pointed out that the policy ought to be stronger on eliminating labour market rigidities, speeding privatization, and removing exchange controls to give clear and unambiguous signals to investors (Nomvete et al. 1997).

GEAR, basically sound though it was, was insufficient to attract the domestic and foreign investment the country required in order to reach the high real GDP growth rates necessary for modernizing the productive economic sectors, improving the social sectors, and making inroads into unemployment. There were several reasons for this.

First, foreign companies which had disinvested in the 1980s were largely wary of the South African 'miracle' and unwilling to rush back to the country. Second, the deteriorating crime situation caused a sense of uncertainty, leading to emigration of skilled individuals, discouraging foreign firms from establishing a presence, and militating against the growth of the tourist sector. Third, a panoply of new labour legislation, heavily biased in favour of the unions, militated against job creation and repelled foreign investors who could find far more favourable labour market conditions elsewhere in a period of growing globalization of production.

The period after 1994 saw a resurgence of capital inflows, but these were mainly short-term portfolio funds rather than long-term investment capital. The latter involved mainly a return of companies that had disinvested rather than the entry of new companies. In the lexicon of globalization, South Africa came to be regarded as an emerging market. By comparison with other emerging markets, however, South Africa's share of FDI was disappointing: US$32 per capita between 1994 and 1999 as against US$106 for Brazil, US$252 for Argentina and US$333 for Chile (*The Economist*, 24 February 2001: 12). Among the reasons for this were, its distance from Europe, North America and Japan; its relatively small domestic market; the general perception of Africa as a high-risk destination for investment; the overregulation of the labour market; the use of tax incentives which were uncertain and inconsistent with trade policies; and remnants of exchange control.

Exchange controls, operated with increasing severity from 1960 onwards, were considerably liberalized after 1994. Many individuals used the opportunity to invest in hard currencies abroad, while large companies listed on the London Stock Exchange in order to raise capital more cheaply for their expansion, in the case of Anglo American primarily for investment in mining ventures in other parts of the world. Generally, a wide spectrum of South African companies used the foreign exchange liberalization to invest elsewhere in Africa outside the common monetary area.

Effects of labour legislation

Labour legislation passed by the ANC government was politically under-standable but economically ill-conceived. The legislation in essence offered trade union members employment conditions superior to those in other countries with similar labour market conditions and at similar levels of economic development, and wages far in excess of market-clearing levels. The contents of these acts cannot be summarized here: suffice it to say that, by attempting to prescribe to employers a demographic profile (including race, sex and disability) and making it extremely difficult to fire or retrench workers, the legislation discouraged firms – small and large – from taking on staff. For foreign companies there is no intrinsic reason to invest in South Africa when flexible labour markets are operating in developing countries (including South Africa's neighbours).

Labour legislation went hand in hand with two other factors which emerged from the 1980s onwards, namely, a culture of entitlement and a widening income gap within the Black population.

Although the income gap between White and Black started being whittled away during the last period of sustained rapid economic growth – between 1965 and 1974 – it remained wide and was an important source of political discontent. Over the years this manifested itself in a culture of entitlement on the part of disadvantaged youth, workers and political leaders which was exacerbated by a policy of transformation after 1994, especially in the public sector. Financial scandals involving new appointees became commonplace and frequently went unpunished despite media exposure. The culture of entitlement, the policy of transformation and the labour laws together propped up a new elite within the Black population. Trade union membership (only 20 per cent of the total economically active population) became a passport to membership of a club of urban insiders protected against competition in the labour market from (predominantly rural) outsiders as the market mechanism was prevented from operating. This labour market rigidity meant that a key factor market was unfree at a time when the other key factor market – capital – was being liberalized through general macroeconomic reforms. Yet, liberalization of the one without the other would not achieve the desired goals of stimulating investment, creating employment, and helping to reduce the income gap and raise the standard of living of the poorest. Labour market policy was antithetical to the interests of the unemployed masses, and for them there was negligible economic trickle-down effect from political change. Income trends from 1970 onwards were in the right direction – the White share of personal income fell from 71 per cent in 1970 to 54 per cent in 1990 and 44 per cent in 2000 (when Africans accounted for 43.4 per cent) and of the richest tenth of the population from 95 per cent in 1975 to 66 per cent in 2000 by which time 23 per cent of the richest tenth were Africans (*The Economist*, 24 February, 2001:11; *Sunday Times*, 18 March, 2001), but the White:African per capita income ratio remained high at about 7:1. According to the United Nations Development Programme, 6.1 per cent of Africans but only 1 per cent of Whites were poor in 2000 (*Business Day*, 3 April, 2001).

In the *Global Competitiveness Report* which became influential in affecting investor perceptions of a country, South Africa scored well on macroeconomic policies but poorly in terms of human resource development and productivity. The education policy of the NP government led to lowered standards in African schools and failed to produce the high-level manpower skills required in a globally competitive economy. Many industries operated with obsolete technology (mainly owing to sanctions and disinvestment) and the cost of replacement was high owing to the weak exchange rate. A relatively poor work ethic stemming from union militancy and labour legislation also conspired against high productivity in the workforce, raising costs of production in manufacturing industry relative to those in competitor countries, and making South Africa uncompetitive as a location for labour-intensive industry. Not helping the situation was the continued loss of skilled manpower. Emigration became brisker after the Soweto riots of 1976, and political change has not stemmed the tide: the failure to provide adequate personal security, the affirmative action policy and the weakening exchange rate prompted people of all races (but predominantly skilled Whites, Indians and Coloureds) to pursue their careers abroad.

Trade and regional relations
Exchange control liberalizaton was particularly generous so far as corporate inevstment in the Southern African Development Community (SADC) region was concerned. This was symptomatic of an improvement in South Africa's international economic relations in general and its regional relations in particular. The new government from 1994 paid great attention to external trade agreements, concluding a Trade, Development and Cooperation Agreement with the European Union (EU) in 2000 and, in the same year, ratifying the SADC Trade Protocol. The bedrock of trade integration in Southern Africa – the Southern African Customs Union (SACU), the world's oldest suviving customs union – was itself the subject of negotiations starting in 1994, but appeared to take a back seat in South Africa's scheme of things as Pretoria's main attention was focused on the EU and SADC. However, SACU countries negotiated with the rest of SADC to achieve an asymmetrical tariff reduction process which would eventually lead to a SADC free trade area eight years after being implemented. This had not begun by the turn of the century when the end of the SACU renegotiations appeared to be in sight, perhaps to create a new secretariat to handle the affairs of SACU and dilute the influence of South Africa. During the apartheid era Pretoria had been regarded as the regional bully boy; by 2000 the perception had not been entirely erased, and South Africa often found itself in a minority, for example, in proposing a more rational operational structure for the largely ineffective SADC.

By the end of the century intra-regional trade flows remained heavily in favour of South Africa, and the country's transport system continued to serve its SADC neighbours to the north but not as dominantly as in the 1980s when a relatively efficient South African system was all that kept the foreign trade of these countries moving. In the 1990s South Africa led the implementation of cross-border development corridors and spatial development initiatives in the region. However, the flagship Maputo Developnent Corridor had not made the progress expected, partly because of continued inability to establish 'seamless' (one-stop) border-post operations.

Infrastructure – physical and social
The Maputo Corridor encapsulated some of the problems resulting from flawed transport policy reforms instituted by the NP government from the mid-1980s and continued by the new government. Historically, the sector had been highly regulated. The government in 1984 moved to deregulate it, but did so in a way which accelerated the shift of traffic from rail to road, leaving South Africa with a greatly diminished operational railway network and a deteriorating road infrastructure. The transport system in reality was far from what it was generally portrayed as being by those who remembered its role in Southern Africa in the 1980s (see, for example, *The Economist*, 24 February, 2000: 4).

Other physical infrastructure had fared better than transport. The landline telephone network had been extended in the 1990s, although the system as a whole had been thrown a lifeline by the growth of the cellular network. Electricity and water networks were also extended to low-income areas.

However, social infrastructure and services suffered badly in the last two decades of the century. Numbers of schools were destroyed or seriously damaged, and investment could not keep up with the demands of the educational system as a whole. In the transformation process thousands of experienced, qualified teachers took early retirement and could not be adequately replaced. A similar situation occurred in the health sector. Hospitals and clinics could not be maintained at previous levels, and the picture by 2000 was one of seriously eroded educational and health infrastucture in the public sector.

In the late 1990s AIDS began to impose increased costs on society and economy although economic costs could be mitigated by recruiting skilled immigrants. Illegal immigration rose significantly in the 1990s as borders became increasingly porous with controls breaking down; immigrants came to be associated with the drug trade, car and cash heists, and criminal activities in general. Crime was the logical sequel to township violence and the ungovernability strategy of the 1980s. South Africa had a particularly high rate of violent crime which led to adverse media publicity abroad and hampered the growth of the tourism industry which had real potential for job creation. Instead, the security industry became the growth industry in South Africa from the 1980s onwards as the police force became decreasingly able to contain crime levels.

Economic sectors
So far as the economic sectors are concerned, manufacturing growth was very slow (Table 2.4) and the effects of global trade liberalization were keenly felt by the labour-intensive clothing, textile and footwear industries which declined rapidly except for those which could find niche markets. The new

Table 2.4 Mean annual real growth rates of gross value added, manufacturing sector, 1951-2000 (%)

Period	Average	Decade average
1951–55	7.5 ⎫	
1956–60	4.6 ⎭	6.0
1961–65	9.9 ⎫	
1966–70	7.4 ⎭	8.7
1971–75	6.0 ⎫	
1976–80	4.6 ⎭	5.3
1981–85	1.1 ⎫	
1986–90	1.6 ⎭	1.4
1990–95	0.2 ⎫	
1996–2000	1.1 ⎭	0.7

Source: Data provided by Research Department, South African Reserve Bank.

government encouraged the development of industrial clusters, the most notable growth being in the automotive sector where car manufacturers benefited from decisions made by German head offices that all right-hand-drive markets would be supplied from their South African plants. The 'minerals-energy' cluster also held great promise.

In mining, gold output fell as the low world price made many mines unprofitable. Platinum output, however, expanded and had replaced gold by the end of 2000 as the main mineral export. Development in agriculture in the 1990s centred around deregulation and trade liberalization. It was marked by the scrapping of control boards and subsidies. These developments, coupled with adverse weather conditions and market prices, led to changes in land use in some parts of the country, livestock farming giving way to private game reserves. Trophy hunting became a growth activity, and was related to a general trend towards eco-tourism and a concern for the environment. The other major trend was the extension of gambling. The new government adopted a policy of allowing 40 casino licences nationwide. This policy was fraught with weaknesses, one of which was that the expectations were unrealistic: not all the casinos had been built at the end of 2000 but it was already clear that they were creating new social problems. A history of casinos in the decade from 2001 to 2010 might well reveal some spectacular business failures since the number of licences far exceeds the ability of the economy to sustain them. The rapid growth of consumer expenditure on gambling and cellular telephones was cited in 2000 as a major problem for the retail trade.

Information technology was a strong growth sector, and the country developed a significant high-tech industry. The computer revolution transformed the workplace in the last 20 years of the century, and in the 1990s South Africa changed rapidly towards a service economy. The contribution of the primary sector to GDP declined while that of the tertiary sector increased to 65.8 per cent in 1999. The informal sector contribution increased to 7 per cent of GDP in 1999.

Saving and investment

Table 2.3 shows that both gross domestic saving and gross investment as a proportion of GDP fell consistently after the 1970s. The fall in gross domestic saving was attributable mainly to the consistently declining rate of personal savings, that is, personal saving as a proportion of personal disposable income, from an average of 9.3 per cent in the 1960s to 8.4 per cent in the 1970s, 4.2 per cent in the 1980s and 2.7 per cent between 1990 and 1997. The main reasons were the sharp increase in direct and indirect taxes, consistently high inflation rates for much of the period, negative real deposit rates in certain years which reduced the incentive to save, and ever-increasing levels of debt as households attempted to maintain living standards (du Toit 1996). Another important factor was the phenomenon of government dissaving as public sector expenditure exceeded revenue: this had reached 7.3 per cent of GDP in 1992 but was reduced by fiscal discipline after 1994 to 2.6 per cent of GDP in 1999/2000 with a zero figure projected by 2002. This helped to reduce South Africa's borrowing requirements and to lower debt costs.

The rule of thumb for gross domestic fixed investment (GDFI) is 25 per cent of GDP. In South Africa the ratio was below this level from 1984 onwards. The major reasons (du Toit 1996) included low levels of domestic saving, the deteriorating security situation, adverse labour market developments and strikes, the impact of sanctions and disinvestment, high real interest rates, the weakening exchange rate which caused the cost of imported capital equipment to rise, lower levels of investment by general government as government current expenditure increased, and the need to improve corporate cash flows in the face of poor economic performance and high inflation, taxes and interest rates. The falling trend in the growth rate of fixed capital stock posed a serious threat to overall economic growth capacity.

Inflation

South Africa experienced double-digit inflation in both producer and consumer prices over the 1974–92 period. Table 2.5 shows the consumer price index for the 1971–2000 period. Double-digit inflation peaked in 1986, and was the result mainly of inadequate fiscal discipline (negative interest rates and a high rate of monetary expansion), wage increases outstripping growth in

Table 2.5   Overall consumer price index, 1970-2000

Year	% Δ over 1 year
1970	5.1
1971	6.4
1972	6.1
1973	9.4
1974	11.6
1975	13.5
1976	11.2
1977	11.2
1978	11.0
1979	13.2
1980	13.8
1981	15.2
1982	14.7
1983	12.4
1984	11.5
1985	16.3
1986	18.6
1987	16.1
1988	12.9
1989	14.7
1990	14.4
1991	15.3
1992	13.9
1993	9.7
1994	9.0
1995	8.7
1996	7.4
1997	8.6
1998	6.9
1999	5.2
2000	5.3
Mean annual percentage increase	
1971–1980	11.0
1981–1990	14.6
1991–2000	8.2

Source: Data provided by Research Department, South African Reserve Bank.

labour productivity, and exchange rate depreciation. From 1993 inflation fell to single digits because of tight monetary policy (that is, relatively high interest rates); increased foreign competition as a result of tariff liberalization which restrained local price increases; lower inflation rates of major trading partners; and a relatively stable dollar price of oil. In 1999, however, the dollar price of oil started to rise and remained at high levels, being partly responsible for a slight increase in the inflation rate in 2000. The government had introduced inflation targeting with a goal of between 3 and 6 per cent by 2002: critics claimed that it restricted economic growth and job creation, but it was generally supported by economists.

2.5   THE POSITION IN 2000

South Africa's international credit ratings improved after 1994, and it was classified as an 'investment grade' country by 2000. The International Institute for Management Development (IIMD, 2000) ranked South Africa 42nd out of 47 countries in both 1999 and 2000 in its world competitiveness scoreboard, but the *Global Competitiveness Report* (World Economic Forum, 2000) rated South Africa 33rd out of 59 countries in 2000 as against 47th in 1999. The positive and negative factors mentioned in these reports are listed in Table 2.6.

A real GDP growth rate of 5-6 per cent per annum was commonly regarded as being necessary to mop up unemployment over the long term, but this assumed a particular capital/labour ratio which might not obtain in a climate of globalization, trade liberalization and technological change. The private and

Table 2.6   Factors influencing South Africa's international credit and competitiveness ratings

Positive	Negative
Sound fiscal policies	Slow privatization
Independent central bank	Uncertainty/delays in policy implementation
Low inflation	Unfavourable labour legislation
Stock exchange	Emigration (loss of skills)
Advance financial services sector	Poor education system (lack of skills)
Economic creativity	Crime/insecurity
Growth of cellular telephony	AIDS
Growth of Internet	High unemployment

Sources: IIMD, *World Competitiveness Yearbook 2000*, ww.imd.ch/wcy; World Economic Forum, *Global Competitiveness Report*, 2000, 196–7.

public sectors worldwide had downsized in order to improve efficiency and competitiveness. Capital intensity generally had risen, and in South Africa was exacerbated by labour market rigidities. Thus, a 5-6 per cent rate might not be an accurate estimate. However, if employment were to be created in small and medium-sized establishments and tourism (as it had been overseas), then high economic growth would be necessary. Moreover, only economic growth would create the fiscal resources necessary for redistribution.

At the end of the twentieth century the prospects for the first decade of the next century were mixed. The expectations set in train in the early 1990s had not been met, and a meanness had crept into society. Links between the government and the unions had been strained by GEAR, privatization and hints of labour reforms, but the government needed to put growth first. Economic growth would not be the sole saviour but it would be necessary for generating income to reallocate towards restructuring an efficient economy and improving the standard of living of the poor in order to avoid further political and social turbulence which would have severe economic repercussions. Just as the rapid economic growth of 1946-74 broke legislated apartheid and hastened Black upward mobility, so too would rapid economic growth in the 2000s be the efficient way to Black empowerment by creating opportunities for new firms and forcing further upward mobility. South Africa had already lost 25 years, and it could not afford a repetition of this experience.

REFERENCES

Development Bank of South Africa (DBSA) (1989), *Report of the Panel of Experts on the Evaluation of the Regional Development Programme as an Element of the Regional Development Policy in Southern Africa*, Halfway House: Development Bank of Southern Africa.

Du Toit, J. (1996), *The South African Economy*, Johannesburg: ABSA Bank.

Giliomee, H. (1997), 'Surrender without defeat: Afrikaners and the South African "miracle"', *SAIRR Spotlight*, **2**, Johannesburg: South African Institute of Race Relations.

Goedhuys, D. (1994), 'South African monetary policy in the 1980s: years of reform and foreign financial aggression', *South African Journal of Economic History*, **9** (2), 145-64.

Hofmeyr, J. (1996), 'The South African labour market: historical trends', in D. Innes (ed.), 'The South African Labour Market: An Analysis of Trends, Challenges and Policy Implications', Unpublished paper, Cape Town: Africa Institute for Policy Analysis.

Horwood, O.P.F. and J.R. Burrows (1962), 'The South African economy: the relevance of the competitive *laissez-faire* model', in C.B. Hoover (ed.), *Economic Systems of the Commonwealth*, Durham, NC: Duke University Press, 462-500.

IIMD (2000), *World Competitiveness Yearbook*, Lausanne: International Institute for

Management Development.

Jenkins, C. (1995), 'Adjusting to economic sanctions in South Africa', in O. Morrissey and F. Stewart (eds), *Economic and Political Reform in Developing Countries*, London: St. Martin's Press, 97–122.

Maasdorp, G. (1975), *Economic Development for the Homelands*, Johannesburg: South African Institute of Race Relations.

Maasdorp, G. (1985), 'Coordinated regional development: hope for the Good Hope proposals?', in H. Giliomee and L. Schlemmer (eds), *Up Against the Fences: Poverty, Passes and Privilege in South Africa*, Cape Town: David Philip, 219–33.

McCarthy, C. (1985), 'Industrial decentralisation and employment creation', in H. Giliomee and L. Schlemmer (eds), *Up Against the Fences: Poverty Passes and Privilege in South Africa*, Cape Town: David Philip, 210–18.

Mohr, P. (1993), 'Will South Africa fall into the populist trap?', Occasional Paper No. 5, Johannesburg: Economic Policy Study Group.

Mohr, P. (1999), 'The South African balance of payments in the 1970s', *South African Journal of Economic History*, **14** (1&2), 309–40.

Mohr, P., M. Botha and P. Hawkins (1994), 'South Africa's balance of payments in the 1980s', *South African Journal of Economic History*, **9** (2), 127–44.

Nomvete, B.D., G.G. Maasdorp and D. Thomas (eds) (1997), *Growth with Equity*, Cape Town: Francolin Publishers.

South African Institute of Race Relations (SAIRR) (2001), *Fast Facts*, April, Johannesburg: SAIRR.

Urban Foundation (UF) (1994), *Public Works Programmes in South Africa: A Key Element in Employment Policy*, Johannesburg: Urban Foundation.

Williams, W. (1990), *South Africa's War Against Capitalism*, Kenwyn: Juta & Co.

World Economic Forum (annual report, 2000), *Global Competitiveness Report*, Oxford: Oxford University Press.

3.   Macroeconomic policy, 1970–2000

P.D.F. Strydom

3.1   INTRODUCTION

South African economic policy during the period under consideration was characterized by major changes. First, an explicit change from non-market-related controls towards market-orientated policies. Second, a major transformation from a siege economy during apartheid to an economic framework which had to support a democratic political framework after the election in 1994. Our analysis concentrates on macroeconomic policy, that is, monetary and fiscal policies with some emphasis on labour market reforms because of their effect on employment. Our exposition is concerned with the major objectives and policy instruments coupled with the effectiveness of these policies in achieving their goals. Finally, we assess the present policy framework of the South African government in terms of its Growth, Employment and Redistribution (GEAR) framework.

3.2   INTERNATIONAL SETTING

The changing economic policies in South Africa from 1970 to 2000 have to be assessed within an international economic environment because the evolution of economic policy together with the changing institutional framework has to a large extent been influenced by global developments. Moreover, during the 1990s South Africa emerged from an era of trade and cultural isolation into a world that was rapidly integrating in terms of trade, technological innovation, globally driven production and distribution processes. Within this environment the country was taking its place as an emerging market which meant that its economic policies had to deal with the economic disruptions that were closely related to developments in these countries. In many instances the South African economy has more sophisticated financial institutions and relatively well-developed markets in comparison with many emerging countries. Unfortunately South African financial markets are severely affected by instabilities in these countries as has been illustrated by the Asian contagion.

Although South Africa has flirted with outward-orientated policies during the 1970s it remained committed to inward-orientated policies with high and complicated tariff structures. The country became committed to an outward-orientated policy in 1990 when it participated in the Uruguay Round of the General Agreement on Tariffs and Trade (GATT), which became the World Trade Organization (WTO). This agreement became effective in 1995 and South Africa introduced substantial revisions of its controversial tariff structures and protectionist measures. The dual exchange rate system was terminated in 1995, which effectively abolished foreign exchange control on non-residents. South Africa's integration with the world economy gained momentum after the election in 1994.

Apart from these developments associated with the opening up of the economy, certain international developments were important in shaping South African monetary and fiscal policies. Towards the end of the 1970s, the major industrial countries embarked on financial market reforms that gained momentum during the 1980s. Significant changes followed in respect of monetary policy in the sense that market-orientated policies were adopted while direct controls were abolished. Moreover, the fixed exchange rate system of Bretton Woods was abandoned in 1971. South Africa adopted many aspects of this new market-orientated approach towards monetary policy as has been evident in terms of the De Kock Commission of Inquiry into the Monetary System and Monetary Policy in South Africa, which submitted its report in 1985.

Fiscal policy was equally influenced by international reforms. During the 1980s, fiscal policy in the major industrial countries experienced important changes in favour of less government intervention, which led to the selling of state assets through privatization, tax cuts and a slowdown in government spending. During the 1990s, the European Union (EU) compelled participating member countries to introduce far-reaching fiscal reforms, reductions in fiscal deficits and lower government debt ratios. Changes in South Africa's fiscal policy were, no doubt, modelled on these global tendencies, particularly after 1994 under the democratically elected government.

3.3   POLICY AIMS AND INSTRUMENTS

It has been a long tradition in the literature to associate macroeconomic policies as well as its components, that is, monetary and fiscal policy with an extensive list of policy aims such as economic growth, full employment, balance of payments equilibrium, distribution issues, a competitive exchange rate and a low inflation rate. The simultaneous achievement of these aims is not always feasible in the real world for they are not mutually exclusive. We are not adhering to this approach but associate monetary policy with the final aim of price stability (or a low inflation rate) and fiscal policy with economic growth which is closely associated with employment. We follow a similar approach to Britton (1991). The aim of monetary and fiscal policy has not always been defined in these strict terms by the South African authorities. We shall nevertheless try to focus our exposition on narrowly defined aims, which means that we are concerned with two targets and two policies.

3.4 MONETARY POLICY

During the 1970s and 1980s, that is, until the submission of the report by the De Kock Commission (1985), monetary policy consisted mainly of direct controls. Certain financial reforms in favour of more liberalized and market-orientated measures had already been introduced in 1979. Prior to these changes, monetary policy was mainly conducted through interest rate controls, liquid asset requirements as well as cash reserve requirements. Direct credit controls in the form of credit ceilings were enforced through moral suasion. These measures were analysed by Strydom (1974), Strydom and Koopmans (1974), Meijer (1976, 1995), the De Kock Commission (1985) and Goedhuys (1994). They were aimed at controlling the growth in the monetary aggregate with a view to combating inflation.

The cash reserve requirement was a variable deposit of banking institutions with the Reserve Bank. The liquid asset requirement forced banks to invest in liquid assets that the Reserve Bank could alter from time to time. These assets comprised Reserve Bank notes, coin, gold coin, cash balances with the Reserve Bank and a large number of financial assets such as Treasury Bills, government stocks, bankers' acceptances and trade bills. Internal contradictions and instrument inefficiencies plagued these policy measures. A major problem was the liquid asset requirement, which featured prominently in monetary policy (Meijer, 1995). During economic expansions or contractions the supply of these assets followed the pattern of the business cycle and banks would have little difficulty in complying with the variable liquid asset requirement imposed by the Reserve Bank. More importantly, banks could easily convert advances into liquid assets and comply with the policy requirement. Banks could easily substitute cash for liquid assets and vice versa which means that their cash base escaped the intended effects of the policy instruments. Monetary policy was ineffective in effecting the cash base or the cost of credit. Moreover, the effectiveness of the instrument was severely obstructed because of interest rate controls that were introduced from time to time.

An important motive behind the liquid asset requirement was that the financial sector was to finance those sectors that issued the liquid assets at reduced (non-market-related) interest rates. Monetary policy induced allocation effects by favouring particular sectors, such as agriculture, exports and the government. Moreover, monetary policy introduced a bias towards relatively low interest rates via the liquid asset requirement. In view of these internal contradictions and ineffficiencies monetary policy was ineffective in controlling the monetary aggregates effectively and the authorities imposed credit ceilings on the banks to restrain credit growth. Within this framework of extensive controls there was little scope for financial markets to develop. It is not surprising that this system was characterized by extensive disintermediation from time to time.

International disruptions, such as the downfall of the Bretton Woods system of fixed exchange rates in 1971 coupled with the two oil crises in 1973–74 and 1979–80, were important challenges to such a rigid policy framework. The effect of these disruptions together with South Africa's particular policy stance became evident in the inflation rate. During the 1970s, South Africa's inflation started rising at a rapid rate and it developed out of step with that in its major trading partners. The prime reasons for this inflationary tendency were cost-push factors as indicated by Strydom (1976). Escalating administered prices and the successive devaluation of the rand were important cost elements. Moreover, the devaluations of the currency were not complemented by restrictive fiscal and monetary policies in order to reap the full benefit of the devaluations. The authorities followed expansionary policies instead (Strydom 1976). The inflationary cycle started to accelerate from an average rate of 4.3 per cent in 1970; by 1975 it was 15.7 per cent before decelerating to 8.7 per cent in 1978. Moreover, as indicated by the United Bank (1991), South African monetary policy appeared to have been primarily expansionary throughout the 1970s and 1980s. The international commodity boom and the rise in the gold price during this period protected South Africa against the harsh effects of the oil crises. We nevertheless hasten to add that South Africa was not very dependent on oil as an energy source and the only activity that relied heavily on oil was transport. Mining and manufacturing were dependent on coal-based electricity.

It is against this background that the De Kock Commission was appointed in 1977. Its final report was released in 1985 with great emphasis on the need for a market-orientated monetary policy and more effective instruments to achieve the goals of economic policy. The Commission recommended the abolition of direct controls, that is, interest rate as well as credit controls as discussed by Meijer (1984/85). A major step forward was the introduction of a managed floating exchange rate system for the rand in early 1979 while monetary policy was to rely more on cash reserve requirements and supporting open market operations. These reforms allowed interest rates to follow market signals and from 1980 onwards interest rates adjusted towards higher levels, signalling a definite break with the rigid control system of the 1970s with its bias towards low interest rates. The new monetary framework explicitly identified a stable price level or the control of inflation as the ultimate goal of monetary policy while the control of the monetary aggregate featured as an intermediate target. Growth targets for the monetary aggregate M3 were defined on an annual basis. These targets were to be achieved through changing interest rates. Monetary targeting was introduced in 1986 with the explicit understanding that these targets were not to be interpreted in a rigid way. Discount policy and supporting open market operations emerged as the main policy instruments of the Reserve Bank. The bank rate featured as the principal operational variable in conducting monetary policy while the banks were allowed unlimited access to liquidity through the discount window by discounting eligible paper with the Reserve Bank. The Reserve Bank, therefore, conducted monetary policy within an explicitly discretionary framework. The liquid asset requirement became a mere prudential element as opposed to an active instrument of monetary policy. The Reserve Bank could alter the cash reserve requirement in order to support its discount policy.

The M3 variable tended, on average, to overshoot its target range from its inception in 1986. Exceptions were the years 1987, 1990, 1992 and 1993 (Du Toit, 1998). The main reason for this is probably the fact that the process of liberalizing the financial sector affected the behaviour pattern of M3. Furthermore, through trade liberalization and the integration of the international economy it became clear that monetary aggregates, as policy targets, were gradually losing their significance as intermediate policy targets. For a different explanation of these events the reader is referred to Moll (2000).

Measured in terms of inflation, the new policy framework contributed towards dampening the sharp upward spiralling of the inflation rate, which occurred during the 1970s. In 1975 the inflation rate reached a high of 15.7 per cent on a year-on-year basis and it accelerated to 16.6 per cent in 1981. The inflation rate peaked in January 1986 when the consumer price index was 21 per cent up on the previous year. Thereafter it followed a well-established downward pattern to reach a low of 1.5 per cent in October 1999. These patterns probably confirm the lagged effects associated with monetary policy. The consistency and credibility of monetary policy were probably the main elements that contributed towards a dampening of inflation expectations during the 1990s. The other major factors that contributed towards a slowdown in the inflation rate are the increased competition and cost-cutting procedures that were imposed by the opening up of the economy and the benefits from economies of scale, which followed. Furthermore, private sector companies embarked on a restructuring process, which resulted in more efficient and cost-effective firms with stronger balance sheets. Fiscal restraint, which became a specific feature of fiscal policy under the new government, played an important anti-inflationary role.

Developments in the foreign exchange market did not augur well for the new policy framework. As indicated by Strydom (1986) the exchange rate policy was plagued by two problems. The first was a logical inconsistency in the policy perspective in the sense that the exchange rate policy was inspired by monetarist thinking while the control of inflation was based on Keynesian principles. The second problem is associated with the fact that the authorities were rushing ahead in liberalizing the financial sector while real sector reforms were overlooked. This means that the problem of sequencing has not been taken into account and several aspects of the reform process failed (Strydom 1995). In similar vein, Goedhuys (1994) discussed the complicated circumstances under which the reforms were introduced. One important example of this discrepancy between the reforms in the financial sector and those in the real sector is evident in the policy aim, at the time, to allow the free floating rand exchange rate to depreciate in order to stimulate exports. During the 1980s and early 1990s the South African economy was adhering to the rules of an inward-looking policy. Outward-looking policies followed in the 1990s, particularly after the 1994 election of the new government. This means that, at the time, the real sector was not in a position to react to the incentives coming from the financial markets, such as a weaker rand exchange rate. In a different direction, liberalized markets are unlikely to be sustainable in a non-liberalized political system.

South Africa adopted a dual exchange rate system in January 1979 with the commercial rand being a market-related rate of exchange for current account and loans transactions. The financial rand was a freely floating exchange rate for equity capital flows. The dual exchange rate regime was terminated during February 1983 together with an abolition of exchange controls on non-residents. A unitary floating exchange rate with Reserve Bank intervention was introduced. The unitary exchange rate system has put up a dismal performance. Political unrest, the infamous Rubicon speech by the then State President P.W. Botha followed by the declaration of a state of emergency in July 1985 played havoc with the foreign exchange market seen in volatile capital movements and leads and lags in terms of import payments and export receipts followed suit. In 1985 the debt standstill was announced when South Africa imposed repayment restrictions on its foreign debt when certain foreign banks (mainly in the US) refused to roll over short-term loans (see Goedhuys, 1994). The index of the weighted nominal value of the rand dropped from a level of 428.4 in September 1983 to 155.6 in August 1986, that is, depreciating over the period at a rate of 3 per cent per month.

In 1989 Dr Chris Stals became governor of the Reserve Bank and during his tenure at the Bank the aim of monetary policy was explicitly directed towards the protection of the value of the currency. Moreover, the exchange rate of the rand became a more important anchor in monetary policy (see Stals, 2000 and Bruggemans, 2000a). During the Asian contagion in 1998 the Reserve Bank appeared to be reluctant to allow the rand exchange rate to absorb the adjustments associated with the depreciation of the South East Asian currencies in a region important for South African exports. This rigid approach resulted in a speculative attack on the South African foreign exchange market with devastating effects on the exchange rate and interest rates. The outcome was an unstable currency, a marked depreciation in the rand exchange rate with the resultant inflationary effects and a high interest rate level to such an extent that the economic expansion was slowed down markedly (Schaling and Schoeman, 2000).

In the new political dispensation the Reserve Bank's independence became enshrined in the South African Constitution and the Bank started following an eclectic approach towards monetary policy. This implied that although the Reserve Bank's final objective was concerned with the control of inflation and monetary aggregates were considered to be intermediate targets, the Reserve Bank did not change its policy stance automatically when the monetary aggregates were not adhering to their growth targets. It followed an eclectic approach based on an in-depth analysis of the factors responsible for inflation. Monetary policy was, therefore, conducted within a long-term framework where inflation and several financial variables were consulted instead of concentrating merely on M3 as an intermediate target. In March 1998 this approach was extended by the introduction of the repurchase-based auction system. This was a flexible accommodation procedure in terms of which banks were offered the opportunity of tendering on a daily basis for a fixed amount of central bank funds through repurchase transactions. The average rate of the tender system is referred to as the repurchase rate (repo rate for short). Together with this the discount window facility was replaced with the marginal lending facility where overnight loans or loans for a few days were to be provided to banks at the marginal lending rate. Banks have unrestricted access to this facility against the collateral of approved securities. The marginal lending rate is fixed at a certain margin above the repurchase rate. Banks were no longer required to maintain the minimum cash reserve with the Reserve Bank on a daily basis but on a monthly basis (SARB, 1998).

In his first annual address to shareholders in 1999, Governor Tito Mboweni indicated that the Reserve Bank was ready to abandon the eclectic approach to monetary policy and to implement a formal inflation targeting approach (SARB, 1999). The Minister of Finance formally announced an inflation targeting approach in his budget speech of 23 February 2000. The inflation target was set at 3 to 6 per cent for the year 2002. The target inflation rate is the overall consumer price index for metropolitan and other urban areas excluding mortgage interest costs. The new policy framework did not exclude discretion on the part of the Bank. Moreover, the Reserve Bank appeared to be fully aware of the significance of achieving and maintaining sustainable high economic growth while taking cognizance of the inflationary effects of exchange rate fluctuations (SARB, 2000a). The new policy framework is no longer obsessed with the exchange rate as an anchor and the exchange rate of the rand is regarded as a function of supply and demand on the foreign exchange market (see Mboweni, 2000). As opposed to other countries, such as the United States, South Africa did not exclude the volatile energy prices from its inflation target. Thus the Reserve Bank could be confronted with difficult situations (Bruggemans, 2000b).

Inflation targeting implies that the Reserve Bank is abandoning M3 as an intermediate target. The international liberalization of financial markets and the globalization of the world economy rendered the system of intermediate targeting ineffective as indicated by Dos Santos and Schaling (2000). More importantly, the acceptance of an inflation targeting framework and the abandoning of monetary aggregates as an intermediate target signals an important shift in central bank thinking. The overall importance of money in the explanation of inflation is abandoned while there is an explicit recognition of the independent influence of cost-push factors in explaining inflation. Inflation targeting implies that the Reserve Bank has lost its target independence. It nevertheless commands instrument independence within a policy framework that is littered with many difficulties (Strydom, 2000).

The outcome of this exposition is that monetary policy has evolved from a non-market approach, with extensive direct controls in the 1970s and early 1980s, towards a market-orientated system. Institutional rigidities and political upheavals hampered the introduction of this system. The success of the policy was inhibited by internal contradictions and it displayed little appreciation of the significance of sequencing in introducing reforms. After the 1994 democratic elections the system developed into a fully fledged market-orientated policy framework which has been successful in bringing the inflation rate down from double- to single-digit numbers. We nevertheless hasten to add that several disinflationary processes were supporting monetary policy in achieving a slowdown in inflation.

3.5   FISCAL POLICY

Before we embark on an analysis of fiscal policy, some observations on the fiscal characteristics of South Africa are in order (see Browne, 1983; Du Toit,

1998; Heyns, 1994). Government expenditure is dominated by current expenditure and of this, consumption expenditure comprises approximately 64 per cent. Salaries and wages comprise approximately 72 per cent of consumption expenditure. This has increased from approximately 50 per cent in 1978 to present levels. Interest expenditure has increased from approximately 8 per cent of current expenditure in 1970 to 20 per cent in 1999. These magnitudes clearly confirm a high debt ratio. During June 2000 the debt ratio comprised 48.3 per cent. It is evident that, from the expenditure perspective, government is fairly limited in its policy options. New fiscal policy challenges, such as the fighting of poverty, can only be pursued if the authorities are successful in cutting back current expenditure, that is, given the explicit constraint imposed by the present government to reduce the tax burden and to bring down the budget deficit.

The revenue side of the state budget is dominated by income tax, which comprises approximately 59 per cent of total state revenue. A strong reliance on direct taxes has always been a feature of South African government finance. The value-added tax, which is the most important indirect tax, comprised 27 per cent of total revenue in June 2000. This ratio has gradually increased to present levels. The real bias in South African taxation is evident from the fact that the share of income tax on individuals in total state revenue comprised approximately 44 per cent in 2000. This ratio has gradually increased through time. In 1980 it amounted to approximately 17 per cent. Company taxation is presently approximately 15 per cent of total revenue. The tax burden is primarily carried by a relatively small percentage of individuals. Income tax on individuals, as a percentage of total revenue, increased from 16.8 per cent in the 1980/81 fiscal year to 43.6 per cent during fiscal year 1999/2000. (For a review of South African tax policy, see Heyns, 1994.)

Current expenditure by government, as a percentage of GDP, has followed a strong upward trend since 1970. This went hand in hand with a rising tax burden and large budget deficits. Moreover, the government sector was characterized by a strong dissaving pattern (Heyns, 1995a). The expansion in government spending is partly explained in terms of an overoptimistic assessment of the economic potential of the country by the authorities during the 1980s (De Kock, 1980). The more important factor responsible for the acceleration in government spending, particularly during the 1980s, was the rising cost burden of the apartheid system. Current expenditure peaked in 1992 at a rate of 32 per cent of GDP. Thereafter it declined and by 1999 had fallen to 30 per cent of GDP. This slowdown in the growth rate of current expenditure was complemented by more effficient revenue collection procedures, under the new government. The result of these efforts were passed on to the private sector in tax cuts while budget deficits were reduced from a peak level of 7.3 per cent of GDP in 1993 to 2.6 per cent in 2000. The fiscal discipline, which the new government imposed, resulted in a flattening-off pattern in the growth rate of government debt, which peaked in 1995 at 51.4 per cent of GDP.

In analysing the effectiveness of fiscal policy over the period under consideration we are adhering to our analysis, introduced above, of limited aims as opposed to assessing fiscal policy in terms of a whole spectrum of aims. In our analysis economic growth is considered to be the prime objective of fiscal policy. Our exposition is concentrating on those aspects of fiscal policy that could contribute towards economic growth whether directly or indirectly in the sense of being growth conducive. In view of the fact that economic growth and employment are interrelated one could also consider employment as a policy objective of fiscal policy. Of course this does not imply that government should create employment directly. It refers to those processes and elements of fiscal and labour market policy that are conducive to employment.

Employment creation by the formal non-agricultural sectors of the economy has followed a declining tendency since 1989 (SARB, 2000b). In terms of the October Household Survey released by Statistics South Africa (2000) the rate of unemployment was 23.3 per cent in 1999. From 1989 to 1999 the non-agricultural private sector has reduced its employment opportunities by 20 per cent (SARB, 2000b). Major job losses occurred in the mining, construction and manufacturing sectors. Moreover, the October Household Survey of 1997 established a curvilinear relationship between unemployment and education. Unemployment is the highest among unskilled people (Statistics South Africa, 1999).

The loss of employment opportunities is partly explained by major adjustments in the South African economy. The mining industry has been under pressure to reduce costs and, owing to the decline in the gold price, marginal mines have had to be closed. These adjustments resulted in a 45.6 per cent loss in employment opportunities in the mining sector from 1989 to 1999 (SARB, 2000b). The opening up of the South African economy to international trade during the 1990s exposed a previously protected and inward-looking manufacturing industry to international competition. Rationalization, internationalization and the development of new markets resulted in an 18.3 per cent employment loss in manufacturing during the past decade. Concurrently job losses in the construction industry reached the high level of 43.9 per cent. High domestic interest rates and falling public sector investment in infrastructure explain this. Rationalization in the public sector with a view to improving the efficiency of government resulted in further substantial job losses. Approximately 102 000 jobs were lost in the public sector between 1989 and 1999 (SARB, 2000b).

Adjustments in the South African economy went hand in hand with the job losses. These adjustments led to the establishment of new industries, particularly in export industries and in information technology. Apart from the fact that South African statistics should be treated with caution in respect of observations at industry level (Statistics South Africa, 1999), there are primarily two reasons why these new industries have been unsuccessful in showing higher employment rates. The first is associated with the fact that the domestic labour market is characterized by a shortage of skilled people. We have already indicated above that unemployment is primarily among unskilled people. From a fiscal policy perspective this outcome of the analysis is rather disturbing because South Africa has gradually increased expenditure on education from 17.7 per cent of total expenditure in 1983 to 22 per cent in 1997. This means that the delivery system in education is ineffective and that fiscal policy as such can do little to address the problem. The ineffective education system is also demonstrated by the human quality index developed by Crafts (2000). It would appear that South Africa's human development index is falling short of that of its major trading partners. In 1995 the human development index for South Africa was 89 per cent of that in Latin America, 77 per cent of that in Australia and Western Europe and 76 per cent of that in North America. Moreover from 1950 to 1995 the human development index advanced much more slowly in South Africa than in Africa, East Asia and China. The second reason why new industries have been unsuccessful in employing more people is related to the rigid labour market. The rigidity of the domestic labour market is associated with centralized bargaining and unrealistic labour standards imposed by labour legislation (Barker, 1999). Moreover, high costs of hiring and dismissal are also important features of labour maket rigidity in South Africa. These non-wage costs have important inhibiting effects on employment creation (Black and Rankin, 1998). These cost-enhancing effects in respect of labour are notorious in encouraging a substitution of capital for labour as has been evident, for instance, in Chile (Edwards and Edwards, 2000). The Reserve Bank reported a rise of 60 per cent in the capital–labour ratio over the past decade which clearly confirms a substitution of capital for labour (SARB, 2000b). The high non-wage costs imposed by the new labour laws are inhibiting employment growth.

In summary, during recent years the South African economy has shown a poor performance in terms of economic growth as well as employment. Structural changes, the high cost of apartheid and economic disruptions from abroad were important factors in explaining this poor performance. There are, nevertheless, other important reasons that require a closer analysis. In order to conduct this analysis an exposition on growth factors is in order.

Recent research confirms that economic growth is determined or enhanced by several factors that appear to work simultaneously in order to achieve sustainable growth (Temple, 1999). Openness or international trade is an important growth factor (Edwards, 1998). Fixed investment, including government spending on infrastructure, human capital development in terms of education and health, coupled with effective macroeconomic stabilization policies are significant factors in determining economic growth. Factors that are robustly related to a poor growth performance include weak institutional structures, lack of depth of financial intermediation, political instability, wars, market distortions and rigidities, corruption and high income inequality. In an analysis of the relationship between economic growth and income inequality Aghion et al. (1999) came to the conclusion that, under conditions of imperfect capital markets, high income inequality has a negative effect on economic growth and that redistributive policies are likely to affect economic growth favourably.

An analysis of the effect of fiscal policy on these various factors, or the support for them from other government policies, would demonstrate how growth conducive fiscal policy has been over the period under consideration. The following aspects need to be considered: macroeconomic stabilization; openness of the economy; redistribution; human capital development; investment in infrastructure; and privatization.

We have already shown that, viewed from a macroeconomic stabilization perspective, South African fiscal policy should be regarded as very successful in the sense that, under the new government, the growth in current expenditure has been contained while budget deficits have been falling on a sustainable basis. This resulted in a flattening off in the government debt ratio. Moreover, these fiscal achievements have been supported by credible monetary policies. During recent years the inflation rate has fallen on a sustainable basis and the effectiveness of monetary policy has been enhanced through the introduction of inflation targeting procedures. Economic stabilization policies are well placed to support economic growth.

South Africa has been successful in opening up the economy to international trade. During the 1990s the domestic trade policies have changed radically from a protectionist and inward-looking approach towards an outward-looking approach coupled with trade liberalization. Since 1994 South Africa has reduced its protective tariffs and, with a few exceptions, the average weighted import tariffs are below the requirements of the WTO (Du Toit, 1998). Moreover, the openness of the economy, as measured by its trade ratio, has followed a sustained upward tendency since 1993. The downward tendency in this ratio, evident since 1980, has effectively been reversed. It is evident that the foreign trade policy has been supported by fiscal policy in creating an environment conducive to economic growth.

Fiscal policy under the new government has been explicitly concerned with the redistribution of income and expenditure in favour of the poor (see Heyns, 1995b). Unequal income distribution is a prominent feature of the South

African economy (McGrath, 1996). Moreover, the unequal income distribution has a strong racial dimension as is evident from the high Gini coefficient which remained unchanged from 1975 to 1991 (McGrath, 1996). This phenomenon is also evident from the fact that the share of income accruing to the poorest 40 per cent of households declined after 1975. By 1991 they earned less than 4 per cent of total income (McGrath, 1996). The different expenditure categories of the state budget have changed markedly since 1994. Defence expenditure has been reduced from 14.2 per cent of total expenditure in 1983 to 6.5 per cent in 1994 and 6 per cent in 1997. Expenditure on general public services has been reduced from a high of 12.7 per cent of total expenditure in 1994 to 8.2 per cent in 1997. Public expenditure in favour of agricultural support fell from almost 4 per cent to less than 1 per cent of total expenditure in 1997. Expenditure items that are contributing towards a more equal income distribution, such as health, have been maintained at previous levels. Health care has, nevertheless, been focusing more on primary health care since 1994. The previous health-care system tended to favour Whites (MERG, 1993). In similar vein expenditure on education has been increased from 17 per cent in 1984 to 22 per cent of total expenditure in 1997. The composition of the latter has changed in the sense that, prior to 1994, education expenditure was primarily aimed at White schools. MERG (1993) indicated that Whites received as much as 33 per cent of government spending on education in 1990. Social security is another component of expenditure, which has changed markedly in favour of a more equal income distribution. This category has increased from 6 per cent in the 1980s to almost 10 per cent of total expenditure in 1997. In his budget speech of 23 February 2000 the Minister of Finance summarized the progress of fiscal policy towards a reduction of inequality as follows. Apart from a highly progressive income tax system, government expenditure is gradually shifting towards supporting the poor. Approximately 57 per cent of government spending is aimed at the poorest 40 per cent of society. The share of government spending going to the top 20 per cent of income earners is less than 9 per cent. Moreover social spending on the poor increased by 34 per cent between 1993 and 1997 while per capita spending on the rich declined by more than 20 per cent. From this exposition it is evident that fiscal policy has changed significantly in favour of a more equal income distribution and in this respect it is conducive to growth.

From a human capital point of view we have already argued that fiscal policy is allocating respectable amounts of money towards education but the delivery system appears to be ineffective. Public policy is failing in respect of investment in human capital and South Africa's growth performance is inhibited in this respect. The employment-securing aspect of public policy is disappointing. It does not secure a stable supply of skilled people demanded by the new industries which are now evolving in the wake of major structural changes in the economy over the past decade. Economic growth is not supported by present policies regarding the development of human capital.

Investment in infrastructure by government appears to be an important element in the growth process. Apart from its direct contribution towards economic growth it also stimulates growth indirectly via favourable effects on gross domestic fixed investment in the private sector. Expenditure on economic infrastructure in real terms by government followed a rising trend during the 1960s and 1970s. This trend peaked in 1976. Thereafter it declined and by 1999 it was 47 per cent below its 1982 level. This fall in investment expenditure, measured in absolute numbers, is alarming. Fiscal policy has been ineffective in reversing the long-established decline in infrastructure investment. This element of fiscal policy appears to be particularly growth inhibiting, and it is not surprising that employment in the construction industry has declined in the past decade. Moreover, private sector investment growth has also been following a long-term downward trend since 1990.

Privatization or the selling of state-owned enterprises has been an important means, in developed as well as in emerging markets, of reducing the share of government in the economy. In emerging markets it has proved to be an important means of enhancing foreign direct investment. It is also an effective means of international technology transfer. Privatization could be an important element through which fiscal policy could support the growth process. The potential for privatization in South Africa is considerable. For years the government expanded its commercial activities. It went hand in hand with investment in electricity supply, in transport, in telecommunications, in broadcasting, in forestry, in water supply, in the postal services and in the arms industry (see Du Toit, 1988).

When the new government announced its intention in 1994 of privatizing state assets, its policy appeared to be consistent with its outward-looking approach. Unfortunately privatization has been conducted half-heartedly and the process has been delayed in order to satisfy the socialist aims of the labour federation Cosatu and the South African Communist Party, the political partners of the present government. As indicated by Du Toit (1998) the privatization process, measured in terms of proceeds, is significantly smaller in South Africa than in other emerging market countries. Between 1994 and 2000 the sale of assets by government through privatization amounted to R8 600 million (SAF, 2000). This is approximately 5 per cent of the estimated value of state corporations in South Africa.

The lack of performance in the area of privatization has deprived fiscal policy of opportunities to become more flexible through the release of tied-up resources. Furthermore, the allocation of privatization proceeds towards debt relief could be an important means of relieving the budget from high interest payments. Privatization could also be an effective instrument in supporting the government's outward-looking trade policies, for it has proved to be an effective method of obtaining foreign direct investment and the transfer of technology to emerging markets in Eastern Europe. The poor performance of fiscal policy on this score has inhibited economic growth.

In sum, fiscal policy appeared to be expansionary and in many instances not supportive of monetary policy during apartheid. The phrase fiscal discipline featured prominently in budget speeches during this period (see Horwood, 1980). It would appear that fiscal discipline was achieved by cutting back on investment in infrastructure. In the new political dispensation fiscal policy developed elements that were conducive to economic growth. It proved to be an effective stabilization instrument while contributing to more equal income distribution. Unfortunately fiscal policy, and public policy in particular, has failed to support employment creation as a result of rigid labour market policies and ineffective human development policies. Fiscal policy has also inhibited economic growth through a lack of investment in infrastructure and the poor performance in respect of privatization. All in all, fiscal policy has probably failed to support economic growth over the period under review.

3.6   THE NEW POLICY FRAMEWORK (GEAR)

The South African government conducts its macroeconomic policies in terms of an integrated strategy referred to as GEAR, that is, Growth, Employment and Redistribution. This policy document which was released in 1996 (RSA, 1996) does not carry the full support of government's political partners, the labour federation Cosatu and the South African Communist Party. The major objectives of GEAR are to achieve sustainable economic growth coupled with the creation of employment at a rate of 270 000 new jobs by the year 2000. The original growth target was a real GDP growth rate of 6 per cent by the year 2000. In 1998 the government launched the Medium Term Expenditure Framework, according to which revisions and forward planning of fiscal policy were made three years ahead. In terms of the revisions reported in the budget speech of 23 February 2000, a real GDP growth rate of 3.4 per cent on average is envisaged for the coming three years. In order to achieve these closely related targets (as analysed above) the following strategies were envisaged in the GEAR document.

Fiscal reforms were aimed at budget deficit reductions to such an extent that, in terms of current projections, the budget deficit should be 2.2 per cent of GDP in 2002. Fiscal policy was to concentrate more on redistribution. Privatization through the selling of state assets featured prominently in GEAR. Infrastructure investment growth was envisaged to reach an average of 2.4 per cent in 2000. Closely related to these fiscal reforms the government envisaged the development of a flexible labour market together with skills development programmes to encourage job creation.

Monetary policy objectives were to maintain a stringent policy in order to reduce inflation. With the introduction of inflation targeting in 2000, the government agreed on an inflation target of 3 to 6 per cent, which was to be achieved by 2002. Growth targets for M3 have not been achieved.

The opening up of the economy, the liberalization of international trade and international economic cooperation were high on the GEAR agenda. While the government has been successful in opening up the economy through tariff reductions and reform, trade agreements and regional economic cooperation have also been expanded since 1994. The openness of the economy, measured in terms of its trade ratio, followed a declining tendency from 1981 to 1992. This was reversed after 1993.

In terms of the GEAR targets, fiscal policy has been successful in reducing the share of government current expenditure as a percentage of GDP. The budget deficit has been a consistently lower percentage of GDP since 1994 and the debt ratio has started to flatten out since 1996. The public sector borrowing requirement, as a percentage of GDP, has declined markedly since 1998. Unfortunately government has been unsuccessful in reversing its dissaving pattern and on this score it has been unable to meet the GEAR target of positive government saving. Fiscal policy has been unsuccessful in achieving the GEAR targets in terms of privatization. This has affected economic growth adversely because South Africa missed opportunities of direct foreign investment and the transfer of international technologies. Fiscal policy has in itself made a contribution towards investment in human capital in view of the relatively large share of education expenditure in total outlays. The lack of support for public policy has, no doubt, been a significant factor in the government's failure to achieve the GEAR targets.

Fiscal policy has definitely failed to achieve the GEAR targets in respect of investment in infrastructure. The government has been unable to reverse the decline that has taken place since 1977. This disappointing performance is an important factor in explaining the failure to achieve sustained high growth rates in South Africa. The failure to achieve the GEAR targets in respect of economic growth and employment is strongly related to the rigid labour market conditions that the present government has instituted. The prohibitive regulations coupled with excessive cost in the hiring and dismissal of people are notorious for their devastating effects on employment. The labour market rigidities appear to be typically insider–outsider phenomena and apart from their inhibiting effect on employment, they are discouraging both domestic and foreign direct investment.

The outcome of this exposition is that the government has been unable to meet its economic growth targets. Similarly, its policies were not conducive to employment creation. The government has been successful in establishing respectable macroeconomic stabilization policies that have reduced the inflation rate in a meaningful way while addressing excessive current government spending. There has been progress in the redistribution of income through government spending and taxation. Furthermore, the government has been successful in opening up the economy and in its efforts to replace the inward-looking trade policies with an outward-looking approach. The failure of government to comply with the overall GEAR strategy is partly explained by its inability to perform in the area of upgrading human quality. The lack of human quality in this country is impacting negatively not only on economic growth but also on employment. The unemployed are to a significant extent unskilled people. The next major reason why the GEAR strategy is unsuccessful is the failure to invest in the infrastructure. Dithering over privatization has added to the problems. We appreciate that the government has made progress in terms of macroeconomic stabilization and the redistribution of income, but the government's obsession with stabilization and redistribution is unlikely to assist it in achieving the GEAR policy targets. Fiscal policy has to shift to a more growth-orientated strategy with privatization and infrastructure investment. A reform of the labour market in the direction of greater flexibility is imperative. Sustainable high growth rates are unlikely to be achieved as long as we maintain these rigidities. Finally, public policy needs to be reversed in terms of the development of human capital. On this score there appears to be an important contradiction between fiscal and public policy in the sense that the budget allocates substantial funds towards education but the delivery system is failing. The elimination of this contradiction is imperative if a high sustainable economic growth rate is to be achieved.

3.7   SUMMARY

This exposition on economic policy concentrated on monetary and fiscal policies while taking cognizance of other elements of public policy that were conducive to the achievement of the aims of these policies. We associated monetary and fiscal policies with the two aims, namely price stability (or the containment of inflation) and economic growth. Moreover, economic growth is closely associated with employment. The analysis was concerned with the effectiveness of two policies in achieving the two aims indicated above. International developments in respect of these policies have had a definite effect on the evolution of macroeconomic policies in South Africa and we integrated these developments into the analysis. Monetary policy evolved from a non-market and interventionist policy that was characterized by several contradicting elements and inefficiencies towards a market-orientated system. The implementation of monetary policy was complicated by institutional rigidities and a lack of a democratic political framework to support a fully-fledged market-orientated system. After the first democratic election in 1994 monetary policy and its institutional framework developed rapidly. Monetary policy contributed towards controlling the rate of inflation during this period. Finally, in 2000, monetary policy opted in favour of inflation targeting which signalled an important shift in policy making in the sense that government announces the targets. Furthermore, this approach recognizes the importance of cost-push factors in the inflation process and the fact that they are beyond the control mechanism of monetary policy.

Fiscal policy developed more independently of monetary policy over the period under consideration in the sense that the close relationship between the two policies that characterized the earlier part of the period became less evident during later years. This is evident from the fact that fiscal policy started developing its own target framework. In South Africa these targets were concerned with budget deficits, the tax burden, the public sector saving ratio and the public debt ratio. During the early part of the period under consideration fiscal policy appeared to be expansionary in terms of current expenditure. A major reason for this was the high demand of the costly apartheid system on the resources of the country. Fiscal policy started featuring more effectively as a macroeconomic stabilization instrument under the new political dispensation. Our analysis shows that fiscal policy has also been instrumental in changing the unequal income distribution pattern in this country during recent years. From a growth point of view fiscal policy has been ineffective in supporting a sustainable high growth rate. Several reasons are responsible for this failure on the part of fiscal policy, particularly within the GEAR policy framework. These reasons were analysed and the outcome of the exposition is that fiscal policy appears to be too obsessed with stabilization and redistribution to stage an effective economic growth policy.

REFERENCES

Aghion, P., Caroli, E. and García-Peñalosa, C. (1999), 'Inequality and economic growth: the perspective of the new growth theories', *Journal of Economic Literature*, **37**: 1615-60.

Barker, F.S. (1999), 'On South African labour policies', *South African Journal of Economics*, **63**: 307-31.

Black, P.A. and Rankin, N. (1998), 'On the cost-increasing effects of the new labour laws in South Africa', *South African Journal of Economics*, **66**: 452-63.

Britton, A. (1991), *Macroeconomic Policy in Britain 1974-87*, Cambridge: Cambridge University Press.

Browne, G.W.G. (1983), 'Fifty years of public finance', *South African Journal of Economics*, **1**: 143–73.

Bruggemans, C. (2000a), 'The inaugural address of Dr. Chris Stals', *Weekly Comment*, 28 August, http://www.fnb.co.za/economics.

Bruggemans, C. (2000b), 'A high octane global economy', *Weekly Comment*, 23 August, http://www.fnb.co.za/economics.

Crafts, N. (2000), *'Globalization and growth in the twentieth century'*, IMF Working Paper WP/00/44.

De Kock, G.P.C. (1980), 'The new South African business cycle and its implications for monetary policy', *South African Journal of Economics*, **48**: 349–58.

De Kock Commission (1985), *Final Report of the Commission of Inquiry into the Monetary System and Monetary Policy in South Africa*, RP.70/1984, Pretoria: Government Printer.

Dos Santos, T. and Schaling, E. (2000), 'Inflation targeting in South Africa', Johannesburg: Department of Economics Research Paper, Rand Afrikaans University.

Du Toit, J. (1998), *The Structure of the South African Economy*, Halfway House: Southern, 2nd edition.

Edwards, S. (1998), 'Openness, productivity growth: what do we really know?', *Economic Journal*, **108**: 383–98.

Edwards, S. and Edwards, A.C. (2000), 'Economic reforms and labour markets: policy issues and lessons from Chile', http://www.anderson.ucla.edu/faculty/sebastian.edwards.

Goedhuys, D.W. (1994), 'South African monetary policy in the 1980s' years of reform and foreign finance aggression', *South African Journal of Economic History*, **9** (2): 145–64.

Heyns, J. v.d. S. (1994), 'South African tax policy in the 1980s', *South African Journal of Economic History*, **9**: 165–83.

Heyns, J. v.d. S. (1995a), 'The dimension of government saving in South African fiscal policy', *South African Journal of Economics*, **63**: 307–31.

Heyns, J. v.d. S. (1995b), 'Equity and redistribution in South Africa: some fiscal federalism perspectives', *South African Journal of Economics*, **63**: 150–72.

Horwood, O.P.F. (1980), 'Die Huidige Fiskale en Monetêre Beleid in Suid-Afrika' [The Present Fiscal and Monetary Policy in South Africa], *South African Journal of Economics*, **48**: 359–69.

Macroeconomic Research Group (MERG) (1993), *Making Democracy Work: A Framework for Macroeconomic Policy in South Africa*, Belleville: Centre For Development Studies.

Mboweni, T.T. (2000) Address Delivered at the Diplomatic Forum, Rand Afrikaans University, http://www.resbank.co.za.

McGrath, M. (1996), 'Income inequality and poverty in South Africa', in Maasdorp, G. (ed.), *Can South and Southern Africa become Globally Competitive Economies?*, London: Macmillan: 69–78.

Meijer, J.H. (1976), 'Monetary policy: principles and South African issues', in Truu, M.L. (ed.), *Public Policy and the South African Economy: Essays in Memory of Desmond Hobart Houghton*, Cape Town: Oxford University Press: 143–64.

Meijer, J.H. (1984/85), 'Monetary policy in South Africa: notes on the new monetary control system', *Finance and Trade Review*, **15**: 1–22.

Meijer, J.H. (1995), 'Monetary policy and the instruments of monetary policy', in Falkena, H.B., Fourie, L.J. and Kok, W.J. (eds), *The South African Financial System*,

Halfway House: Southern: 333–433.

Moll, P.G. (2000), 'The demand for money in South Africa: parameter stability and predictive capacity', *South African Journal of Economics*, **68**: 190–211.

Republic of South Africa (RSA) (1996), *Growth Employment and Redistribution: A Macroeconomic Strategy*, Pretoria: Republic of South Africa.

Schaling, E. and Schoeman, C. (2000), '*Foreign exchange market intervention in South Africa during the Asian contagion: leaning against the wind or causing a hurricane?*' Johannesburg: Department of Economics Research Paper, Rand Afrikaans University.

South African Foundation (SAF) (2000), *Perspective*, Spring, Johannesburg: SAF.

South African Reserve Bank (SARB) (1998), *Annual Economic Report 1998*, Pretoria: SARB.

South African Reserve Bank (SARB) (1999), 'Seventy-ninth ordinary general meeting of shareholders', http://www.resbank.co.za.

South African Reserve Bank (SARB) (2000a), 'Governor's address at the eightieth ordinary general meeting of shareholders', http://www.resbank.co.za.

South African Reserve Bank (SARB) (2000b), *Annual Economic Report 2000*, Pretoria: SARB.

Stals, C.L. (2000), 'A macroeconomic model for the implementation of monetary policy: inaugural address', Johannesburg, Rand Afrikaans University.

Statistics South Africa (1999), *October Household Survey*, 4 November, http://www.statssa.gov.za.

Statistics South Africa (2000), *October Household Survey*, 3 July, http://www.statssa.gov.za

Strydom, P.D.F. (1974), 'Monetary legislation in South Africa: an analysis', *South African Journal of Economics*, **42**: 1–11.

Strydom, P.D.F. (1976), 'Inflation in South Africa 1: Institutional aspects', *South African Journal of Economics*, **44**: 115–38.

Strydom, P.D.F. (1986), 'A critical assessment of the equilibrium approach to the rate of exchange', *South African Journal of Economics*, **54**: 55–65.

Strydom, P.D.F. (1995), 'Liberalising foreign trade: the interaction between the real and monetary sectors', *Investment Analyst Journal*, **41**: 37–47.

Strydom, P.D.F. (2000), 'Inflation targeting: some critical observations', http:/www.fnb.co.za/economics.

Strydom, P.D.F. and Koopmans, A.J.G. (1974), 'Monetary policy in South Africa', *Finance and Trade Review*, **11**: 1–46.

Temple, J. (1999), 'The new growth evidence', *Journal of Economic Literature*, **37**: 112–56.

United Bank (1991), *Economic Perspective: The Expected Stance and Impulse of Monetary Policy in 1991*, Johannesburg: United Bank.

4. Agriculture, 1970–2000

Nick Vink and Stefan Schirmer

4.1 INTRODUCTION

Dramatic transformations occurred in South African agriculture during the period from 1970 to 2000. Government policies towards farmers shifted in a number of ways, farmers' characteristics changed, labour relations on the farms were transformed and the sector as a whole became more efficient than it had ever been before. The details of these changes are often still only vaguely understood and much research remains to be done in this field. This chapter draws on existing research to outline some of the broader patterns of change that occurred from 1970 to 2000.

4.2 THE POLITICAL ECONOMY OF CONTROL OVER AGRICULTURE: THE 1970s

Four events between 1973 and 1976 created a security crisis in South Africa that was serious enough to threaten what Terreblanche (1998, p. 37) calls the 'accumulation and legitimation aims of the white hegemonic order'. These were the 'unlawful' strikes by Black trade unions in the Durban region in 1973; the OPEC (Organization of Petroleum-Exporting Countries) oil crisis of 1973; the *coup d'état* in Lisbon in April 1974 that resulted in the abortive invasion of Angola by South Africa in 1975; and the Soweto unrest of June 1976. Desperate attempts by the ruling elite to prolong the existing order lasted for no more than 20 years after these events, and were doomed to failure.

  By 1976 (coinciding with the Soweto unrest) the economy had moved into a serious recession caused by the OPEC oil-price hikes and a global slowdown in growth. However, South Africa's recession turned into a period of prolonged stagflation that lasted until 1994. Terreblanche (1998) shows that, over time, the National Party had shifted from an exclusive focus on the interests of the Afrikaners (the eras of Prime Ministers Malan and Strydom) to a broader focus on the interests of Whites (the latter days of Prime Ministers Verwoerd and the Vorster period). However, after the crisis events of the early

1970s the era of the 'Total Strategy' was ushered in by P.W. Botha's regime, ostensibly to protect the continued existence of all South Africans against what was elsewhere called the evil empire. One concrete result in South Africa was a doubling of the defence budget from 2.4 per cent of GDP in 1971/72 to 4.8 per cent in 1977/78.

The shift towards urban interests had important implications for agriculture. Increased defence and education spending resulted in a radical cut in the budget of the Department of Agriculture from 1.5 per cent to only 0.6 per cent of GDP. However, an increasing part of the total agricultural budget was allocated to the homeland governments, with the result that White farmers got a smaller and smaller proportion of the available funds (Vink and Kassier, 1991). The fact that the government was unable (and perhaps also unprepared) to maintain the high level of subsidies for agriculture has traditionally been regarded as an important reason for the split in the National Party in February 1982 and the creation of the Conservative Party under Dr Andries Treurnicht.

The South African economy grew at above 5 per cent per annum to 1970 and above 3 per cent to 1980, both well above population growth rates during this period. Real per capita incomes declined, however, after 1974. The economy was characterized by a number of negative features that have been ascribed to apartheid and bad economic policies (Kritzinger-van Niekerk et al., 1992). The most important in terms of their impact on agriculture were the rise in the inflation rate from the early 1970s (Moll, 1993) and increasing concentration in the agro-industrial complex. The latter was largely a result of industrialization through import substitution (see, for example, Board of Tariffs and Trade, 1992; Brand et al., 1992; Kassier Report, 1992). By the beginning of the 1980s these distortionary influences on prices, together with a range of farm-specific policies, had created an agricultural sector that desperately needed to be reformed (Kassier and Groenewald, 1992).

The main structural features of the agricultural economy during this era were the mechanization of field crop harvesting in commercial farming, increased pressure on food production in the homelands, tight control over the marketing of agricultural products under the consolidated Marketing Act of 1968, the shift away from a small-farmer-friendly policy in commercial agriculture, and attempts to address the environmental consequences of agricultural policies.

4.2.1   Capital and Labour in Agriculture

The experience in the commercial maize farming areas illustrates an important trend in capital and labour substitution in the agricultural economy as a whole (Van Zyl et al., 1987). The total number of farm employees grew to 1970, and then fell between 1970 and 1980. Despite the decline in the latter period, farm employment was higher in 1980 than it had been in 1950. More detailed analyses of farms in the maize-producing areas show a turning point around 1970, with the growth rate in employees per 1000 ha dropping faster than that per 1000 ha cultivated land in the 1970–85 period as compared to 1945–70. This turning point around 1970 is graphically illustrated by De Klerk (1983), who showed that while 16 per cent of the maize crop was harvested with combine harvesters in 1968, this had increased to 81 per cent by 1977. The area planted to maize increased from 1945 to 1970 as tractors were introduced on a large scale. This increased the demand for labour to harvest the bigger crop. When combines were introduced from the late 1960s, the demand for labour fell and farmers increasingly made use of temporary or seasonal labourers, most of whom were women and children (Marcus, 1989). While not unrelated to changing employment patterns on the farms, the state's decision to ban the labour tenant system and to destroy Black settlements in areas designated as White contributed in their own right to the rapid overcrowding in areas designated as Black.

4.2.2 Food Production in the Homelands

Homeland consolidation and Trust land purchases occurred throughout the 1970s but could not curb the related processes of overcrowding and agricultural decline. In this context, government intervention in homeland agriculture was mainly directed towards physical 'betterment planning' and administrative control (De Wet, 1987). Despite a real improvement in the standard of living of homeland households able to access wage incomes, a growing number of households became increasingly destitute as they could find neither jobs nor arable land (Simkins, 1981). By 1985 homeland production defined as non-market or subsistence contributed a measly average of R171 per annum to households budgets and agricultural earnings were a mere 10 per cent of total household earnings (Cobbett, 1987). The absence of commercial farming in the homelands was ascribed by the state to a lack of managerial and entrepreneurial ability among Black farmers, despite a long history of evidence to the contrary and the continued existence of pockets of enterprise and accumulation (Bundy, 1979, Matsetela, 1981, Surplus People Project, 1984). This served to justify the use of public institutions and expatriate management to 'develop' agriculture, resulting in large-scale centrally managed projects with little or no community participation. In a later adaptation, some of these schemes were adjusted to settle selected labourers as 'project farmers' under the control of central management. The farmer settlement approach became the mainstay of agricultural development efforts in these areas in the 1970s and early 1980s (Van Rooyen et al., 1987).

The original Marketing Act of 1937 was revised, and the subsequent amendments were consolidated into a new act in 1968. By this time, control over marketing throughout the supply chain was almost complete. For example, under the Wheat Scheme millers and bakers had to be registered with the Wheat Board, their only supplier. The Wheat Board set prices between the farmer and the Board, the Board and the miller, the miller and baker and the retail price. All prices were pan-territorial and pan-seasonal. Bakers were licensed in terms of the quantity, shape, geography and price of bread and other products that they sold. Similar controls existed in virtually all other branches of the agricultural sector.

4.2.3   The Bias towards Large Farmers

After gaining power in 1948 the National Party had placed particular emphasis on assisting poorer White farmers by, for example, pushing up the prices set within the marketing system (Lazar, 1987). Throughout the 1950s the government sustained its commitment to keeping these farmers on the land. This commitment culminated in a Commission of Enquiry set up in 1957 to discover new ways to halt the depopulation of the countryside (Union of South Africa, 1960b). However, by the time the Commission published its report in 1960 changes were beginning to take place within government attitudes towards keeping poorer, invariably smaller farmers on the land. Although the report had made numerous recommendations on how to stop the weaker White farmers from losing their land, the only recommendation that received serious consideration was the one that opposed land subdivisions. This recommendation, which was later taken up by the Du Plessis Commission of 1962/63 and culminated in the 1970 Sub-division of Land Act, reflected a growing bias within the state against small farms (Lipton, 1986). This changing attitude within government circles coincided with a substantial shrinkage in White-owned farm numbers and a concomitant increase in the average farm size.

4.2.4   Soil Conservation

Changes in the state's approach to soil conservation also manifested themselves in the 1970s. Officials began in the 1960s to reduce the independence of soil conservation committees and to centralize the inspection and enforcement of soil conservation practices. Inspection tours were undertaken and attempts were made to train district committee members, but by 1968 the Board was still not satisfied with its ability to control these committees. To achieve more centralized control, a formal Inspectorate was established by means of the Soil Conservation Amendment Act of 1969. This act allowed policies to be implemented from within the Department of Agriculture and gave greater scope for forcing farmers to adopt certain practices (Delius and Schirmer, 2000). However, while these moves might have increased the effectiveness of the soil conservation bureaucracy, the continuation in the 1970s with a broader policy of subsidizing the maize price effectively promoted overproduction and the ploughing up of unsuitable land. Soil erosion and low yields remained serious problems in the 1970s. Nevertheless, successes were achieved and fears that soil erosion was continuing unabated were exaggerated. During the period from 1982 to 1988, dry weather probably reduced the value of field crops by nearly half their previous value. Grazing lands also deteriorated and it was reported in 1991 that no less than 60 per cent of the country's grazing was in poor condition (De Klerk, 1991). Falling prices for grazing land lent support to the argument that there was some deterioration, but recent findings suggest that very little permanent degradation of commercial grazing land had taken place. By the late 1990s most areas were not permanently degraded and some areas had actually improved (Hoffman and Todd, 2000).

In an earlier review, Vink (1999) concluded that for the agricultural sector the 1970s represent the confluence of a number of different trends. These include the expected and unexpected consequences of heavy direct state intervention in the sector; the consequences of apartheid policies for Black farmers – access to land and their influence on the price of farm labour; and the increasing financial and environmental cost of intervention in the sector. In this sense the decade represents the end of an era, leading in the early 1980s to a process of deregulation that has left South African farmers with levels of state support that are as low as their counterparts in Australia and New Zealand, traditionally low subsidizing countries.

Agricultural policy in the period up to the late 1970s can thus be characterized as a combination of segregation of land ownership and a two-track approach to access to support services. This had a number of major effects on the farming sector as a whole. First, it resulted in extraordinary institutional duplication with attendant high fiscal cost (Vink and Kassier, 1991; Lipton, 1993). South Africa ended up with 11 agricultural departments by 1980 (14 by 1984) and with internal barriers to trade in farm commodities through duplication of control over marketing. Second, it created 'two agricultures' (Lipton, 1977) which differed in access to land and support services, productivity, and so on. Third, it created the anomaly of a country that regularly exported food 'surpluses' while most of the population lived well below minimum levels of living. In addition, the food self-sufficiency index showed exports of field crops and imports of red meat while the country has a poor arable resource base (McKenzie et al., 1989). Fourth, there was much evidence of severe environmental damage to fragile land resources in both the commercial farming areas and the homelands (McKenzie et al., 1989). Fifth, the combination of subsidies and distorted prices led to high rates of growth in farmland prices. By the beginning of the 1980s the farm sector had become inflexible and it has been argued that these farm policies made the sector particularly vulnerable to the disastrous drought that struck the subcontinent in the early 1980s (Van Zyl and Groenewald, 1988). Sixth, the processes of forced removals and homeland consolidation created a high level of uncertainty among individual farmers, both Black and White, as to the protection of existing property rights, with predictable economic consequences in some of the ecologically most vulnerable parts of the country.

4.3   THE 1980s: A TIME OF CHANGE

South African farm policy changed emphatically in the period around 1980, although some of the policy shifts were initially quite gradual. Vink (1993) has demonstrated that the process started outside the sector itself. First, starting in the late 1970s the South African financial sector was extensively liberalized following the publication of the De Kock Commission Report (1985). The most immediate effect on agriculture came from changes in the external value of the currency and in the interest cost of farm borrowing. As the rand started a decade-long decline in value, farm input prices, which have a relatively large import component, rose faster than farm output prices. As part of the financial sector reforms the reserve requirements of the banking sector were changed, making it impossible for the Land Bank to continue subsidizing farmers' interest rates. The use of interest rate policy by the Reserve Bank saw interest rates rise to very high levels during the widespread drought of 1983/84. Interest rapidly became the single largest cost of production in agriculture. Second, many of the existing controls over the movement of labour in South Africa were lifted by the mid-1980s, setting in motion vast population movement from the farms and the homelands to the towns and cities (Urban Foundation, 1991). This was accompanied by migration of people from most parts of Southern Africa to the rural and urban areas of South Africa. Third, considerable microeconomic deregulation took place, also starting in the late 1970s and early 1980s and leading to a significant increase in activity in the informal economy (Kirsten, 1988; May and Schacter 1991, Moll, 1993). One of the most visible effects was the increase in informal marketing of farm products in the urban areas (for example, Karaan and Myburgh, 1992).

In the midst of these economic transformations farmers confronted climatic challenges that rank alongside the late 1920s and early 1930s as the most difficult in the twentieth century. Initially, the state did not leave White farmers to deal with these circumstances alone. The state provided farmers with debt consolidation subsidies that added up to R344 million between 1981 and 1987. The state disbursed crop production loans worth R470 million, paid interest on consolidated debts, issued drought relief worth R120 million and provided farmers with subsidies to convert maize fields on marginal land into planted pastures. The state also stood as guarantor of consolidated debts to the value of R900 million. It is possible that this assistance allowed almost half of South Africa's White farmers to survive on the land (De Klerk, 1991).

By this time, however, the state was not simply concerned to keep Whites on the land. Within the existing framework of support, the state undertook policy shifts designed to improve the efficiency and viability of agriculture, largely in the interest of fiscal sustainability. The problem started in 1981 because the record maize harvests of that year meant that the government had to pay the sum of R0.5 billion to export the surplus at low prices while paying farmers the price set by the Maize Board (Lipton, 1996). The drought that followed led to larger problems. At a time of increasing fiscal pressure the government thus found itself having to provide massive transfers to farmers both when natural conditions were favourable and when they were unfavourable.

In response to this situation the White Paper on Agricultural Policy issued in 1984 argued that 'orderly marketing' was a positive factor only if the forces of supply and demand were taken into consideration. It was regarded as desirable to keep a substantial number of White farmers on the land but these were to be financially sound farmers able to improve the soil and to participate 'optimally' in international markets (Williams et al., 1998). The desire to keep inefficient farmers on the land had declined during the 1960s and 1970s and was even weaker in the 1980s as the government faced numerous economic and political threats to its survival.

In 1985, the Minister of Agriculture refused to approve a further increase in the producer price of maize and in 1987 the government stopped new subsidies to the maize price. Uniform and guaranteed prices were maintained but had to be paid for from the revenues of the Maize Board, which would therefore have to fix prices in accordance with projected market conditions rather than estimated costs of production. Producers now had to fund any losses incurred on the export of surplus grain. The reduction of indiscriminate subsidies also led, inevitably, to a degree of decentralization within the marketing process. State policy thus succeeded in putting pressure on farmers to become more competitive. At the same time the state gave farmers the support that allowed them to survive through difficult times.

These examples illustrate the general trend towards deregulation and liberalization within the existing framework of the Marketing Act. Other examples include the elimination of restrictive registration of processors in the red meat industry; the abolition of most controls on domestic marketing of deciduous and citrus fruit; the abolition of production quotas in the wine industry; deregulation of the grain sorghum and leaf tobacco single channels;

further envisaged deregulation of the mohair and maize schemes; and the eventual abolition of some control schemes, particularly in the banana, wool, egg and chicory industries. The main effect of these steps was to decrease the scope for micro-management in most of the subsectors in agriculture. The report of the Kassier Committee can be regarded as a milestone in this process.

Other important policy shifts included a change in tax treatment of agriculture, a shift to the farmer support philosophy in the homelands away from estate-type farming schemes and the tariffication of farm commodities, mainly as a result of the pressures arising from the Uruguay Round of the General Agreement on Tariffs and Trade (GATT).

4.4   ENTERING A PERIOD OF RADICAL CHANGE: THE 1990s

Deregulation and liberalization were a fact of life in the agricultural sector of South Africa during the 1980s.[1] That process was, however, characterized by change within an existing institutional structure, as the main role players involved in the sector remained in place despite the general relaxation in state intervention. This changed with the election of the Government of National Unity in 1994, although in agriculture at least some direct policy changes had to wait until 1996, that is, until after the withdrawal of the National Party from the Government of National Unity. The most important policy initiatives taken subsequent to this time included land reform, institutional restructuring in the public sector, the promulgation of new legislation, including the Marketing of Agricultural Products Act and the Water Act, trade policy and labour market policy reform. The purpose of these policy reforms was to correct the injustices of past policy, principally through land reform, to get the agricultural sector on a less capital-intensive growth path and to enhance the international competitiveness of the sector.

While the 1980s saw a state that continued to help White farmers cope with the challenges provided by markets and nature, the 1990s witnessed a wholesale withdrawal of this assistance. By 1997 all of the control boards, for example, had ceased to function, and all domestic agricultural markets, with the sole exception of sugar, had been fully deregulated. Government subsidies to commercial farmers had also virtually ceased. A prominent feature of this process was the extent to which it was undertaken in isolation from agricultural interest groups, in contrast to the close cooperation that had existed with commercial farm lobby groups in earlier times.

While the strong influence of agricultural interest groups on the policies formulated by previous governments led to fiscal waste and inefficiency, the lack of cooperation in the formulation of post-1994 policies produced different kinds of problems. It meant that the state was unable to draw directly on real experiences in the formulation and implementation of policy, nor could the state make people feel part of the policy process and thereby ensure their support. The lack of consultation also provoked knee-jerk opposition from groups who might otherwise have been induced to be more supportive. Lastly, the lack of interest groups that have an influence at the level of the state means that there has been little pressure on the government to deliver on its promises. These problems have been reflected in the progress of the various initiatives launched as part of the pre-1999 Land Reform Programme.

4.4.1 Land Reform

The Department of Land Affairs, successor to the Department of Regional and Land Affairs, completed the process of land reform policy design with its White Paper (RSA, 1997) while implementation of the programme had started in 1994. Land reform was to consist of the land restitution, the redistribution and the tenure reform programmes. Dissatisfaction, especially with aspects of the redistribution programme, resulted in a redesign of the programme during 2000.

The land issue has always played a central role in the struggle for democracy in South Africa, and one of the first steps after 2 February 1990 was the repeal of racially based land legislation. The debate gained momentum with a 1992 workshop in Swaziland where the World Bank brought together various groups from South Africa as well as scholars and practitioners from other countries in Southern Africa and elsewhere (published as World Bank, 1993). The next milestone was the rural restructuring study of the World Bank, presented at the 'Options for land reform' conference of the Department of Economics and Planning of the African National Congress in Johannesburg in 1993.

These 'options' included a proposal by the Development Bank of Southern Africa (DBSA) for equity-sharing projects, and a wide range of these have subsequently been implemented. The first of these projects to be implemented, the DBSA-funded Whitehall Project, was formally evaluated at an early stage (Eckert et al., 1996).

A large proportion of the analytical work that supported the policy positions taken during these debates was subsequently published in Van Zyl et al. (1996). More recently, the debate has shifted to progress with the implementation of the land reform programme (Plewman et al., 1995; Department of Land Affairs, 1997; Hall, 1998; Kirsten et al., 1996; Kirsten and Van Zyl, 1999; Graham and Lyne, 1999).

International experience has shown that market-assisted land redistribution programmes tend to perform better than those administered by the public sector. Reliance on the market mechanism stems from the observed weakness of non-market-orientated programmes that typically vest too much control in public sector bureaucracies, which tend to develop their own set of interests that are often in conflict with the rapid redistribution of land. None the less, a well-functioning land market is not a sufficient condition for the subdivision of large, mechanized and relatively inefficient farms into smaller family farms, specifically where economic and institutional distortions favour large farms. Therefore, non-market interventions in the form of grants and post-settlement support are necessary. Executing land reform through grants or vouchers to beneficiary groups who buy from willing sellers also obviates the need for a land reform/settlement agency, and thus reduces the opportunities for bureaucratic rent seeking. The cost and delays of expropriation proceedings are also avoided.

In South Africa, a pilot land reform programme was designed, more or less in accordance with the guidelines of the market-assisted approach. In practice, however, beneficiary households usually had to pool their meagre grants in order to buy land from a willing seller. The reason was at least partly due to the fact that the Subdivision of Agricultural Land Act (Act 70 of 1970) has yet to be repealed, which would have enabled the subdivision of farms into affordable pieces of land.

The Department of Land Affairs has spent a lot of time and effort in mobilizing communities and assisting them in accessing government grants to acquire land. However, the Department's own research shows that, in most cases, farms financed with land grants and settled by groups of households, were too small to support all of the beneficiaries as full-time farmers. Thus, a new approach to land reform has been proposed after extensive consultation and planning during the course of last year (RSA, 2000). In providing for an extended scale of grants, dependent on an increasing own contribution, it fits directly with the new vision of the ministry to benefit the rural poor and to assist in the establishment of a class of commercial black farmers. This initiative will, however, also fail unless efforts to implement the programme are well planned and well coordinated, unless support services for agriculture are in place to provide the environment for a vibrant and successful agricultural sector, and unless the problem of bureaucratic centralization is addressed.

4.4.2   Institutional Restructuring in the Public Sector

One of the main features of South African agricultural policy in the 1990s was the extent of institutional restructuring that took place. There were generally three reasons for these processes. Some institutions (for example, the

Development Bank, the Land Bank, the Agricultural Research Council, the Department of Regional and Land Affairs, the development corporations in the former homelands, and so on) were believed to be too closely aligned with apartheid policies aimed at 'development' of the former homeland areas or at favouring commercial farmers (see, for example, Callear and Mthethwa, 1996 and DBSA/LAPC, 1997). Such institutions were subjected to restructuring programmes aimed at realigning them to a new mandate in support of the development priorities of the new government.

In the second case, the public sector agencies supporting the agricultural sector were subjected to the same processes of 'provincialization', which came about with the adoption of the Interim Constitution. In the case of agriculture, the former 'own' and 'general affairs' departments were amalgamated to form the core of the new National Department of Agriculture, there was a redeployment of functions and staff from the former homeland departments of agriculture to the new National Department and to the new provincial departments. During this process a change was also effected in the relationship between the national and provincial departments of agriculture and farmer lobby groups.[2]

In the third instance, agricultural institutions in the public sector were reorientated to fit in with new policy directions. The most radical of these changes occurred in the changes to agricultural marketing policy (see below).

4.4.3 The Promulgation of the Marketing of Agricultural Products Act, No. 47 of 1996

This new act represented a radical departure from the marketing regime to which farmers had become accustomed in the period since the 1930s (Groenewald, 2000). While far reaching, the deregulation that had taken place since the 1980s was piecemeal, uncoordinated, and accomplished within the framework of the old Marketing Act, with the result that any policy changes could easily be reversed. The new act changed the way in which agricultural marketing policy would henceforth be managed in South Africa.

The recommendations of the Kassier Committee (Kassier Report, 1992) were based on the premise that a stronger, more centralized and more representative authority was required to override the vested interests in the regulated marketing system as it existed at the time. The main purpose of the recommended 'Agricultural Marketing Council' would, therefore, be to manage deregulation. This principle of a managed transition was carried over into the new act, which, however, went further in building safeguards to protect the disempowered. This was accomplished through the ingenious definition of the goals of the act, the conditions under which intervention could take place and the process for allowing this to happen (see Vink, 1998).

Commercial farmers reacted to these changes in a wide range of different ways, some of which are described below. It is, however, ironic that the earlier attempt to provide marketing support services for small farmers under the BATAT programme (see, for example, Van Reenen, 1997) foundered, and it is not clear that small farmers are any better off now than under the previous regime. Yet there has been some research on ways in which their access to markets could be improved (see, for example, Bayley 1996; Madikizela and Groenewald, 1998; and Matungul, 1999).

4.4.4   The promulgation of a new Water Act, No. 36 of 1998

An earlier lack of research on the economics of water use in South Africa was partly rectified during the process of the drafting of the White Paper on water (a process described by Carter, 1996). As can be expected, economists emphasized the desirability of water markets. Backeberg (1995, 1997) argued that increasing scarcity and competition for water resulted in a recognition that public policies must change to manage water as an economic commodity. Another example of this genre can be found in the work of Armitage (1999), who studied the demand side for water by investigating how water markets can lead to more efficient use of water. Hassan et al. (1996), Louw and Van Schalkwyk (1997) and Van Zyl and Vink (1997) also address the efficiency of water use.

Changes resulting from the new act that were expected to impact most severely on agriculture include the higher priority afforded to water used by humans and the environment, the termination of the riparian principle of water rights, the implementation of an integrated catchment management system, the termination of subsidized water prices and greater cross-border cooperation between Southern African countries. Slow progress in the implementation of the act has, however, minimized the impact to date.

4.4.5   Trade Policy Reform

The new South African government embarked on a process of trade policy reform that aimed to reverse decades of 'inward industrialization' strategies. The distinguishing characteristic of these reforms was a willingness to expose businesses in the country to tariffs that were often below the bound rates negotiated in the Uruguay Round of the GATT. Whereas agricultural trade had been managed through quantitative controls, the Marrakech Agreement called for the tariffication of all agricultural goods, and a phased reduction in the tariffs. South Africa also participated in the renegotiation of the Southern

African Customs Union treaty, agreed to the new South African Development Community (SADC) trade protocol, and negotiated a free trade agreement with the European Union. In all these cases, the country agreed in principle to liberalize agricultural trade further. Finally, the country gained membership of the Cairns Group, thus signalling its intention unilaterally to liberalize its trade regardless of the progress made by the developed countries in withdrawing farm support programmes. These policies have had a marked affect on the sector, as will be discussed below.

4.4.6   Labour Market Reform

While labour legislation governing working conditions, wage rates, and so on has progressively become applicable to the agricultural sector over a period of more than a decade, certain aspects of the land reform programme have also impacted on the manner in which labour is managed in the agricultural sector. Here specific mention should be made of the introduction of legislation that governs the occupational rights of workers who live on farms. Further labour market reform is also expected, especially with the application of the Basic Conditions of Employment Act to agriculture.

4.5   CONCLUSIONS

South African agriculture began the era discussed here as a highly regulated sector in which both natural and fiscal resources were wasted. In addition, large, capital-intensive farms were becoming increasingly dominant. Those, both White and Black, who practised agriculture on a smaller scale were exiting in growing numbers. The former suffered from neglect while the latter were pushed out by deliberate apartheid regulations. In the 1980s the state gradually reduced its regulations. Much of this was forced on the state by potent economic and political challenges. White farmers, in turn, struggled to deal with the hazards of drought and financial liberalization, but they could still count on fairly substantial amounts of state aid to help them through. Black farmers, by contrast, were controlled and coerced in the name of 'betterment', but at the end of the decade a few were able to benefit from the initiation of more helpful farmer support programmes. In the 1990s, market deregulation and land reform were supposed to reverse the trends of the previous decades. Significant successes were achieved in making the sector more efficient and some Black farmers benefited from land reform, equity schemes and other transfers. However, by the year 2000, a radically new farming sector, dominated by small-scale, labour-intensive farmers of all races, had not yet materialized.

NOTES

1. See Vink et al. (2000) for a review of recent South African literature on the process and results of deregulation in agriculture in the period since the early 1980s.
2. Until the 1990s the policy of the Department of Agriculture was to negotiate with only one representative body of farmers, namely the South African Agricultural Union (SAAU, now known as Agriculture South Africa or Agri-SA).

REFERENCES

Armitage, R.M. (1999), 'The allocation of water through a water market', Unpublished MScAgric thesis, University of Natal, Pietermaritzburg.

Backeberg, G.R. (1995), 'Die politieke ekonomie van besproeiingsbeleid in Suid-Afrika' (The political economy of irrigation policy in South Africa), Unpublished PhD thesis, University of Pretoria.

Backerbeg, G.R. (1997), 'Water institutions, markets and decentralised resource management: Prospects for innovative policy reforms in irrigated agriculture', *Agrekon*, **36** (1).

Bayley, B. (1996), 'Improving market access: some options', Working Paper 34, Land and Agriculture Policy Centre, Johannesburg.

Board of Tariffs and Trade (1992), *An Investigation into the Price Mechanism in the Food Chain*, Pretoria: Board on Tariffs and Trade.

Brand, S.S., N.T. Christodoulou, C.J. van Rooyen and N. Vink (1992), 'Agriculture and redistribution: growth with equity', in Schrire, Robert (ed.), *Wealth or poverty? Critical choices for South Africa*, Cape Town: Oxford University Press: 353–75.

Bundy, C. (1979), *The Rise and Fall of the South African Peasantry*, London: Heinemann.

Callear, D. and T. Mthethwa (1996), *South African Agricultural Development Corporations: Where to from here?*, Johannesburg: Land and Agriculture Policy Centre.

Carter, R.C. (1996), 'Policy development in the water sector – the South African experience', in Abrams, L.J. and P. Howsam (eds), *Water Policy: Allocation and Management in Practice. Proceedings of International Conference*, Cranfield University, UK.

Corbett, M. (1987), 'The land question in South Africa: a preliminary assessment', *South African Journal of Economics*, **55** (1): 63–77.

Delius, P. and S. Schirmer, 'Soil conservation in a racially ordered society: South Africa, 1930-1970', *Journal of Southern African studies*, **26** (4): 719–42.

De Klerk, Michael (1983), 'Technological change and employment in South African agriculture: the case of maize harvesting in the Western Transvaal, 1968-1981', Unpublished MA thesis, University of Cape Town.

De Klerk, M. (1991), 'The accumulation crisis in South African agriculture', in Gelb, S. (ed.), *South Africa's Economic Crisis*, Cape Town: David Philip: 198–227.

De Kock Commission (1985), *Final Report of the Commission of Inquiry into the Monetary System and Monetary Policy in South Africa*, RP 70/1984, Pretoria: Government Printer.

De Wet, Chris (1987), 'Betterment planning in South Africa: some thoughts on its history, feasibility and wider policy implications', *Journal of Contemporary African*

Studies, **6** (1/2): 85-122.

Department of Land Affairs, DANIDA/EC/UK-DFID (1997), *Mid-term Review of the Land Reform Pilot Programme*, White Paper, Pretoria.

Development Bank of Southern Africa/Land and Agricultural Policy Centre (DBSA/LAPC) (1997), *The Reorganisation of State-run and Parastatal-run Agricultural Projects*, Midrand: DBSA/LAPC.

Eckert, J.B., J.N. Hamman and J.P. Lombard, (1996), 'Perceptions of a new future: empowering farm workers through equity sharing', *Development Southern Africa*, **13** (6): 693-712.

Graham, A. and M. Lyne (1999), 'Land redistribution in KwaZulu-Natal: an analysis and comparison of farmland transactions in 1997 and 1998', *Agrekon*, **38** (4): 512-525.

Groenewald, J.A. (2000), 'The Agricultural Marketing Act: a post-mortem', *South African Journal of Economics*, **68** (3): 364-402.

Hall, R. (1998), 'Design for equity: linking policy with objectives in South Africa's land reform', *Review of African Political Economy*, **25** (77): 451-62

Hassan, R., J. Berns, A. Chapman, R. Smith, D. Scott and N. Ntsaba (1996), 'Economic policies and the environment in South Africa: the case of water resources in Mpumalanga', Land and Agriculture Policy Centre Working Paper, 24.

Hoffman, M.T. and S. Todd (1999), 'A national review of land degradation in South Africa: the influence of biophysical and socio-economic factors', Unpublished seminar paper, Oxford, p. 5.

Hoffman, M. and S. Todd (2000), 'A national review of land degradation in South Africa', *Journal of Southern African Studies*, **26** (4): 734-58.

Karaan, M. and A.S. Myburgh (1992), 'Food distribution systems in the urban informal markets: the case of red meat markets in the Western Cape townships', *Agrekon*, **31** (4): 289-93.

Kassier, W.E. and J.A. Groenewald (1992), 'The agricultural economy of South Africa', in Csaki, C., Th. J. Dams, D. Metzger and J. van Zyl (eds) (1992), *Agricultural restructuring in Southern Africa*, Proceedings of the International Association of Agricultural Econonomists (IAAE) Interconference symposium, Windhoek: 84-100.

Kassier Report (1992), *Report of the Committee of Inquiry into the Marketing Act*, Pretoria: National Department of Agriculture.

Kirsten, J.F., C.J. Van Rooyen and S. Ngqangweni (1996), 'Progress with different land reform options in South Africa', *Agrekon*, **35** (4): 218-23.

Kirsten, J.F. and J. Van Zyl (1999), 'Comparing notes on the approaches and progress with land reform in southern Africa: the South African land reform programme', *Agrekon*, **38**: 326-42:

Kirsten, M.A. (1988), 'n Kwalitatiewe en kwantitatiewe perspektief op die informele sektor' (A qualitative and quantitative perspective on the informal sector), Unpublished MA thesis, University of Stellenbosch.

Kritzinger-van Niekerk, L.K., J.B. Eckert and N. Vink (1992), 'Toward a democratic economy in South Africa: an approach to economic restructuring', Development Bank of South Africa, Unpublished report.

Lazar, J. (1987), 'Conformity & conflict: Afrikaner nationalist politics in South Africa, 1948-1961', Unpublished PhD thesis, Oxford.

Lipton, Merle (1977), 'South Africa: two agricultures?', in Wilson, F., A. Kooy and D. Henrie (eds), *Farm Labour in South Africa*, Cape Town: David Philip: 72-85.

Lipton, M. (1986), *Capitalism and Apartheid: South Africa, 1910-1986*, Cape Town:

David Philip.

Lipton, Merle (1993), 'Restructuring South African agriculture', in Lipton, Merle and Charles Simkins (eds) (1993), *State and Market in Post Apartheid South Africa*, Johannesburg: Witwatersrand University Press: 359–408.

Lipton, Merle (1996), 'The politics of rural reform in South Africa', in Lipton, M., M. de Klerk and M. Lipton (eds), *Land, Labour and Livelihoods in Rural South Africa. Vol. 1: Western Cape*, Durban: Indicator Press: 409.

Louw, D.B. and H.D. Van Schalkwyk (1997), 'The true value of irrigation water in the Olifants river basin, Western Cape', *Agrekon*, **36** (4): 551–60.

Madikizela, S.P. and J.A. Groenewald (1998), 'Marketing preferences and behaviour of a group of small-scale irrigation vegetable farmers in Eastern Cape', *Agrekon*, **37** (1): 100–109.

Marcus, Tessa (1989), *Modernizing Super-exploitation: Restructuring South African Agriculture*, London: Zed Books.

Matsetela, T.J. (1981), 'Rural change among Africans in the Ventersdorp district of 1910–1935: a case study of Bakwena-ba-ga-Mogopa', Unpublished M.A. dissertation, School of Oriental and African Studies, University of London.

Matungul, M.M.P. (1999), 'Marketing problems faced by emerging farmers in South Africa: a case study of transaction costs in KwaZulu-Natal', Unpublished PhD thesis, University of Natal, Pietermaritzburg.

May, Julian and Mark Schacter (1991), 'Minding your own business: deregulation in the informal sector', *Indicator SA*, **10** (1), Summer: 53–8.

McKenzie, C.C., D. Weiner and N. Vink (1989), 'Land use, agricultural productivity and farming systems in Southern Africa', Unpublished research report, Development Bank of South Africa.

Moll, Terence (1993), 'Macroeconomic policy in turbulent times', in Lipton, Merle and Charles Simkins (eds) (1993), *State and Market in Post Apartheid South Africa*, Johannesburg: Witwatersrand University Press: 235–70.

Plewman, T., M. Aliber and L.A. Coetzee (1995), 'A monitoring and evaluation system for land reform in South Africa', Land and Agriculture Policy Centre Briefing Paper No. 7.

Republic of South Africa (RSA) (1997), *White Paper on South African Land Policy*, Pretoria: Government Printer.

Republic of South Africa (RSA) (2000), *Integrated Programme of Land Redistribution and Agricultural Development in South Africa*, Version 1, Pretoria: Ministry for Agriculture and Land Affairs.

Simkins, C. (1981), 'Agricultural production in the African reserves of South Africa, 1918–1969', *Journal of Southern African Studies*, **7** (1): 256–83.

Surplus Peoples Project (1984), *Forced Removals in South Africa*, 5 vols., Johannesburg: Surplus Peoples Project.

Terreblanche, S.J. (1998), 'Empowerment in context: the struggle for hegemony in South Africa', in Kirsten J., J. van Zyl and N. Vink (eds), *The Agricultural Democratisation of South Africa*, Cape Town: Francolin: 13–60.

Union of South Africa (1960), *Report of the Commission of Enquiry into European Occupation of Rural Areas*, Pretoria, p. 3.

Urban Foundation (1991), *Rural Development: Towards a New Framework*, Johannesburg: Urban Foundation.

Van Reenen, E. (1997), 'The BATAT marketing drive: improving market access for small scale farmers', *Agrekon*, **36** (4): 648–53.

Van Rooyen, C.J., N. Vink and N.T. Christodoulou (1987), 'Access to the agricultural market for small farmers in Southern Africa: the farmer support programme', *Development Southern Africa*, **4** (2): 207-3.

Van Waasdijk, T. (1954), 'Agricultural prices and price policy', *South African Journal of Economics*, **22** (1): 160-73.

Van Zyl, J. and J.A. Groenewald (1988), Flexibility in input substitution: a case study of South African agriculture', *Development Southern Africa*, **5** (1): 2-13.

Van Zyl, J., J. Kirsten and H.P. Binswanger (eds) (1996), *Agricultural Land Reform in South Africa: Policies, Markets and Mechanisms*, Cape Town: Oxford University Press.

Van Zyl, J. and N. Vink (1997), 'The effects of water policies on the farm sector in the Western Cape', *Agrekon*, **36** (4): 573-84.

Van Zyl, J., N. Vink and T.I. Fènyes (1987), 'Labour-related structural trends in South African maize production', *Agricultural Economics*, **1** (3): 241-58.

Vink, N. (1993), 'Entrepreneurs and the political economy of reform in South African agriculture', *Agrekon*, **32** (4): 153-66

Vink, N. (1998), 'The political environment', in Spies, P.H. (ed.), *Agrifutura 1997/98*, University of Stellenbosch, Agrifutura Project: 1-68.

Vink, N. (1999), 'South African agriculture in the 1970s', *South African Journal of Economic History*, **14** (1&2): 90-113.

Vink, N. and W.E. Kassier (1991), 'Agricultural policy and the South African state', in De Klerk, M. (ed.), *A Harvest of Discontent: The Land Question in South Africa*, Cape Town: IDASA: 213-37.

Vink N., J. Kirsten and L. Hobson (2000), *Agricultural and Agribusiness Sector Policy in South Africa: A Review of the Literature*, Pretoria; USAID.

Williams, G., J. Ewert, J. Hamann and N. Vink (1998), 'Liberalising markets and reforming land in South Africa', *Journal of Contemporary African Studies*, **16** (1): 165-94.

World Bank (1993), *Experience with Agricultural Policy: Lessons for South Africa*, Washington, DC: International Bank for Reconstruction and Development.

5. The mining sector, 1970-2000

I THE YEARS OF TURBULENCE, 1970-1990
Stuart Jones

5.1 INTRODUCTION

In the last three decades of the twentieth century the mining industry's contribution to the South African economy fluctuated dramatically. After experiencing a steady erosion in its contribution to GDP in the 1960s, from 12.7 per cent in 1960 to 9.0 per cent in 1970, the decade of the 1970s witnessed an abrupt reversal of this trend and by 1980 mining's share of GDP had risen to 21.5 per cent. This then declined to 9.7 per cent in 1990 and 6.5 in 2000. The decline in the 1990s was faster than that of the 1960s and by 2000 mining's proportion of GDP was at its lowest level since the formation of the Union in 1910. Mining's importance to the economy did not decline as fast as its contribution to GDP, because of the key role it played in supporting the balance of payments by earning foreign exchange.

In these two decades, 1970-1990, the mining industry experienced first a boom in gold mining, as a result of the gold price rise in the 1970s, and then a slump, as a result of the fall in the gold price in the 1980s. Coal exports became a major feature of the 1980s, while platinum was steadily increasing in importance. Job reservation remained throughout the 1970s and 1980s but the prohibitions on trade unions fell away in the 1980s. Concurrently with these developments foreign labour in the gold mines was replaced with local South African labour. Mining, however, continued to be controlled by a handful of powerful mining-finance houses presided over by the Anglo American Corporation.

5.2 CONTRIBUTION TO GDP

The contribution of mining to GDP was dominated by the experience of the gold mines, with gold reaching a price of US$850 per ounce in 1980. It was this phenomenal increase in the price of gold that led to the regression in the shape of the economy with mining's share of GDP climbing to 21.5 per cent.

Table 5.1 Contribution of mining to GDP and of individual minerals to total mineral sales, 1970–1990

Mineral	Proportion of GDP (%)					Share of total sales (%)				
	1970	1975	1980	1985	1990	1970	1975	1980	1985	1990
Gold	7.1	10.2	18.9	13.5	8.2	53.1	61.9	69.2	58.9	50.6
Coal	0.9	1.3	1.0	4.4	3.5	7.2	7.6	7.6	19.3	21.4
Diamonds	0.6	0.7	1.0	0.6	n/a	4.8	4.2	3.7	2.7	n/a
Iron ore	0.2	0.2	0.5	0.4	0.5	1.9	1.0	2.0	1.8	2.8
All mining	13.4	16.4	26.5	23.0	16.1	n/a	n/a	n/a	n/a	n/a

Source: Chamber of Mines and South African Statistics

Then, when the price of gold fell the authorities in Pretoria permitted the rand to depreciate in order to preserve the rand value of gold, which inevitably contributed significantly to inflation of these years. It was the declining gold price that led the industry to seek other outlets for its product than central banks. Demand from the jewellery industry accounted for 54 per cent of the total demand for gold in 1980 and 82 per cent in 1989.[1]

The move into gold coins in the form of the Kruger rand was also successful. First minted in 1967, it was in 1970 that the Chamber received permission from the Minister of Finance to market the coins. Sales rose rapidly, reaching a peak of 6012293 ounces in 1978. Anti-South African campaigns then disrupted sales. Even so, by 1996 more than 46.6 million ounces of gold had been sold in this way and the Kruger rand had become the most successful gold coin in the history of the world.[2]

The gold mines also contributed to GDP with their forward and backward linkages. Inputs on a large scale were provided by the electricity and mechanical engineering industries. One gold mine consumed as much electric power as a city the size of Bloemfontein. Hundreds of thousands of miners needed to be provided with food, clothing, housing and medical treatment and, according to the Chamber of Mines' calculations, the intermediate multiplier led to a further expenditure amounting to 80 per cent of the value of the goods directly supplied to the mines. Yet, by 1990, the direct contribution of mining to GDP at 9.7 per cent was a third that of manufacturing and electricity production and around two-thirds that of the financial sector. However, this 9.7 per cent contribution to GDP provided the bulk of the country's exports (see Chapter 9).

5.3 GROSS DOMESTIC FIXED INVESTMENT

In the 1970s mining and quarrying's contribution to gross domestic fixed investment rose steadily from 5.8 per cent to 9.6 per cent and this trend continued in the 1980s, reaching 14.8 per cent in 1987. Long lead times in the investment in new mines meant investment continued into the depressed years after 1985. By 1987 16 new gold mining developments and six platinum ventures had been undertaken costing almost R5 billion. Buoyant world commodity prices maintained this high level of fixed investment. Gross fixed investment in mining had risen from R180 million in 1970 to R7 176 million in 1990. In constant prices investment had risen three-and-a-half-fold.

5.4 MARKET CAPITALISATION

In current prices the market capitalization of almost all the mining companies rose massively. In 1970 the market capitalization of the diamond companies exceeded that of the gold mines (Table 5.2) by over 20 per cent. This state of affairs did not last long. By 1973 gold was moving ahead, more than treble that of diamonds in 1975, quadruple in 1980 and almost five times as large in 1985. Thereafter diamonds caught up and by 1995 the market capitalization of the diamond counters had once again overtaken those of the gold mines. Even after taking into account inflation, enormous wealth had been created, as the value of the listed gold mines rose by 2 262.3 per cent, diamonds by 1 458.4 per cent and coal by 2 626.0. In terms of growth rates, coal was the star performer in the 20 years from 1970 to 1990.

Table 5.2 *Market capitalization of mines on the Johannesburg Stock Exchange 1970–2000 (Rm)*

Year	Gold	Diamonds	Coal	Platinum
1970	1 739.7	2 094.3	148.3	–
1975	5 808.0	1 672.0	343.5	–
1980	22 306.0	4 968.0	2 545.9	–
1985	37 450.0	7 878.0	3 545.0	–
1990	41 097.0	32 638.0	4 042.6	932.6
1995	51 261.0	54 627.0	15 159.0	16 362.0
2000	43 584.2	81 195.4	41 272.9	138 706.9

Source: Johannesburg Securities Exchange.

The values provide some evidence that, in the 1980s, the combination of inflation and sanctions was hurting the economy, for in real terms the value of both the gold and coal mines fell sharply. Consumer prices quadrupled, but the market capitalization of gold and coal counters barely doubled.

The rise in the prices of gold triggered an investment boom across a broad range of minerals. In the 1970s there was investment in coal and diamonds as well as in two new gold mines. In the following decade platinum came in and pushed up investment. Between 1970 and 1990 capital investment in the mines rose from R125.5 million to R4 933.0 million, an increase of almost 4 thousand per cent, which was about three-and-a-half times the rate that prices had increased (see Table 5.3). There was therefore a significant rise in real investment in the mining sector in these 20 years, but it had occurred in the 1970s. In the 1980s prices rose faster than investment, which provides further evidence that sanctions were damaging the economy in the 1980s, the decade in which South Africa lost its preeminent position in mining.[3]

Table 5.3 *The capital expenditure of South African mining companies, 1970-1990*

Year	Expenditure
1970	125.5
1975	407.3
1980	1 417.7
1984	2 517.0
1990	4 933.0

Source: South African Statistics.

5.5 LABOUR

Mining for gold was labour intensive and the gold mines employed over three-fifths of mine workers in the 1970s, which fluctuated between 620000 and 720000. In the 1980s the number rose to over three-quarters of a million. Widespread rationalization programmes after 1986 led to the number falling, as the mines struggled with rising costs and a declining gold price. Sanctions campaigns did not hurt the gold mines, but they harmed the coal mines, which from 1986 also began to shed labour. Open cast coal mines were more amenable to mechanization than the deep level gold mines and labour reduction in coal mines was accompanied by rising productivity.

The rise in the price of gold also made it possible for the gold mines to raise wages, which in real terms in 1970 were still about the same as in 1910. Not surprisingly, few South Africans would work for such low wages and by the early 1970s the gold mines had become dependent upon foreign labour supplied by neighbouring countries primarily Lesotho, Mozambique and Malawi. In the mid-1970s both Malawi and Mozambique suspended recruitment of workers for the South African mines, just at the time that the rise in the price of gold made it possible to pay higher wages and recruit local people. Within little more than a decade the proportion of South Africans working in the gold mines rose from 25 to 55 per cent of the total labour employed.

It was also a time of considerable labour unrest in the country at large. Between 1972 and 1975 over 50 riots occurred, resulting in 132 deaths.[4] This had subsided by 1975; but its impact led the government to appoint the Wiehahn and Rickert Commissions. The former examined industrial relations and the latter investigated legislation affecting labour utilization not covered by Wiehahn. Their reports recommended fundamental changes in government policy and the recognition of Black trade unions, the ending of racial discrimination and an acceptance of the free enterprise system.

This may perhaps be seen as a return to normal economic conditions, in which factor movements responded to signals coming out of the market, something that was impossible while the United States maintained gold at an artificially low price and the South African state prevented the development of normal labour relations.

One of the most far-reaching consequences of employing local labour in the gold mines, at a time when the authorities in Pretoria were relaxing their rigid apartheid policies, was the sudden development of trade unions. Cyril Ramaphosa rose to power as a miners' leader in the 1980s – a time of renewed violence in the mines, when many aspirant union leaders were murdered (strangled by metal coat hangers). The emergence of powerful trade unions led to further increases in wages and labour increased its proportion of the net value added to the gold mining sector from below 50 per cent in 1970 to over 67 per cent by the end of the 1990s.[5] Real labour costs rose in all mining sectors in the 1980s, after having fallen in the second half of the 1970s,[6] despite the increase in wages that then took place. This repatriation of labour in the gold mines was accompanied by a large increase in the number of workers employed. The number rose from 655 346 to 724 587 in 1985. Thereafter it declined and by 1990 had fallen to 692 900. (See Table 5.4.)

Wages rose rapidly (see Table 5.5). Over the decade of the 1970s real wages trebled for Black mine workers, while the minimum wage rose tenfold. In 1975 for the first time the Black share of the total wage bill overtook that of Whites and by 1990 it was well over 60 per cent of the total. In current prices the Black wage bill had risen by 2 174 per cent, which was about twice as fast as the rise in the consumer price index. It was, therefore, in the 1980s that Black purchasing became a major factor in the country's retail markets.

Table 5.4   Labour employed in the South African Mines, 1970–1990

Year	Total*	White	Black
1970	655 346	62 372	588 851
1975	639 473	63 249	568 100
1980	709 042	72 329	625 259
1985	724 587	78 202	636 982
1990	692 900	–	–

Note: The total includes Coloureds and Indians.

Source: South African Statistics.

Table 5.5   Salaries and wages in the mining sector, 1970–1990 (R)

Year	Total*	White	Black
1970	399.2	266.4	126.6
1975	1 003.2	482.5	504.9
1980	2 237.7	902.3	1 290.5
1985	4 778.6	1 825.5	2 879.2
1990	10 268.3	–	–

Note: The total includes Coloureds and Indians.

Source: South African Statistics.

5.6   GOLD

5.6.1   The Situation in 1970

Compared with the 1960s when eight new gold mines were opened, the 1970s were a time when the rewards of earlier investment were realized. Gold mines have a diminishing lifespan and the closure of old mines, which had been such a feature of the 1960s, ceased in the 1970s. At the same time the economic centre of gravity of gold mining was moving westwards and the importance of mines of the East Rand and Central Rand diminished rapidly. The East Rand, which had produced 30 per cent of the country's gold output in 1957, accounted for only 3 per cent in 1977, while the Central Rand had seen its share fall from 14 per cent to 1 per cent.

Rising costs were becoming a major problem. The mining companies' response to this situation was to concentrate on high-grade ores. By 1970 five mines were able to keep going only because they also produced uranium and 19 of the 48 producing mines were being subsidized by the government. In 1970 only ores with a grade of 12 grams of gold per ton were being mined and the future looked increasingly bleak as American hostility to an increase in the price of gold threatened the economic viability of almost all the mines.

5.6.2   The Rise in the Price of Gold

In theory a two-tier system of pricing gold was in existence in 1970, with the official price remaining at US$35 per fine ounce and a free market price that was supposed to reflect supply and demand. This had been introduced in 1968 and had initially led to the price rising to US$42 per fine ounce, but by 1970 it had fallen back to US$35. This, however, did not last very long and in 1971 the price had begun to rise before the US Treasury suspended its practice of selling gold to other countries' central banks at US$35 per fine ounce. The United States had kept the price of gold artificially low for 20 years for political reasons, but such a policy depended upon a worldwide shortage of dollars. This situation no longer existed in 1971 and economic imperatives finally prevailed. America had begun its long march into sustained balance of payment deficits.

The rand price of gold rose at a faster rate than the dollar price, because of the devaluation of the rand. While balance of payments difficulties were the driving force behind this, the mines were the chief beneficiaries. In 1971 the average rand price of gold per ounce had been R28.64; two years later it had risen to R65.08. The following year, the year of the first great oil-price rise, saw gold rise to over R100 per ounce. Thereafter worldwide inflation swept all before it, carrying the price of gold to its peak of US$850 in January 1980. This led to a 2 217 per cent increase in the value of output between 1970 and 1990 with the quantity produced decreasing by 40 per cent. Yet by 1990 gold's proportion of total mineral sales was little changed from that of 1970, 50.6 per cent as opposed to 53.1 per cent.

In the 1980s the response of the mining companies to the falling price was to maximize output in order to maintain their cash flow. The peculiar structure of the mining industry encouraged this development. A handful of mining finance houses controlled the mines. In 1970 there were seven of them

Table 5.6   Value of the principal minerals produced in South Africa, 1970–1990 (R)

Mineral	1970	1975	1980	1985	1990
Gold	830.3	2 560.4	10 369.6	15 139.7	19 239.3
Coal	109.9	316.1	1 143.4	4 962.3	8 149.2
Platinum	–	–	851.2	1 998.5	5 164.2
Diamonds	75.5	174.2	553.0	702.0	n/a
Iron ore	29.0	42.1	295.1	472.4	1 076.5
Copper	139.1	146.3	309.9	535.9	1 063.0
Manganese	26.6	102.1	145.0	298.8	848.3
Nickel	–	61.6	112.3	284.4	655.6
Chrome ore	10.6	40.8	84.4	231.7	421.1
Asbestos	34.6	91.5	114.4	139.2	194.8
Zinc	–	14.9	19.7	77.3	191.5

Source: South African Statistics.

dominated by the Anglo American Corporation. The other six were: Goldfields of South Africa, Union Corporation, General Mining, Johannesburg Consolidated Investment Company, Anglo Vaal and Rand Mines. The last mentioned had ceased prospecting for new ore bodies and in 1970 was a shade of its former self. These seven mining houses had historically raised capital for individual mines and then provided them with technical assistance and management. In 1970 the mines, which they controlled, were tied to them by management contracts that paid the mining houses fees irrespective of the profitability of the mines. As a result, the controlling shareholders had little economic incentive to press for productivity raising changes that might come up against established ways of doing things. It was inefficient. Before 1970 low labour costs had allowed it to continue and in the 1970s the higher gold price reduced the pressure to change. Even in the 1980s, when the need to reduce costs was growing, sanctions campaigns and a depreciating rand diverted attention away from considering any radical change to the structure. The losers were the shareholders of the individual mines, who were, in effect, disenfranchised by the existence of management contracts. In 1990 politics not corporate governance was making the headlines and another decade of low gold prices was to pass before the fruits of reform were realised. However, the number of mining finance houses had been reduced to five, with the acquisition of Union Corporation by the Afrikaner-controlled General Mining and the fading away of Rand Mines. The attempt by Anglo American to gain control of Consolidated Gold Fields, with its bid for Consolidated Gold Fields, came perilously close to giving Anglo American a dominance in gold mining comparable to its position in diamonds; but American courts blocked this move, the rationale for which was never satisfactorily explained by the Oppenheimers. Had it succeeded, the power of the mining finance houses would have been greater than ever and reform even more difficult.

5.7   DIAMONDS

In 1970 diamonds formed only a minor proportion of South Africa's mineral output. Historically important because the discovery of diamonds at Kimberley triggered the mineral boom in the second half of the nineteenth century, by 1970 they had been overtaken by gold, coal and copper. Twenty years later in 1990 coal was far ahead and iron ore had caught up with copper. De Beers dominated both production and sales and in 1970 were poised to discover the world's greatest diamond pipe – Jwaneng in Botswana. De Beers had already invested in 'sea mining' off the coasts of South West Africa and Namaqualand and continued to operate the Kimberley Mine in the Cape and the Premier Mine (which had produced the Cullinan Diamond) in the Transvaal; but it was the discovery of the Botswana pipes that transformed the situation. This was particularly important for De Beers which was facing competition from the Soviet Union in the 1970s and from Australia in the 1980s.

De Beers was transformed in the third quarter of the twentieth century, as its monopoly over production was changed into a monopoly over buying. The name Central Selling Organisation did not come into general use until the later 1950s, when South Africa became a major importer as well as exporter of diamonds.[7] The sorting of diamonds was transferred to South Africa before 1970, influenced by the high tax policies of the British Labour government. As a result, at the beginning of our period, De Beers was importing almost two-fifths of the world's diamond production to South Africa and paying 70 per cent of its profits to the government.

While the total output of diamonds barely grew in the 1970s, rising from 8 112 carats in 1970 to 8 522 carats in 1980, the value of sales more than quintupled to R553 million. In 1987, the last year for which sales figures were published by the government, the value of the diamond output was still above that of copper and iron ore but their share of total mineral output had fallen to 3 per cent. In these 20 years De Beers had displayed considerable skill in managing the price, in stockpiling diamonds when the secondary market collapsed in the early 1980s and in preparing for political difficulties by the division of De Beers into two companies, Centenary based in Switzerland and the original De Beers in South Africa.

5.8 COAL

Coal mining underwent the greatest changes in the last third of the century. In 1970 little was exported. Power generation and the railways were the biggest consumers of coal, followed by the Iron and Steel Corporation. The country possessed abundant supplies of coal, mainly in the Transvaal, much of which could be mined by open cast operations. This, together with low labour costs, made South African coal very cheap by international standards, one-eighth the pithead costs in Britain and Germany.

Before 1970 the demand for coal had been growing slowly, as the declining demand from the railways counterbalanced the increased demand from Escom. Government control over marketing and prices had also held back the growth of the industry. This control was relaxed in the 1970s to facilitate exports. The pricing structure had made no allowance for either the cost of producing coal or its market value. It was based on depreciated historical capital investment that made sense only to Pretoria bureaucrats. Not surprisingly little investment in new mines took place in such an environment.

'The general climate in the price-controlled sector remained one of survival in a progressively less favourable environment.'[8] It was this somewhat dismal background that led to the appointment of the Petrick Commission in 1970 to investigate the coal industry and to its report that recommended a review of the pricing structure, which led eventually to the triumph of market forces and to five new collieries being brought into production in 1978. Today, before the weight of African National Congress/Communist Party propaganda, it is forgotten how deeply entrenched were anti-market attitudes and practices in the era of National Party rule.

Export markets became a practical possibility in the last quarter of the century as a result of two developments within South Africa and two without. The first of these occurred in the 1960s when improved washing techniques enabled South African coal, with its high ash content, to be used in the iron and steel industry. Already by 1970 South African coal producers had signed a contract with Japanese steel producers. The second development within South Africa was the decision to build a new railway line from the Eastern Transvaal to the coast at Richards Bay specifically for exports. Richards Bay possessed a good natural harbour and the government built the necessary bulk handling facilities. Exports began in 1976 and have been expanding ever since. The external events which made the export of coal on a large scale economically viable were the rise in the price of oil, which made coal more attractive as a source of power, and the development of bulk ore carriers that made it possible to transport coal from places as far away as South Africa and Australia to the steel industries of Europe and Japan.

Exports rose rapidly. From 1.3 million tons in 1970 exports rose to 6 million tons in 1976, when the Richards Bay Railway Line opened. By 1978 exports had doubled again and work was in progress to handle 20 million tons and plans were afoot to double capacity again. By 1980 exports had risen to over 29 million tons and in 1987 reached 45.5 million tons. South Africa had become the third largest exporter of steam coal in the world, after Australia and the United States, despite the sanctions introduced by the United States, France and Denmark which had removed a quarter of the existing export market in 1986. In the process the Richards Bay coal terminal had become the world's largest and most modern. Coal output had risen from 54.6 million tons in 1970 to 185.4 million tons in 1990, its value from R109.9 million to R8 149.2 million. By 1990 coal was second to gold both in the value of production and in the value of its exports.

5.9   OTHER MINERALS

In the long run one of the most striking features of the mining industry has been diversification into minerals other than gold. The very success of the coal industry in developing its export markets and in providing the domestic electricity and iron and steel industries with their basic inputs in the 1970s and 1980s tends to reinforce this belief, yet it would be incorrect to apply knowledge of what happened in the 1990s back to the 1970s and 1980s. In 1990 the share of gold in total mineral production was still above its 1970 level and it would seem reasonable to assume that the share of diamonds was not greatly changed from 1985. The increase in that of coal, from 0.9 per cent to 3.5 per cent, consequently occurred at the expense of the other minerals. There was no pronounced trend towards broadening the mineral base in the 1970–90 period.

Significant changes, however, did occur within this sector as copper, asbestos and zinc declined in importance while iron ore, manganese and chrome began their long march up the production table. Iron ore and manganese benefited from the expansion of the Iron and Steel Corporation of South Africa as well as from the opening up of export markets. By 1990 iron ore accounted for 2.8 per cent of mineral production and manganese was close on its heels with 2.2 per cent of mineral sales. Output of manganese had increased by 46 per cent. The Bushveld Igneous Complex north of the Witwatersrand contained the world's largest known reserves of platinum and platinum group metals such as palladium and rhodium and, in the 15 years after 1975, platinum output increased by 506 per cent. (See Table 5.7.)

Table 5.7   Increase and decrease in the output of selected minerals (by volume), 1970–1990

Mineral	Increase (+) or decrease (−) (%)
Coal	+240.0
Platinum	+506.7
Manganese	+46.0
Iron ore	+232.0
Chrome ore	+192.0
Diamond	+6.4
Copper	+20.2
Nickel	+12.3*
Gold	−40.0
Asbestos	−43.8
Zinc	−41.6**

Notes: *Since 1980; **Since 1975.
Source: South African Statistics.

In the 1970s inflation benefited a number of the base metals. In constant prices the real value of the sales of coal, iron ore and chrome rose faster than their output.[9] In the 1980s developments in the infant platinum industry attracted much attention with the metal attracting support as a hedge against inflation and currency depreciation and as a vital component in reducing pollution in the automobile industry. A minor platinum boom followed in 1987 with seven new projects initiated that would increase output by over one and a half million ounces.[10] Overproduction ensued and led to the abandonment of many of these projects in the early 1990s. All in all the other minerals sector was one of potential, rather than actual, achievements in the 1970–90 period.

Some idea of the importance of South Africa's mineral production may be obtained from Table 5.8, prepared by the South African Minerals Bureau in 1980.

Table 5.8   South Africa's share of world mineral production, 1980

Mineral	Western World		World	
Platinum group metals	1	9	1	48
Gold	1	71	1	55
Vanadium	1	62	1	34
Chrome ore	1	61	1	39
Andalusite/sillimanite	1	46	1	39
Manganese ore	1	41	2	22
Vermiculite	1	32	2	31
Antimony	2	29	3	20
Diamonds	2	23	3	18
Titanium	4	22	5	20
Zirconium	3	19	3	17
Fluorspar	2	15	3	11
Uranium oxide	3	14	–	–
Asbestos	3	13	3	6
Coal	4	7	7	4
Iron ore	8	5	10	3
Phosphate	5	3	7	3
Lead	6	3	10	2
Copper	9	4	13	3
Nickel	5	4	8	4
Tin	8	1	11	1

Source: South African Minerals Bureau.

II TRANSFORMATION IN THE 1990s*
Stuart Jones and Roger Baxter

5.10 INTRODUCTION

The 1990s can be characterized as a period of considerable change for the South African mining industry. Three key developments have driven the forces of change: the advent of democracy in South Africa, globalization and commodity prices. Democracy has opened up the sector to the world but has at the same time resulted in an almost complete rewrite of the statute book in South Africa. From labour market legislation to minerals policy, the changes have been considerable. At the same time the new access to the global economy and the strong forces of globalization led South African mining companies not only to change the way that they traditionally operated, but also to diversify their operations geographically, to change their financing methods and to restructure their head offices. As a result they have, in many cases, become significant global players. The Chamber of Mines, which is in many respects a microcosm of the mining industry, has also experienced significant change. The chamber has evolved into being the preeminent business lobby and advocacy organization in South Africa, while shedding all the associated service companies into stand-alone entities.

The functioning of commodity markets has also been influenced by commodity cycles over the decade. This has resulted in certain companies diversifying their commodity profile while others have become more commodity focused. In the gold sector in particular, the decline in the gold price and the rise in production costs resulted in significant changes including: revised work practices and a tremendous focus on human capital development, both of which have led to improvements in productivity but also significant job losses. While gold's direct contribution to the economy has declined during the 1990s, the industry has moved down the value chain with the result that, from a multiplier and indirect effect, the minerals complex remains the cornerstone foundation of the economy.

5.11 MINING: THE CORNERSTONE OF THE ECONOMY

South Africa is a veritable minerals treasure trove with mineral deposits only matched bythe countries of the former Soviet Union. Perhaps the two most important commodities that do not occur in South Africa in large quantities are

*Part II has relied heavily on information provided by the Chamber of Mines.

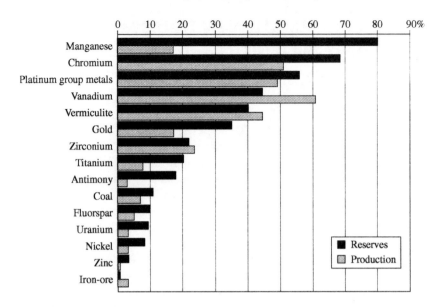

Source: Chamber of Mines.

Figure 5.1   South Africa's role in global mineral resources and production, 1999

crude oil and bauxite. Figure 5.1 shows South Africa's role in global mineral reserves and production.

The mining industry has been the mainstay of the South African economy for over a century. Both diamonds and gold are two highly valued commodities, which were largely instrumental in the development of the country's infrastructure and the establishment of secondary industry during the first half of the twentieth century. Associated with the development of mining and beneficiation activities, South Africa has been an exporter of an ever-increasing number and quantity of minerals and metals for more than one hundred years. In 1999, more than 60 different minerals were produced and exported to some 90 countries, the major destinations being Europe and the Far East.

5.11.1   Contribution to GDP

While the contribution of mining to GDP declined to 6.5 per cent in 2000, the non-gold sectors grew to exceed that of gold during the decade (see Figure 5.2).

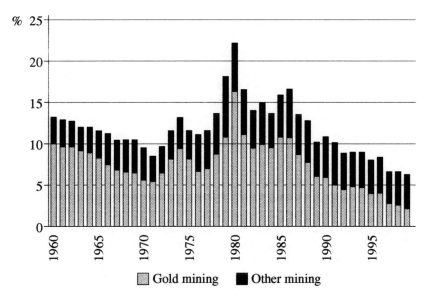

Source: South African Reserve Bank/Chamber of Mines.

Figure 5.2   Contribution of mining to GDP, 1960–1999

Although the relative importance of gold mining has fluctuated over the last decade with the performance of the gold price, gold mining still contributes just under 3 per cent directly to GDP. Taking into consideration the indirect contribution to the economy and the multiplier effects, mining's total contribution to GDP is closer to 10 per cent. These multiplier effects include:

- *Backward linkages*, arising from the purchase of goods and services by the mining industry which stimulate industrial production and the provision of services (for example, gold mines consume 15 per cent of all electricity generated in South Africa).
- *Forward linkages*, arising from the use of mineral products in other domestic industries, such as electricity generation where 95 per cent of all electricity generated comes from coal-fired power stations.
- *Social multipliers*, stemming from the role of mining in the development of human resources and infrastructure such as schools, colleges, clinics, roads and housing.
- The *primary incomes multiplier* which emanates from household expenditures of primary incomes derived from mining.
- The *employment multiplier*, which derives from the employment created in other industries as a result of mining. This multiplier includes

the benefits of the provision of employment for workers from deep rural communities and the transfer of funds back to these areas.

- The *income terms-of-trade multiplier* which results from the positive impact that mineral export earnings have on the balance of payments, foreign reserves, monetary policy and ultimately upon the general level of business activity in the country.
- The *capital formation multiplier* which arises from mining's influence in attracting foreign capital to the country (via the JSE[11] or via direct investment), and in domestic capital formation.

5.11.2   Gold

The long dominance of gold was broken in the 1990s by the rise in the output of platinum group metals, which, for a time in 2000, overtook gold in the value of sales. This occurred because both the output and price of platinum group metals were rising rapidly and because both price and output of gold were falling. Between 1979 and 1989 the production of gold had declined by 13.9 per cent, from 705.4 metric tons to 607.5 metric tons, a decline that accelerated to 26 per cent in the 1990s. By the end of the twentieth century South Africa's proportion of Western World gold production had fallen to the level of 1895. In the 30 years covered by this book the output of gold had more than halved, the country's proportion of Western World gold production had fallen from 79 per cent to 21 per cent and South Africa's prominence in gold mining had become part of history.

The value of the gold output kept on increasing in rand terms because of the constant depreciation in the value of the currency. In this way, in the 1990s, the average rand value of a fine ounce of gold continued to rise until 1997. Then, in that year, it fell from R1 664 in 1996 to 1523, the first time that it had fallen in rands. Although it rose in 1998 it did not regain its 1996 level until 1999 and by then it was too late to save many of the marginal mines, which had been faced with steadily rising costs. Averaged grades being mined were falling from 13.28 grams per ton in 1970 to 4.62 grams per ton in 1999. The richer seams were being worked out rapidly and it was only the rise in the price of gold in the 1970s that had enabled many of the mines to continue in operation. When the fall in the average grade mined coincided with a decline in the inflation–adjusted price of gold and wage increases, the writing was on the wall for many of the marginal mines. This explains the sharp decline in the physical volume of gold produced (see Table 5.9).

5.11.3   Coal

Coal output, which had been rising rapidly in the mid-1970s, experienced

Table 5.9   Gold production, employment and working costs, 1970–1999

	1970	1975	1980	1985	1990	1995	1999
Value (Rm)	831.20	2 560.40	10 374.70	15 139.70	19 239.30	23 218.60	24 679.00
Metric tons treated (m)	80.00	75.10	93.30	123.80	129.40	101.50	89.40
Fine gold (kg 000)	1 000.40	713.40	672.80	670.80	602.00	522.40	449.50
Working revenue (metric ton R)	11.24	34.45	120.56	139.22	163.50	219.00	272.20
Working costs (metric ton R)	7.34	16.71	35.53	68.76	130.34	185.15	229.63
Average grade mined (grams/ton)	13.28	9.42	7.28	6.09	5.05	4.87	4.62
Average number of employees in service (000)	416.80	370.60	469.30	513.80	474.90	377.10	221.80

slower growth in the 1990s. The increase of 83.2 per cent between 1979 and 1989 was succeeded by one of 22.6 per cent between 1989 and 1999. Prices dipped slightly in the overseas markets in real terms even when converted into rands. The domestic market was even more sluggish.

Between 1989 and 1999 the volume of output consumed at home increased from 131.1 million tons to 155.0 million tons – a rise of 18.2 per cent, while the value of sales rose by 130 per cent. In real terms the value of coal sales had declined, in response to the difficulties facing the domestic economy. The industry was very dependent on the electricity industry for its sales. Power generation took 55 per cent of domestic sales and industry a further 38 per cent in 1999. Domestic consumers took a mere 3 per cent in 1999. In this decade domestic consumption declined in 1991, 1992, 1998 and 1999, increasing pressure was placed on margins and the industry responded by cartelizing into two main groups, one controlled by Anglo American, the other by Gencor, now Billiton.

Export markets offered a possible escape from the depressed conditions in the domestic economy; but in the 1990s the growth of these markets also slowed down, as a result of both increased competition and the recession in Japan and South East Asia. The Australian currency depreciated and by the end of the decade both Australia and Indonesia remained lower cost exporters of steam coal than South Africa. Transport costs to Europe worked in South Africa's favour and gave South African coal a competitive edge in the European markets. Australia, the United States and Canada dominated the hard coking coal markets, leaving South African exporters to concentrate on steam coal exports at a time of falling demand from the iron and steel industry and an expanding world output. Despite these disadvantages, the improved facilities at Richards Bay for coal exports and closer proximity to Europe, together with the ending of sanctions, enabled the coal exporters to increase their shipments. In only one year, 1999, did the volume of coal exports decline. From 48.9 million tons in 1989 exports rose to 65.7 million tons in 1999. This increase in volume of 34.4 per cent was matched by an increase in sales of 140.3 per cent. By 1999, 63 per cent of exports totalling R9 330.5 million were going to Europe, 17 per cent to the Far East, 13 per cent to the Middle East and 5 per cent to South America.

Between 1970 and 1999 the value of coal sales had risen by 15923 per cent. The market had been freed from excessive government regulation and South Africa had established itself as one of the world's leading coal exporters. Coal, in 1999, accounted for 2.5 per cent of the country's GDP.

5.11.4   Other minerals

Platinum metals were often listed with other minerals until almost the end of the century. Their rise to preeminence occurred rapidly, in two years, 1999 and 2000, though platinum production had been rising since 1980. Between 1980 and 1990 it increased by 24.1 per cent, between 1990 and 1999 by 58.3 per cent. The price of platinum group metals (platinum, palladium and rhodium) rose very rapidly on two occasions, in 1990 and then in 1999–2000, when for a while it seemed that the value of platinum production would surpass that of gold.

Demand from the jewellery industry was the principal driving force behind the growth of the industry, followed by that for autocatalysts and investment. The 1999 rise in the price from US$350 an ounce to US$520 an ounce was triggered by the Russian decision to withhold supplies from the market. The price continued to rise throughout most of 2000, making it likely that platinum investment and output will continue to rise. A handful of firms dominated production. Two firms, Anglo Platinum and Impala Platinum, accounted for three-quarters of production in 1999, when the total output was 3.9 million ounces valued at R14 901 million.

The palladium price rose even more rapidly than that of platinum, more than doubling to US$800 an ounce in February 2000. In value it is still less than half that of platinum, though demand from the automobile industry for autocatalysts and from the electronic industry has proved to be consistently strong. Rhodium followed close behind, with an output in 1999 of 410 000 ounces and the price reached US$2 525 an ounce in February 2000. Together the platinum group metals are likely to overtake gold early in the new century.

Gold, coal and platinum group metals dominated output in 1999. Together they accounted for over three-quarters of the value of mineral production. The only other minerals with sales of more than a million rand were iron ore, copper and nickel, though chrome ore and manganese were about to join that club. As for the notion that South Africa's mineral base broadened considerably in this period, we have already shown that this did not happen in the 1970–90 period. In the following decade there is some evidence of this happening as a result of the unparalleled decline in the gold output. In 1990 gold, coal and platinum accounted for 85.6 per cent of production: in 1999 for 74.8 per cent. An increase in the proportion of total sales by coal of 1.6 per cent and platinum of 5.9 per cent was more than counterbalanced by the fall in the share of gold from 50.6 per cent to 32.3 per cent. Iron ore marginally increased its proportion of total sales from 2.8 per cent to 2.9 per cent, but copper decreased by 1.0 per cent, nickel by 0.2 per cent and manganese by 1.5 per cent and even chrome only managed to increase its share by 0.1 per cent. Since zinc and asbestos also experienced sharp falls in output, the reason for the increase in sales did not occur either in the precious metals or in the ordinary minerals. It was the result of the increase in the value of the miscellaneous groups, which includes strategic minerals.

Table 5.10   Principal mineral sales, 1990–1999 (Rm)

Commodity	1990	1995	1999
Gold	19 239.3	23 218.6	24 679.0
Coal	8 149.6	12 817.8	17 609.4
Platinum	5 164.2	6 164.2	14 901.0
Iron ore	1 076.5	1 657.9	2 206.0
Copper	1 063.9	1 678.7	1 392.6
Nickel	655.8	850.0	1 142.2
Chrome ore	421.1	590.6	956.1
Manganese	848.3	686.8	934.5
Total sales	38 046.5	54 180.3	76 471.2

Source: South African Statistics and the Chamber of Mines.

It is the addition of the R8 257.5 million in the miscellaneous category that provides support for the view that South Africa's mineral base broadened considerably in these years. But what were these strategic minerals? It seems reasonable to argue that they were diamonds. Diamond output increased by 16.4 per cent to 10 642 carats, which was still below the level of 1985. There is no evidence of broadening here. We do know, though, that taxation on the diamond mines rose from R40.1 million in 1990 to R366 million in 1999 and that diamond sales in 1999, according to the *Annual Report 1999-2000* of the Chamber of Mines, were US$766 million, which would account for a sizeable proportion of the miscellaneous category. Since diamond production was lower in 1999 than ten years earlier this cannot be considered evidence of a

Table 5.11   Changes in the volume of mineral output, 1990–1999

Commodity	Decrease/increase (%)
Gold	Decreased by 25.5
Coal	Increased by 21.6
Platinum group	Increased by 58.3
Iron ore	Decreased by 2.6
Copper	Decreased by 19.6
Nickel	Increased by 18.9
Chrome ore	Increased by 14.9
Manganese	Decreased by 29.5

Source: South African Statistics.

broadening in the mineral base and our conclusion must be that, with the exception of platinum, there was no pronounced trend towards broadening the mineral base of South Africa in the 1990s.

5.11.5 Contribution to Exports

In the 1990s the contribution of primary minerals continued to account for the largest portion of total export earnings. During 2000, despite the 4.5 per cent decline in gold production, the contribution of primary minerals to total merchandise exports increased for the first time since 1993. This was as a result of the significant rise in platinum group metal (PGM) prices with the result that PGM exports of R24.6 billion nearly matched gold exports of R25 billion. While the contribution of primary exports to total merchandise exports has generally declined during the decade, beneficiated mineral exports (that is, ferro alloys, chemicals from coal and so on) bring the total contribution of the minerals complex to 59 per cent of total merchandise exports.

Mineral production was heavily geared to export markets (see Table 5.12). Of the 12 leading mineral commodities exported, five depended on external markets to take over 90 per cent of their output and another two to take over

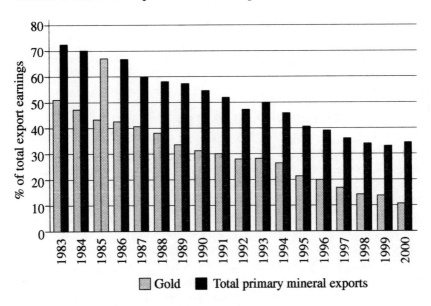

Source: South African Reserve Bank/Chamber of Mines.

Figure 5.3 Contribution of gold and total primary minerals to South Africa's merchandise exports, 1983-2000

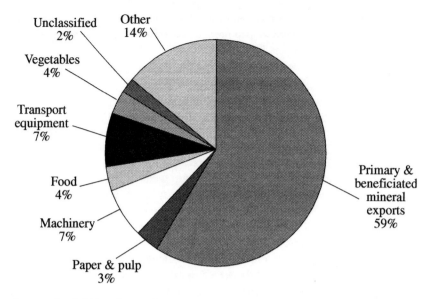

Source: South African Reserve Bank/Chamber of Mines.

Figure 5.4   Breakdown of merchandise exports, 2000

70 per cent. They were all narrowly focused, being either in the precious metals category, or inputs for the iron and steel industry.

5.12   FORCES OF CHANGE IN THE 1990s

The ending of apartheid in the early 1990s was a significant political and economic factor that influenced South Africa's mining industry during the decade. Suddenly the world was opened to an industry that had been, to a large extent, confined to South African shores by financial and trade sanctions. The industry found itself behind its global competitors in terms of best practice. The legacies of apartheid in education, job reservation laws, archaic work practices, the lack of access to global finance and technology were apparent. The lack of a global outlook was a severe constraint. Change was rapid. New leaders emerged in the industry to change the face of the industry for ever. From Gilbertson at Gencor, to Swanepoel at Harmony and Godsell at Anglogold (to mention but a few names) the leadership of the industry changed. Mines were increasingly run as businesses. The management philosophy of production maximization in the 1980s changed to shareholder value maximization in the 1990s.

Table 5.12 Principal mineral exports of South Africa in 1999

Commodity	Exports (Rm)	Percentage of sales
Gold	14 769.1	99.1
Platinum group	13 982.4	93.8
Coal	9 330.5	53.0
Iron ore	1 721.4	78.0
Copper	723.6	52.0
Manganese	615.2	65.0
Nickel	494.7	43.1
Chrome ore	310.3	21.0
Silver	146.6	95.5
Fluorspar	141.3	91.7
Lead	88.6	87.0
Asbestos	35.0	94.6

Source: Chamber of Mines, *Annual Report, 1999-2000.*

5.12.1 Labour

The most striking feature of the labour employed in the mines in the 1990s is the sharp fall in numbers at a time of growing unemployment (see Figure 5.5). There are a number of different reasons for this development. Foremost among these was the reduction in the number employed by the gold mines. This fell from 505 271 in 1989 to 221 848 in 1999. In the 1990s the gold mines were shedding labour at the rate of 8.7 per cent a year, bringing about a collapse of 56.1 per cent in one decade. The unionization of the mine workers, together with the exhaustion of richer seams and a falling rand price of gold, made the closure of uneconomic marginal mines essential. It also encouraged the mines to replace labour with capital wherever possible and to utilize existing labour more efficiently. Between 1989 and 1999 working costs per kilogram of gold increased by 111.3 per cent, but productivity also rose substantially. Kilograms of gold per employee rose from 1.3 in 1991 to 2.5 in 1999.

Employment in other mines fell as a response to mechanization or falling output. The production of manganese, iron ore and copper all declined, while coal mines accelerated the process of mechanization. Anti-capitalist attitudes among trade union leaders combined with regular wages increases encouraged this development in coal mines and was possible because many of them were geologically suited to mechanization in ways which were not possible in the gold mines.

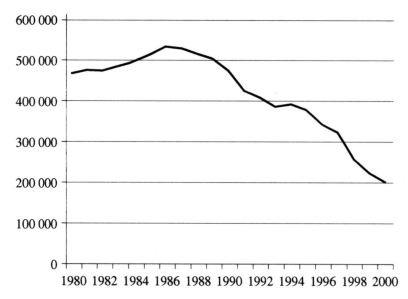

Notes: Gold mines that are members of the Chamber of Mines.

Source: Chamber of Mines.

Figure 5.5 Labour employed in the South African gold mines, 1980-2000

Work practices on mines underwent thorough change. The collapsing of management hierarchies into narrower bands, incentivizing the workplace and introducing more appropriate management practices were common themes. At the same time significant attention was focused on human capital – which had historically been treated mostly as a cost. With the emergence of career paths, training programmes aimed at equipping workers with the necessary skills to progress along such career paths were developed. The Chamber and the unions signed an agreement on adult basic education and training; and significant progress has been made in this regard. Concurrently the adoption of a new Mines Health and Safety Act was adopted and much more attention was placed on these issues. The result has been a significant improvement in fatality and accident rates to their lowest levels ever recorded (see Figure 5.6).

The development of the human capital element does not mean that the industry neglected the natural capital and social capital elements. The globalization of the shareholder base of mining companies, combined with greater public awareness and legislative change in South Africa, has resulted in a significant improvement in the industry's environmental performance. The 1991 Minerals Act, which for the first time provided for statutory environmental management programmes to be submitted by mines, a set of

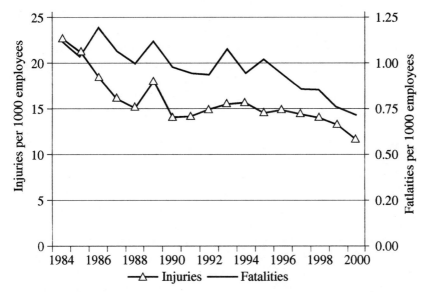

Source: Chamber of Mines.

Figure 5.6   Injuries and fatalities in South African mines, 1984-2000

guidelines developed by industry and government, and the National Environmental Management Act adopted in 1997, all assisted in this process. The mining industry's contribution to corporate social investment has increased significantly during the 1990s. From contributions to the Business Trust and Business Against Crime, to clinics in rural areas and health education facilities for disadvantaged communities, the contribution of the industry runs into hundreds of millions of rands per year.

5.12.2   Capital and the Mining Houses

The traditional function of the mining houses in the early 1990s has changed from that of an entity providing all the technical, financial and human capital expertise for mining projects, to being a much more streamlined conduit for maximizing shareholder value. Foreign listings and bench marking against international best financial practices has been one of the forces driving this change. In addition, the services provided by the mining houses have to all intents and purposes been subcontracted out with a supervisory level of residual expertise remaining in the mining head offices.

The shareholding structure of the mining houses has also changed drastically. In the early 1990s the mining houses with significant cross-holdings were ostensibly controlled by a fairly small number of South African families. Today over 60 per cent of the industry's market capitalization is owned by foreigners and the remainder by South African financial institutions on behalf of millions of South African pension fund holders and investors, but control is different. The Oppenheimer family still controls a very significant portion of mineral production.

The dominance of the traditional mining finance houses ended in the 1990s. Rand Mines finally faded away, the fate of any mining company that refuses to engage in exploration, JCI unbundled with Anglo American cherry picking the platinum mines that became Anglo Plats, Anglovaal also unbundled and separated its manufacturing business from its mining, and Goldfields of South Africa was merged with the former Gencor gold mines to form a new Gold Fields that focused only on gold mines. The rest of the former Gencor base minerals were placed into Billiton and then listed on the London Stock Exchange. Anglo American followed them. In this way, in barely half a decade, the sanctions era disinvestment campaigns were completely turned around, with both Anglo American and Billiton now based in London and managing their South African operations as foreign investments. As a consequence of these changes power has passed to those in charge of the gold mines, which has resulted in a more hands-on approach and an ability to turn loss-making mines into profitable ones – a feat which the mining houses were unable to do, but which Harmoney was able to achieve within a couple of years.

The market capitalization of the mines reflected these changes (see Table 5.2, above). While the rise in the value of the coal mines is striking, the most remarkable feature in the table is the rise in the value of diamond shares that overtook gold in 1995, providing further indirect evidence that it was diamond sales that were pushing up the value of total mineral sales and not the widening of the mineral base. By the end of the decade the market capitalization of the platinum mines was more than treble that of the gold mines and the capitalization of the diamond mines almost doubled that of the gold mines. The coal mines, though, had been subsumed into larger holding companies and were no longer listed separately.

Gross domestic fixed investment in the mining industry continued on a fairly large scale. It rose from R7 176 million in 1990 to R10 601 million in 2000 in current prices. In real terms, though, it had declined considerably and the figure for 2000 was lower than that for 1990. The decline had taken place between 1990 and 1993, when new investment had fallen by 45 per cent. The political changes of 1994 had then led to renewed confidence in the economy and an upward movement in investment that lasted until 1997. The recovery was fragile and four years of rising investment were not sufficient to lift new investment back to the level of 1990, when the recovery went into reverse in 1999 and 2000. As a result, fixed domestic capital investment in mining in 2000 was 46 per cent below that of 1990.

Investment in gold mining was more limited, as the profitability of the industry was under threat. Even so the R1.8 billion in 1990 rose to R2.4 billion in 1999 and the industry felt able to raise dividends by 18 per cent to R2.5 billion, after paying a wage and salary bill of approximately R20 billion.

5.12.3   Changing Demand

Over the decade the nature of commodity cycles and prices has also changed. Traditionally the duration and breadth of the rise in the commodity cycle from trough to peak was about five years. This has now narrowed to nearly half that level and applies to commodities in their different cycles. On the gold side, prices are half the level of 20 years ago in dollar terms and the structure of demand has changed. In 2000 the majority of purchases were by millions of individuals around the world buying gold jewellery compared to the dominance of central banks 20 years ago. To illustrate the forces of change, consider how the decline in US$ gold prices forced the South African industry to respond (see Figure 5.7).

The changing nature of commodity cycles has also resulted in a number of

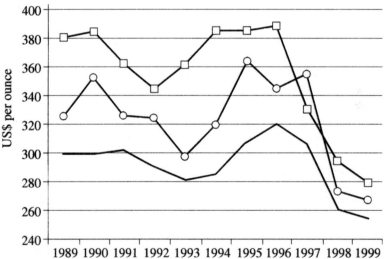

-O- South Africa —— Average Australia, Canada, USA -□- Average gold price

Source: Gold Fields Mineral Services.

Figure 5.7   *Gold production cost trends for South Africa and the average of Australia, Canada and the USA, versus the gold price, 1989–1999*

major mining companies becoming commodity diversified, which enables them to balance good performing commodities against the underperformers within the overall commodity cycle. Good examples of these include Anglo American and Billiton. Other South African mining companies have become purely commodity focused, believing that their comparative strengths of commodity focus outweigh the benefits of diversification effects.

5.12.4   Legislative Change

The pace of legislative change in South Africa during the 1990s has been all-encompassing and a significant driving force behind change in the mining industry. In particular, new competition laws, labour market laws, energy policy laws and the proposed new minerals policy for the country have played a role in shaping the way in which the industry behaves and interacts with the community, government and shareholders. Unfortunately, certain of these laws, especially in the labour market domain, have resulted in the inability of the industry to use its capital assets more intensively with a resultant pressure on unit costs. For example, the inability of the industry to blast on Sundays limits the ability of the mining companies to cover their fairly high fixed cost structures.

It is remarkable that mining is the only industry in South Africa that faces a prohibition of work on Sundays. As a result of other policy changes, such as the liberalization of capital controls on residents, the industry has been able to globalize its operations. Significant South African investment has been flowing into the mining industries of Ghana, Tanzania and Mali as well as into North and South America and Australia.

5.12.5   Challenges Facing the Industry in 2000

While the mining industry continues to be the cornerstone economy of the South African economy, a role which has not really changed during the 1990s, a number of significant challenges face the industry at the start of the new millennium. In the case of HIV/AIDS the impact of the pandemic on productivity rates, absenteeism, compensation claims and on the fabric of South African society are factors that the industry is coming to grips with. The changing nature of commodity cycles will pressure further consolidation at both the local and international mining levels. Within South Africa the economic and investment environment will play a key role in determining future investment in the industry and the ability of the country to reduce unemployment, raise economic growth levels and provide a prosperous future for all its people. Environmental lobbies and pressures from Black empowerment lobbies are also likely to influence future profitability and affect future investment in the mining industry. After the experience of Zaire and Zambia, the importance of good management has been highlighted. This is the essential ingredient that transforms potential profits in the ground into real profits in the bank.

5.13   CONCLUSION

The mining industry experienced considerable change in the last 30 years of the twentieth century, during which the production of gold steadily declined, as the richer and more easily worked seams were exhausted. Three mineral booms occurred, each of which attracted bursts of investment. The first one was associated with gold and the phenomenal rise in its price in the 1970s, which for a while slowed down the long-term decline of the industry. In the 1980s coal was the focus of attention and in the 1990s platinum, but vigorous though their growth was, it was not strong enough to counterbalance the decline in gold which is the main feature of the period.

This led to the contribution of mining to GDP declining from 9.0 per cent in 1970 to 6.5 per cent in 2000. If the indirect contribution of mining to the economy is included then mining was probably responsible for approximately 12 per cent of GDP. It remained vital for the country's balance of payments, accounting, in 1999, for 41 per cent of total exports.

Mining's importance as an employer declined, mainly as a result of the gold mines shedding labour, but also as result of mechanization in order to keep costs down. The gold mines employed 54.7 per cent of the 436 500 people employed in the mining industry in 1999 and wages now accounted for over half the value added. The mines, though, were a diminishing source of wealth to rural areas. The social costs of the decline in the gold-mining industry are serious in the latter part of our period, as the demand for unskilled workers was declining throughout the country.

At the end of the century, in 2000, gold, platinum and coal dominated mineral production and exports with diamonds a poor fourth. With gold demonetized, the market now determines the value of the commodities increasing the importance of the Free Trade Agreement signed with the European Union in 1999. Industrial demand for coal, iron ore and platinum has replaced the monetary role of gold and this perhaps is the most striking change that has occurred to the mining industry in the last third of the twentieth century.

NOTES

1. Chamber of Mines Economics Department, 'The South African mining industry in the 1980s', in Stuart Jones and Jon Inggs (eds), *The South African Economy in the 1980s*, Special Issue of *South African Journal of Economic History*, September 1994, p. 50.

2. Gillian Moncur and Stuart Jones, 'The South African mining history in the 1970s', in Stuart Jones and Jon Inggs (eds), *The South African Economy in the 1970s*, Special Issue of *South African Journal of Economic History*, September 1999, p. 125.

3. Stuart Jones and André Muller, *The South African Economy, 1910–1990*, London: Macmillan, 1992, p. 267.

4. Ibid., pp. 139 and 140.

5. Johannes Fedderke and Farah Pirouz, 'The role of mining in the South African economy', Econometric Research Southern Africa Policy (ERSA) Paper, No. 9, University of the Witwatersrand, Johannesburg, December 2000, p. 33.

6. Ibid., p. 23.

7. Stuart Jones, 'Business imperialism and business history', in Stuart Jones and Jon Inggs (eds), *Business Imperialism in South Africa*, Special Issue of *South African Journal of Economic History*, September 1996, p. 18.

8. Moncur and Jones, op. cit, p. 127.

9. Ibid., p. 136.

10. Ibid., pp. 137 and 140.

11. JSE was formerly the Johannesburg Stock Exchange. Its name was changed in 1999 to the Johannesburg Securities Exchange.

6. The manufacturing industry, 1970–2000

Trevor Bell and Nkosi Madula*

6.1 INTRODUCTION

At the end of the 1960s, after a half century of rapid industrialization, South Africa had a relatively advanced and diversified manufacturing sector. By the standards of today's advanced industrial countries, which feature in Gerschenkron's (1952) seminal analysis, South Africa was a very late industrializer, but it was a very much earlier industrializer than those East Asian countries which have been the stars of the manufacturing growth firmament since the 1960s.

Since the early 1970s, however, South Africa's manufacturing growth performance has deteriorated greatly, and has been especially poor since the early 1980s. This is the central fact which any account of South African manufacturing in the 1970–2000 period must seek to explain.

An account of how South Africa industrialized in the decades before 1970 is necessary for understanding subsequent developments, and the forces which dislodged South Africa from its earlier, robust growth trajectory. Section 6.2 of this chapter thus provides a short description of the main features of South African industrial development from the eve of the First World War through to the beginning of the 1970s. Section 6.3 deals with developments during the 1970s, a decade notable for the great gold-led commodity price boom which began in 1972; and Section 6.4 with the period from the early 1980s through to the late 1990s, during which manufacturing output stagnated and employment declined. In the light of the discussion in earlier sections, Section 6.5 considers some further perspectives on the problems of South African manufacturing over the past 30 years, and their implications for the future sectoral growth path of the economy.

It should be emphasized that the aim of this chapter is to provide an overview of the evolution of South African manufacturing industry as a whole over the past 30 years, and of the larger forces which have resulted in changes in its growth and sectoral structure. Details of the development of particular, individual manufacturing sectors, such as textiles and clothing, or the motor vehicle industry, are therefore not discussed. Furthermore, though the discussion may have policy implications, policies relating to the development of South African manufacturing, and ongoing attempts to formulate an effective response to the decline of this important part of the economy, are not a significant focus of this study.

6.2   THE DRIVE TO INDUSTRIALIZATION THROUGH IMPORT SUBSTITUTION: 1911–1970

Hard data on the rate of growth and structure of manufacturing industry before the First World War are it seems hard to come by. One view, however, is that with some notable exceptions,[1] South African manufacturing industry grew relatively slowly during the first great wave of investment in gold mining, 1886–1911, and at the end of this period was in general of a rudimentary kind. The reasons for the rapid growth of manufacturing which began shortly thereafter are controversial.[2] One probably fundamental factor, however, was the abrupt collapse of new investment in gold mining in 1911 (Frankel, 1967), which until then had absorbed most of the capital and technical expertise available to South Africa (Van Eck, 1961: 101).

The emphasis in South African development shifted, thus, to exploiting the huge scope which existed at the time for industrialization through import substitution. In 1916/17, the ratio of South Africa's imports to its GDP, and the ratio of manufactured imports to the domestic supply of manufactured goods (that is, the ratio of imports to gross output plus imports), both exceeded 50 per cent (Bell and Farrell, 1997: 596). Furthermore, in the case of non-durable consumer goods, generally the focus of industrialization in its early stages, imports consisted to a major extent of products of the most basic kind (De Kock, 1936). There was thus much scope for relatively easy import substitution.

Given the relatively large internal market created by gold, domestic producers took good advantage of the opportunities for profitable import substitution. From the First World War through to the end of the 1960s, South Africa industrialized largely through a process of import substitution.[3]

As Table 6.1 shows, manufacturing value-added (MVA) grew rapidly. The highest MVA growth rate, though not the highest GDP growth rate, in any full decade shown in the table, occurred in the period from 1926/27 to 1936/37, which included the Great Depression.[4] Both the MVA and GDP growth rates, however, reached their peaks at 9.9 per cent and 6.3 per cent during 1960–65, with average annual growth rates during the 1960s as a whole of 5.7 per cent and 8.6 per cent respectively.[5] As a result, the economy diversified considerably, away from primary commodities, towards manufacturing. The

Table 6.1   Average   annual   rates   of   growth   of   GDP,   MVA,   and manufacturing employment in South Africa, 1916-2000

	GDP %	MVA %	Employment %
1916/17–1926/27	4.00	6.80	1.82
1926/27–1936/37	3.90	8.90	5.60
1936/37–1946/47	3.70	6.10	6.38
1946/47–1956/57	5.50	7.50	5.12
1946–1950	4.10	9.03	7.02
1950–1955	4.89	7.48	5.39
1955–1960	4.11	4.56	0.66
1960–1965	6.28	9.85	6.93
1965–1970	5.15	7.38	2.84
1970–1975	3.65	5.93	3.93
1975–1980	3.09	4.47	1.90
1980–1985	1.35	0.95	0.47
1985–1990	1.67	1.59	1.09
1990–1995	0.86	0.15	−1.25
1995–1998	2.43	0.71	−1.66
1995–2000	2.45	1.11	n/a
1950–1960	4.50	6.01	3.00
1960–1970	5.71	8.61	4.87
1970–1980	3.37	5.20	2.91
1980–1990	1.51	1.27	0.78
1990–1998	1.45	0.36	−1.40
1990–2000	1.65	0.63	n/a
1970–1975	3.65	5.93	3.93
1975–1978	1.71	2.05	0.85
1978–1981	5.25	8.55	4.21
1975–1981	3.47	5.25	2.52
1970–1981	3.55	5.56	3.16

Note: Employment growth rate for earliest period is for 1920-26.

Sources: GDP and MVA growth rates calculated for 1916/17–1956/57 from data in T.A. du Plessis (1965), and for 1946-2000 from South African Reserve Bank data. Employment growth rates for years from 1920 to 1970 derived from data in South African Statistics 1990, and for subsequent years from DRI-WEFA database.

percentage share of manufacturing in GDP increased from 6.2 in 1916/17 to 19.4 in 1956/57 (in constant 1956/57 prices) (T.A. du Plessis, 1965), and further to 22.8 per cent (in current prices) in 1970. Manufacturing output also became increasingly diversified.[6]

Also, manufactured exports became an increasingly large proportion of South Africa's total exports, rising from 8.2 per cent in 1916/17 to 26.3 per cent in 1956/57[7] and to 31.4 per cent in 1972 (owing partly to a levelling off of gold exports in 1965-70). The composition of manufactured exports also changed considerably, with the share of non-durable goods (especially food, beverages and tobacco) decreasing substantially in the 30 years to 1956/57; and those of natural resource-based manufactures (such as chemicals, iron and steel, non-ferrous metals, and pulp and paper), and of downstream durable goods industries (fabricated metal products, machinery, electrical machinery and transportation equipment) rising (Bell et al., 1999: 8).

The upshot of these developments was that, as noted earlier, by the early 1970s, South Africa had a relatively mature and diversified manufacturing sector. Comparison with South Korea helps put this in perspective. In 1970, some 58.3 per cent of South Korea's total MVA was still contributed by subsectors producing non-durable consumer goods, higher than for any year in South Africa since 1916/17; and the combined MVA share of fabricated metal products, the various capital goods sectors, and the motor vehicle industry, in South Korea was only 12.4 per cent, compared with 33.3 per cent in South Africa in 1972.[8]

Although with a considerable time lag, and at much lower levels of per capita income, South Africa, like some other natural resource-abundant countries, such as Australia and Canada, had apparently made effective use of the internal market for manufactures, and of the rents, created by its natural resource abundance, to achieve a considerable degree of industrialization.[9]

6.3   THE ONSET OF THE DECLINE IN MVA AND GDP GROWTH DURING THE COMMODITY PRICE BOOM OF THE 1970s

6.3.1   Declining Growth

As noted earlier, the average annual rates of growth of both GDP and MVA reached their peak of 6.3 per cent and 9.9 per cent, respectively, in 1960-65. They fell to 5.2 per cent and 7.4 per cent, respectively, in 1965-70, further (to 3.7 per cent and 5.9 per cent) in 1970-75 and yet further (to 3.5 per cent and 5.3 per cent) in 1975-81 (averaging 3.5 per cent and 5.6 per cent in 1970-81 as a whole) (Table 6.1).[10] These MVA growth rates, in both 1970-75 and

1975–81, were lower than in any earlier full decade or five-year period since the First World War, for which figures are shown in Table 6.1, excepting only 1955–60.

This was the beginning of the decline of growth rates, and of the descent towards stagnation of the economy as a whole, but especially of manufacturing, which has characterized the period since the early 1980s. As is argued later, in so far as factors peculiar to South Africa are concerned, though other factors may have compounded and propagated it, the initial impulse to decline was fundamental change in the South African economy in the years between 1965 and 1975.

Nearer to the surface, and more readily observable, however, the major feature of the 1970s was the great, gold-led commodity price boom which took off from about 1972.

6.3.2 The Commodity Price Boom of the 1970s and the Effect on Relative Prices

Superficially, conditions for growth were very favourable in the 1970s as a whole. The commodity price boom resulted in huge foreign exchange windfalls. Although interrupted by declines in the mid-1970s, the price of gold increased from a yearly average of about US$52 in 1972 to US$613 in 1980, before beginning its descent. Commodity prices in general followed a roughly similar pattern, with a large upswing from 1972 to 1980, interrupted by declines from late 1974 through to 1976–77.

The effect on the foreign currency value of South Africa's exports of goods was dramatic. Whereas total exports of goods (measured in constant US dollars) increased at an average annual rate of 5.03 per cent in 1965–70, in 1970–80 they grew at 12.4 per cent a year.[11] Exports of gold and 'other mining' (coal, diamonds, platinum, iron ore and so on) grew at 16.4 per cent and 15.3 per cent, respectively, between 1970 and 1980 (Table 6A.1) (compared to absolute declines at 0.9 per cent and 1.9 per cent, respectively, in 1965–70) (Bell et al., 1999: Table 1). A major effect of this was a substantial real appreciation of the foreign exchange value of the rand. Relative to its level in 1970–72, the real effective exchange rate (REER) was 9.4 per cent higher in 1974–78, 24.8 per cent higher in 1979–81, and 28.2 per cent higher in 1982–83.

6.3.3 The Effects of the Commodity Price Boom on Manufacturing Industry

Intersectoral differences in export growth rates

The commodity price boom, and the resulting real appreciation of the rand, thus, represented a huge change in relative prices which impacted on manufacturing industry in various ways. One of these is reflected in the rate of growth and structure of manufactured exports. Whereas South Africa's total exports of goods including gold (measured in constant US dollars) grew at rates unprecedented at least since the Second World War, the average annual rate of growth of manufactured exports in the aggregate in 1970–80 (7.2 per cent) (Table 6.2) was slightly lower than in 1960–70 (8.0 per cent) (Bell et al., 1999: Table 1).

This is particularly remarkable considering that (measured in constant US dollars) the export growth rate of natural resource-based manufactures (represented by chemicals, iron and steel, non-ferrous metal basic industries, and pulp and paper) grew rapidly at 11.9 per cent a year in 1970–80 (Table 6.2). (The share of these sectors in total manufactured exports thus increased from 24.3 per cent in 1970 to 37.1 per cent in 1980. Table 6A.2.)

As these figures suggest, the exports of non-natural resource-based, more downstream manufactures grew slowly in 1970–80. For instance, measured in constant US dollars, the export growth rate of the downstream durable goods group of industries (represented in this study by fabricated metal products, machinery, electrical machinery, motor vehicles and other transportation equipment) fell from an estimated 8.0 per cent a year in 1960–70, to 2.1 per cent in 1970–80 (Table 6.2). (Their share in total manufactured exports which had been strongly on the rise before 1956/57, and held steady in the 1960s, fell from 15.7 per cent in 1970 to 9.1 per cent in 1980. Table 6A.2.)

The effect of the commodity price boom on real exchange rates probably contributed to these intersectoral differences in export growth rates. It resulted in a substantial deterioration in the international competitiveness of the more downstream manufacturing sectors. Exporters of minerals and of natural resource-based manufactures were insulated from any adverse effects of the appreciation of the rand on their competitiveness by rising world prices for their output. The price competitiveness of downstream durable goods, however, fell both relative to foreign producers of such goods, and relative to domestically produced primary products and natural resource-based manufactures.[12]

Sectoral allocation of manufacturing investment

The substantial change in relative prices resulting from the commodity price boom also had a significant effect on the sectoral allocation of investment within manufacturing industry. The most striking feature of manufacturing investment, in the 1970s, is that the share of the chemicals sector in manufacturing gross fixed capital formation increased from 7.2 per cent in 1974 to 55.7 per cent in 1979, and remained high for several years thereafter. This remarkable increase was due mainly to investment in two new, large-

Table 6.2 *Average annual rates of growth of South Africa's manufactured exports, 1970–1998*

	Based on exports in constant (1995) US dollars								Based on constant price trade-weighted foreign currency units						
	1970–75 %	1975–80 %	1980–85 %	1985–90 %	1980–90 %	1990–95 %	1995–98 %	1990–98 %	1970–80 %	1980–85 %	1985–90 %	1980–90 %	1990–95 %	1995–98 %	1990–98 %
Chemicals	7.06	13.61	-5.73	10.56	2.09	10.65	-1.91	5.76	8.9	1.47	3.66	2.56	10.92	3.16	7.94
Iron and steel	9.14	18.73	-1.72	16.14	6.84	8.71	1.46	5.93	12.38	5.74	8.89	7.3	8.98	6.7	8.12
Non-ferrous basic metals	17.60	15.80	5.41	3.87	4.64	2.83	11.60	6.04	15.06	13.4	-2.62	5.09	3.08	17.37	8.23
Pulp and paper	2.24	8.68	4.14	14.58	9.23	13.40	-11.83	3.19	4.1	12.02	7.41	9.69	13.69	-7.28	5.32
Total natural resource-based group	8.58	15.31	-1.31	11.73	5.01	8.94	0.35	5.64	10.47	6.2	4.75	5.47	9.21	5.54	7.82
Fabricated metal products	4.29	4.71	-9.18	30.82	9.00	10.09	3.83	7.70	3	-2.23	22.58	9.48	10.36	9.21	9.93
Machinery and equipment	-2.03	2.40	-7.29	20.29	5.61	13.47	-2.45	7.22	-1.16	-0.21	12.76	6.08	13.76	2.59	9.44
Electrical machinery	0.10	5.22	-11.38	24.46	5.02	15.14	0.43	9.39	1.09	-4.73	16.6	5.39	15.41	5.62	11.64
Motor vehicles	3.60	6.23	-2.45	23.70	9.85	14.02	5.36	10.69	3.84	4.94	15.95	10.31	14.3	10.8	12.98
Other transport equipment	4.11	1.93	-10.09	19.35	3.59	10.17	2.85	7.37	1.35	-3.2	12	4.12	10.47	8.2	9.61
Total durable goods group	0.46	3.71	-7.26	23.43	6.99	12.85	1.37	8.40	0.72	-0.02	15.7	7.46	13.13	6.61	10.64
Textiles	-0.70	5.95	-3.92	12.67	4.05	5.94	-2.20	2.81	1.2	3.4	5.61	4.5	6.2	2.86	4.93
Wood and wood-based products	15.89	38.10	-7.76	17.08	3.92	5.01	-2.16	2.26	22.81	-0.96	9.79	4.28	5.31	2.86	4.39
Leather products	-1.66	15.12	1.80	6.52	4.13	19.25	-2.71	10.49	4.33	9.9	-0.1	4.78	19.55	2.32	12.77
Furniture	2.34	41.70	-10.37	35.73	10.30	30.02	5.20	20.09	18.18	-3.18	26.86	10.82	30.38	10.62	22.59
Footwear	5.06	25.90	-11.81	15.77	1.04	11.79	-11.85	2.26	15.75	-4.93	8.33	1.49	11.95	-7.23	4.33
Clothing	4.88	15.41	-5.30	10.76	2.41	6.02	-4.28	2.03	8.27	1.98	3.77	2.87	6.29	0.68	4.15
Total labour-intensive group	1.03	12.78	-4.83	13.57	3.96	10.16	-1.30	5.72	5.2	2.45	6.44	4.42	10.44	3.81	7.9
TV, radio & communication equipment	-2.19	0.33	1.77	21.00	10.96	20.79	8.80	16.15	-1.84	8.97	13.67	11.3	21.18	14.41	18.6
Professional & scientific equipment	-4.54	1.63	-4.38	19.55	6.92	12.18	1.93	8.22	-2.52	3.02	12.04	7.43	12.43	7.19	10.44
Other manufacturing sectors	9.91	2.21	-14.22	14.69	-0.81	4.49	-2.97	1.63	4.68	-7.7	-7.52	-0.38	4.75	2.05	3.73
Total manufactured exports	7.55	6.94	-7.26	14.19	2.91	8.42	-0.38	5.03	5.88	-0.21	7.05	3.36	8.69	4.77	7.21

Source: Calculated from the DRI-WEFA and South African Reserve Bank databases.

scale, capital-intensive synthetic fuel plants, known as Sasol II and Sasol III (Sasol I, as noted earlier (note 5), having been constructed in the early 1950s).

As the discussion in Section 6.2 indicated, by the 1970s, import/domestic supply ratios, and consequently the scope for further import substitution, were considerably lower than in earlier decades. Because of this, and the appreciation of the rand, conditions in general were not conducive to import substitution. One major exception, however, was production of alternative energy sources, that is, of alternatives to imported crude oil. The price of oil had increased fivefold in a short space of time after the 1973 oil crisis, and trebled again after the second, in 1979. Also, when the decisions were taken to construct the Sasol II and Sasol III plants, in 1974 and 1979, respectively, real interest rates in South Africa (as in the world economy in general) were low, indeed, at times negative,[13] and the strong rand made for relatively low prices of imported capital equipment.

Together these three factors (high oil prices, low real interest rates, and a strong rand) resulted in a relatively low user cost of capital. It is debatable whether Sasol II and Sasol III were then, or subsequently, commercially justifiable propositions or should be seen simply as late, gross examples of South Africa's (allegedly inefficient) traditional import-substituting strategy, necessitated now by political circumstances. At the time, however, conditions for them could hardly have been more favourable.[14]

Earlier in the decade, as a result of decisions taken before the major commodity price upswing, another capital-intensive, natural resource-based sector which accounted for a sizeable proportion of manufacturing investment, was the iron and steel industry. This was apparently related to the expansion of ISCOR's steelworks in Pretoria and Vanderbijlpark in 1973, and its completion of a new plant in Newcastle in 1974 (McCarthy, 1999: 150).

Intersectoral differences in value-added growth rates
The effects of the commodity price boom discussed so far were those stemming mainly from the change in relative prices which it brought about. However, it also had a substantial effect on the level of expenditure in the economy. That is, it had spending effects as well as price effects.

The most striking spending effect of the commodity price boom was a substantial increase in gross domestic fixed capital formation, in the economy as a whole, including the large-scale investments in synthetic fuels discussed above. The ratio of economy-wide fixed capital formation to GDP increased substantially between 1970 and 1975, fell through to 1978, but with the cyclical upswing, thereafter, increased considerably again through to 1981 (almost to the 1975 level, the highest GDFI/GDP (gross domestic fixed investment to gross domestic product) ratio since the Second World War) (Figure 6A.1).[15]

The output of the sectors comprising the downstream durable goods group of industries – fabricated metal products, machinery, electrical machinery, motor vehicles, and other transport equipment – consists to a significant extent of capital goods, the demand for which is very sensitive to variations in the level of investment. These are the major capital goods-producing manufactur-ing sectors. The general increase in investment in 1970–81 resulted in rapid growth of value added in this category of manufacturing industries.[16] Despite the much lower export growth rates of these sectors collectively in the 1970s, compared to the 1960s, and to natural resource-based sectors in the 1970s, their average annual output growth, in 1970–81, was relatively rapid, at 7.3 per cent compared to the 6.2 per cent of the natural resource-based sectors (Table 6.3). Any negative effects of the commodity price boom on the price competitiveness of these sectors, and hence on their exports, therefore was much more than offset by the positive spending effects of the boom on their output.

The sensitivity of the rate of growth of these sectors, and hence to a significant extent of total MVA, to the level of investment, evident in 1970–81, is crucial to understanding the stagnation of South African manufacturing industry since the early 1980s. The tendency for the degree of export orientation, and the rate of growth of output of these sectors to be inversely related, remains, but now with relatively rapid export growth, and increasing export orientation, is associated with declining output.

The motor vehicle industry and the last throes of import-substituting industrialization

One subsector among those in the downstream durable goods category which benefited from the spending effects of the commodity price boom, and which should perhaps be singled out for more detailed discussion, is the motor vehicle industry.

A new motor industry policy, the so-called Phase III of the local content programme, was announced in 1969. In terms of this, South African assemblers were required to increase the local content of locally assembled passenger vehicles, in stages, to 66 per cent of the total component weight of vehicles, by 1976.[17]

This would be expected to have resulted in import substitution in the motor industry, and thus perhaps to have contributed to accelerated growth of the sector. The motor vehicle industry was indeed one of the most import-intensive manufacturing subsectors in the early 1970s.[18] It has been estimated that more than a third of the import substitution that occurred in manufacturing industry as a whole, in 1972–80, was contributed by the motor vehicle industry (Bell and Farrell, 1997: 599, Table 16). The motor vehicle industry

Table 6.3   Average annual rates of growth of value added in South African manufacturing industry, 1970–1998

	1970–75 %	1975–78 %	1978–81 %	1975–81 %	1970–81 %	1980–85 %	1985–90 %	1980–90 %	1990–95 %	1995–98 %	1990–98 %
Chemicals	4.54	11.31	8.33	9.81	7.38	6.77	–0.72	2.96	0.37	4.10	1.75
Iron and steel	7.52	0.96	3.11	2.03	4.49	–1.96	0.42	–0.78	3.94	2.98	3.58
Non-ferrous basic metals	16.91	–4.34	12.07	4.54	9.42	4.18	1.33	2.75	6.55	18.45	10.86
Pulp and paper	6.61	2.87	4.11	3.49	4.89	5.21	1.36	3.27	2.01	–2.65	0.24
Total natural resource-based group	5.63	5.31	6.32	5.81	6.19	4.08	0.02	2.03	1.93	4.00	2.70
Fabricated metal products	5.46	–2.04	12.64	5.05	5.23	–2.44	–4.48	–3.46	–0.78	4.06	1.01
Machinery and equipment	8.65	–0.80	13.59	6.15	7.28	–1.83	–2.15	–1.99	0.76	–9.41	–3.18
Electrical machinery	14.33	6.23	9.41	7.81	10.72	1.11	–5.27	–2.13	2.96	–1.66	1.21
Motor vehicles	10.73	–1.12	17.79	7.92	9.19	–4.97	3.54	–0.81	0.43	–5.30	–1.76
Other transport equipment	5.94	–5.63	3.96	–0.95	2.12	–2.17	–6.91	–4.57	–5.92	5.27	–1.87
Total durable goods group	8.62	–0.66	13.60	6.23	7.31	–2.48	1.71	–2.09	0.41	–3.58	–1.11
Textiles	1.81	8.31	8.30	8.31	5.30	§–2.71	–4.30	–3.51	0.84	–1.38	0.00
Wood and wood-based products	3.94	1.79	10.14	5.88	5.00	0.69	–1.99	–0.66	2.38	0.04	1.50
Leather products	5.77	–6.07	8.08	0.75	3.00	5.87	0.14	2.96	1.85	4.38	2.79
Furniture	3.25	1.39	17.23	9.02	6.36	1.52	2.76	2.14	–0.64	1.46	0.14
Footwear	1.15	0.97	4.19	2.57	1.92	2.36	1.58	1.97	–1.89	–9.25	–4.72
Clothing	3.26	2.97	14.10	8.39	6.03	1.37	2.13	1.75	–0.08	–3.04	–1.20
Total labour-intensive group	2.75	3.80	10.66	7.18	5.14	0.15	–0.39	–0.12	–0.36	–1.53	–0.35
TV, radio & communication equipment	8.25	–8.45	6.98	–1.04	3.08	6.95	12.91	9.89	–3.12	9.82	1.54
Professional & scientific equipment	–9.71	–4.40	13.90	4.35	–2.35	14.59	7.21	10.84	2.10	–6.34	–1.15
Other manufacturing sectors	4.21	1.91	4.69	3.29	3.71	1.71	5.49	3.58	–1.28	0.82	–0.50
Total MVA	5.93	2.05	8.55	5.25	5.56	0.95	1.59	1.27	0.15	0.65	0.33

Source: Calculated from the DRI-WEFA database.

108

grew relatively rapidly in 1970–81 (at 9.2 per cent a year), but some other manufacturing subsectors grew even faster ('other chemicals' at 10.2 per cent, plastics 13.7 per cent, and electrical machinery, 10.7 per cent). It is not clear, therefore, to what extent motor industry policy as such contributed to the rapid growth of this sector, as distinct from the spending effects of the commodity price boom on an industry where sales volumes are very sensitive to cyclical movements in incomes (and indeed also to real interest rates which, as noted earlier, were very low in the 1970s).

6.3.4   The Slowdown in the World Economy

The discussion of the 1970s has so far touched on the relative price and spending effects of the commodity price boom on South Africa as a minerals-rich economy. Especially, it has emphasized intersectoral differences in the performance of manufacturing industry caused by the boom. Beneath the surface, however, various real forces were at work slowing the growth of the economy as a whole, including in particular manufacturing industry. As indicated earlier, some of these forces, to be described later, were peculiar to South Africa, and involved fundamental changes in the structure of the economy. One major real factor, external to South Africa, however, was the slowdown in the growth of the world economy in the 1970s.

A deterioration in growth performance in the 1970s was obviously not peculiar to South Africa. The Organization for Economic Cooperation and Development (OECD) recession of 1974–77, was the most severe since the Second World War. Its effects are reflected in the variations in output growth rates in South African manufacturing during the 1970–81 period, noted earlier.[19] This was probably the major *external* reason for the worsening of South Africa's growth performance in the 1970s.

It is now widely accepted that a long-term decline in the growth trajectory of the world economy (of which the mid-1970s OECD recession was a manifestation) took effect from about 1972–73. Pritchett (2000: 224, Table 2), for instance, finds that in the case of developed countries, the average (mean) GDP per capita growth rate fell from 4.26 per cent in 1960–73, to 2.05 per cent in 1973–82, while the median per capita rate fell from 3.97 per cent to 1.79 per cent a year. In developing countries, the mean per capita GDP growth rate fell from 2.68 per cent in 1960–73 to 1.74 per cent in 1973–82, while the median fell from 2.72 per cent to 1.99 per cent. There was, thus, a general decline in per capita growth rates in the 1970s, but with a larger proportional decline in per capita growth rates for developed than for developing countries, in 1973–82, compared to 1960–73.

It is striking, though, that the percentage points decline in South Africa's per capita growth rate was greater than that of developing countries in general. As the figures above indicate, in developing countries the mean per capita growth rate fell by 0.94 percentage points, and the median by 0.73 percentage points. In South Africa, however, the per capita growth rate fell from 2.44 per cent in 1960–73 (roughly the same as the mean and median in developing countries in general in this period) to 0.75 per cent in 1973–82, that is by 1.69 percentage points, significantly more than in developing countries in general. This suggests the possibility of some special factor operating in the case of South Africa, in the 1970s, which made for a larger proportional decline than in developing countries in general. It seems, therefore, that the deterioration in South Africa's per capita growth and hence in the growth of manufacturing industry, in the 1970s, must be explained both in terms of factors which made for the slowdown in the world economy as a whole from about 1973, and in terms of some factor peculiar to itself.

6.4   ECONOMIC CRISIS, THE SHIFT TO EXPORT-ORIENTATED INDUSTRIALIZATION AND THE STAGNATION OF MANUFACTURING INDUSTRY: THE 1980s AND 1990s

6.4.1   The shift to Export-orientated Industrialization under Conditions of Economic Crisis

For a while, between 1965 and 1972, there had been the possibility of South Africa shifting from its traditional strategy of import-substituting industrialization (ISI) to export-orientated industrialization (EOI), in relatively placid economic conditions. As the rapid growth of gold output from 1951 onwards (following the opening of the Orange Free State gold fields) came to an end, gold exports, measured in constant US dollars, reached their peak in 1965 and declined (at a rate of 0.9 per cent a year in 1965–70 (Bell et al., 1999: Table 1). The resulting slow growth of South Africa's exports led to the appointment of the Reynders Commission, in 1969, to inquire into South Africa's export trade. Its report, published in 1972, emphasized the need for diversification into non-gold exports, including manufactures, and proposed the use of direct export promotion measures.

For a moment, thus, there had been the possibility of South Africa making the transition to EOI. The ink had hardly dried on the Reynders Commission report, however, when it was overtaken by events, and, for the time being at least, rendered superfluous by the natural resource boom of the 1970s. A shift to EOI between 1972 and 1981 was neither necessary nor economically feasible.

The problem of sustaining export growth in the face of declining gold exports, however, returned with a vengeance in the early to middle 1980s (Bell et al., 1999).

With the collapse of the commodity price boom, and in the context of the OECD downturn of 1980–83, the exports of all the main sectors of the economy fell sharply. The rand began to depreciate in late 1983, and fell precipitously from mid-1984, culminating in the debt crisis of August 1985, and the rescheduling of foreign debt. As in many other developing countries which had been subjected to such debt shocks in the early 1980s, the immediate effect was a sharp reduction in gross domestic expenditure, particularly investment, which fell by 20 per cent between 1984 and 1986. The most urgent requirement for recovery was accelerated growth of exports, including, especially, manufactured exports, to compensate for the decline of gold and other commodities. The effect of these events was an abrupt, involuntary shift to EOI in conditions of economic crisis.

In a mood of optimism before the debt crisis, a deliberate voluntary process of import liberalization had in fact been instituted in 1983, which resulted in a substantial reduction in quantitative rectrictions (QRs) in 1983–85.[20] The real depreciation of the rand, together with domestic recession, however, were the decisive factors in the shift to a system of incentives less biased towards production for the domestic market, and more favourable to exports. Following the debt crisis, in 1985–90, QRs were relaxed further, systems of duty-free-imports-for-exports were introduced in the motor vehicles, textiles and clothing industries in early 1989, and export subsidies, in the form of the General Export Incentive Scheme, were introduced in April 1990. Between 1990 and 1995, import surcharges, which had been imposed earlier in response to the foreign exchange crisis, were removed. Comprehensive tariff reductions began with the commencement of the Uruguay Round implementation period in January 1995.

6.4.2 The Growth and Changing Structure of Manufactured Exports: 1985–1998

In 1985–90, following the debt crisis and the real depreciation of the rand, and in the context of revival of OECD economics, the average annual rate of growth of manufactured exports, *measured in constant US dollars*, accelerated to 14.2 per cent, considerably faster than the 7.2 per cent growth rate of the 1970s (Table 6.2).

The 1985–90 period, however, was one in which, following the Plaza Accord of September 1985, the US dollar depreciated substantially against other major currencies, especially the yen and the mark. The real increase in the foreign currency value of South Africa's exports, in 1985–90, thus, was not nearly as great as the rate of growth of exports measured in constant US dollars suggests.

To get a truer reflection of the increase in South Africa's capacity to import essential intermediate and capital goods, resulting from export growth, South Africa's exports in rands have been converted into what we shall call constant price trade-weighted foreign currency values.[21] Measured in these terms, South Africa's manufactured exports in the aggregate grew at an average annual rate of 7.1 per cent in 1985–90, only slightly higher than the 5.9 per cent a year rate of the 1970s (Table 6.2).

The question of the effect of export growth on South Africa's capacity to import essential inputs and capital goods is important and we return to it in Section 6.5.2, below. Of particular interest at this point, however, is the change in the sectoral structure of manufactured exports after 1985.

What is striking is that, whereas the average annual rate of growth of the exports of the natural resource-based group of sectors (measured in constant trade-weighted foreign currency) fell to 4.8 per cent in 1985–90, compared to 11.9 per cent in 1970–80; that of the downstream durable goods group accelerated considerably to 15.7 per cent in 1985–90, from 0.7 per cent in 1970–80 (Table 6.2).[22]

In the 1990s, the average annual rate of growth of South Africa's manufactured exports in the aggregate increased to 8.7 per cent in 1990–95 (owing to especially rapid growth in 1993–95, with the revival of OECD economics); but this could not be sustained, and it fell to 4.8 per cent in 1995–98 (a period which ended with the East Asian crisis). Particularly pertinent at this juncture, however, is that in both these parts of the 1990s, as in 1985–90, the durable goods group of industries performed better, in terms of export expansion, than the other major categories of manufacturing industry shown in Table 6.2 – averaging a growth rate, in trade-weighted foreign currency, of 10.6 per cent per annum in 1990–98 as a whole. With the end of the commodity price boom, therefore, it seemed there was a shift in South Africa's comparative advantage within manufacturing towards the down-stream durable goods sectors. This has in effect represented a return to underlying trends which were in operation before the aberration caused by the commodity price boom.[23]

There was also a significant increase in the degree of export orientation in manufacturing industry. The ratio of total manufactured exports to the total sales of manufacturing industry, in the aggregate, fell during the commodity price boom, but thereafter increased from 9.1 per cent in 1983, to 12.7 per cent in 1990, 19.1 per cent in 1995, and 21.1 per cent in 1998. This impressive display of increased export orientation, however, is a sign, not of the success of manufacturing industry, but of its deepseated problems.

6.4.3   Export-orientated Stagnation

As noted earlier, the rate of growth of manufacturing value added in 1970–81, 5.6 per cent a year, was the lowest MVA growth rate in any full decade since the Second World War. It fell considerably further, however, to an average annual rate of 1.6 per cent in 1985–90, and to 0.2 per cent in 1990–95, recovering only slightly to 0.7 per cent in 1995–98 (Table 6.3). The increases in the degree of export orientation of manufacturing industry, as measured by the ratio of exports to total sales, noted above, have thus been largely due to the stagnation of manufacturing output. It is noteworthy, indeed, that since 1985, the very manufacturing category that has experienced the most rapid export growth, and the largest increases in export orientation, has had the lowest output growth rates, and shown the biggest proportional decline in output growth compared to the 1970s.

The output of the downstream, durable goods group of industries – fabricated metal products, machinery, electrical machinery, motor vehicles, and other transport equipment – consists of capital goods to a greater extent than in other manufacturing sectors. These sectors which collectively were the laggards in export growth, but the best performers in terms of output growth, in 1970–81, have had relatively rapid export growth, and the largest increase in export orientation[24] since 1985, but absolute decline in real value added. Value added in these sectors fell at an average annual rate of 2.1 per cent in 1980–90 and at 1.1 per cent in 1990–98. By contrast – a fact of some significance for the future sectoral growth path of the economy – value added in the natural resource-based manufacturing industries (which has increased in every five-year subperiod since 1970), grew at 2.0 per cent in 1980–90 and 2.7 per cent in 1990–98 (Table 6.3).

The decline of value added in the downstream durable goods manufacturing sectors is clearly largely due to the decline in the economy-wide rate of investment, to which demand for their output is particularly sensitive. The significance of these sectors, therefore, is not only that their decline has impeded the growth of manufacturing industry in general, but that they are a barometer of the state of the domestic economy as a whole. By comparison, the natural resource-based category of manufacturing sectors has put in a relatively solid output growth performance.[25]

Just as the downstream, durable goods sectors grew fastest in 1970–81, when the rate of investment rose to unprecedented levels in 1975 and 1981, so they have been hardest hit by the substantial declines in levels of capital formation. Revival of growth in these sectors, and thus in manufacturing as a whole, therefore depends heavily on a revival of the domestic demand for capital goods.

As things are, there is a situation in which South Africa's comparative advantage, judging by shares in exports, has shifted within manufacturing, towards these downstream durable goods sectors, and towards manufacturing in general, but in which both the shares of these sectors in MVA (Table 6A.3), and of manufacturing in GDP, have fallen (Table 6A.4).

Before going on to consider the reasons for the deterioration in the growth performance of South African manufacturing industry since the 1960s, and in particular the decline of investment and the stagnation of the economy since the early 1980s (in Section 6.5), it should be noted that the extent of the decline in South Africa's growth since the early 1980s, has been apparently very much in line with the experience of developing countries in general.

6.4.4   The Slowdown in Developing Countries in General Since the Early 1980s

In Section 6.3.4 it was noted that the per capita growth of both developed and developing countries declined in 1973–82 compared to 1960–73; and that the proportional decline in growth rates was greater in developed than in developing countries. The percentage points decline in South Africa's per capita growth between 1960–73 and 1973–82, however, was significantly greater than for developing countries in general, a fact taken to suggest some factor peculiar to South Africa at that stage. By contrast with the changes at that stage, the per capita growth of develop-ing countries in general has declined considerably further, both compared to the period 1973–82, and especially relative to developed countries.

Easterly (2001: 3) finds that the median per capita growth of developing countries was 2.5 per cent a year in 1960–79, but 0.0 per cent in 1980–98 as a whole, and indeed, in both the 1980s and 1990s separately. The decline in South Africa's per capita growth since the early 1980s, compared to earlier years, has it seems been of about the same order of magnitude as the decline of the median for developing countries in general. Compared to Easterly's 2.5 percentage points decline in the median for developing countries, between 1960–79 and 1980–98, South Africa's per capita growth rate fell from 1.73 per cent to –0.43 per cent, that is by 2.16 percentage points.

It seems, thus, that so far as the relatively large decline in South Africa's per capita growth rate between 1960–73 and 1973–82 is concerned, the causes must be sought in factors peculiar to South Africa, as well as in factors common to both developing and developed countries. Though factors peculiar to South Africa may clearly also partly account for the further decline since the early 1980s, it seems that a crucial question for understanding the case of South Africa concerns the reasons for the deterioration in the growth of developing countries in general relative to developed countries.

In the light of this, the next section is devoted to consideration of possible reasons for the decline of manufacturing industry in South Africa since the 1960s.

6.5 SOME PERSPECTIVES ON THE DECLINE OF MANUFACTURING INDUSTRY IN SOUTH AFRICA

6.5.1 The Decline in the Output of Gold

One factor peculiar to South Africa, which has probably contributed significantly to the decline in the rate of GDP and MVA growth since the 1960s is the decline in the physical volume of gold output. This probably accounts at least partly for the size of the decline in South Africa's growth rate between 1960–73 and 1973–82, relative to the average for developing countries.

With the opening of the Orange Free State gold fields, gold output increased almost uninterruptedly from 348 thousand kilograms in 1951, to a peak of 1 million kilograms in 1970, but at a declining rate from 1965 on, as the maximum output permitted by existing deposits was approached. Despite the huge increase in the gold price in the 1970s, the output of gold in physical terms began falling after 1970, and in the year 2000 was only 43 per cent of its 1970 level.

These changes in the physical output of gold resulted in a significant decline in the rate of growth of real value added in mining as a whole in 1965–70, compared to 1960–65, and a substantial absolute decline in 1970–75 (Figure 6.1 and Table 6A.5).[26] This would clearly have had a significant negative impact on GDP, and probably largely accounts for the 1.50 percentage points decline in the GDP growth rate from 5.15 per cent in 1965–70 to 3.65 per cent in 1970–75.[27] It would have contributed significantly to a sudden lowering of the long-term growth trajectory of the economy in the early 1970s, and made for lower GDP growth in 1973–82 than in 1960–73.[28] While perhaps the whole of the decline in GDP growth between these two periods cannot be explained in these terms, this factor, apparently peculiar to South Africa, seems to account for a significant part of the decline in South Africa's per capita growth in 1973–82, relative to the past, and to other developing countries. Whereas conditions during the commodity price boom of the 1970s seemed favourable, underneath it all real forces were at work to slow the growth of the South African economy, as a whole.

6.5.2 The Problem of Foreign Exchange Constrained Growth Since the Early 1980s

As argued in Bell et al. (1999), there has since the early 1980s apparently been

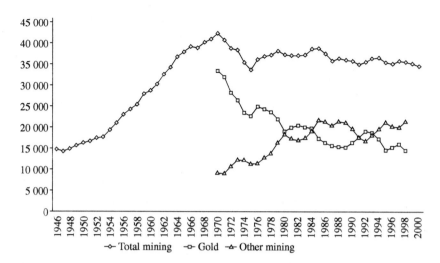

*Figure 6.1   Value added in the South African mining industry (in constant
1995 prices), 1946-2000 (R millions)*

a substantial reduction in the ability of the South African economy to grow
without running into balance of payments difficulties. This is suggested by
evidence of a significant unfavourable change since the early 1980s in the
historical relationship between the rate of growth of the GDP and the ratio of
the current account deficit to GDP. Current account deficit/GDP ratios in the
years since 1994, for instance, have been such as would on average have been
associated with much higher GDP growth rates in earlier decades.

This is seen as suggesting a foreign exchange constraint on South African
economic growth. Since imported intermediate and capital goods are essential
for domestic output and investment,[29] the upper limit on output and investment, and hence on economic growth, has been set by the availability of
foreign exchange, since the early 1980s. There are various possible reasons for
this. One possibility is a decline in the rate of growth of South Africa's
exports. As noted in Section 6.4.1, for a while, between 1965 and 1972, South
Africa faced the problem of sustaining the growth of its total exports and the
prospect of a tightening foreign exchange constraint.[30]

In 1985-90, South Africa's total exports measured in constant US dollars
grew at a relatively good rate (of 5.8 per cent a year) (Table 6.4), but, as
indicated earlier, this gives a misleading impression of the effect of export
growth on import capacity. In constant price trade-weighted currency units, a
more appropriate measure, South Africa's total exports, in 1985-90, fell at
0.8 per cent a year, owing to an 8.2 per cent a year decline in gold exports
(Table 6.4). This aggravated the problems caused by the foreign debt crisis,

which had involved a sudden, massive withdrawal of foreign exchange, and produced a substantial contraction of the economy.

In the 1990s, merchandise exports (that is, exports of goods other than gold), increased at average annual rates of 5.4 per cent and 6.1 per cent, in 1990–95 and 1995–2000 respectively.[31] Both of these growth rates were higher than the average annual rates of growth of merchandise exports in 1950–70. Weighed down by declining gold exports, however, total exports increased at average annual rates of 3.1 per cent and 4.1 per cent in 1990–95 and 1995–2000, respectively, both lower than the average of 4.5 per cent for 1950–70. Following the absolute declines in total exports in the 1980s, these export growth rates, in the 1990s, have not been sufficient to generate the foreign exchange earnings needed to raise GDP and MVA growth rates significantly towards pre-1980 levels.[32]

The problems caused by sluggish growth of exports have been compounded by two other factors which have probably contributed significantly to the reduced ability of the South African economy to grow without running into balance of payments difficulties.[33]

One striking difference between earlier and more recent decades is a significant decline in the rate of import substitution (Bell and Farrell, 1997: 595–9).[34] In earlier decades, the effect of GDP growth on import growth was contained in some measure by rapid import replacement.[35] Since the early 1980s, it seems that there has been a tendency towards import de-substitution, to which trade liberalization may well have contributed in recent years.

Another major difference is that the output–capital ratio for the economy as a whole was more than one-third higher in 1960–65 than in 1995–97. Given the complementarity between domestic resources and imported capital goods in GDFI,[36] this seems to imply that the increase in capital goods imports, as a proportion of GDP, required to support a one percentage point increase in capacity GDP, was about one-third smaller in the 1960s than it is today. For this reason alone, an increase in GDP by one percentage point would exert a substantially greater negative effect on the current account of the balance of payments than was the case in, say, 1964, and thus render completely unattainable capacity output growth rates such as those of the mid-1960s.

Whether a foreign exchange constraint, and a consequent reduction in the ability to grow without running into balance of payments difficulties, is a problem common to developing countries, and hence whether it is a reason for the decline in the average per capita growth rates of developing countries, since the early 1980s, is unclear. That it is at least not unique to South Africa is suggested by Ros (1995) on Mexico.

It is a problem, however, which does seem to apply to South Africa and which probably accounts to a significant extent for the decline in the level of investment, and hence in the rate of growth of the economy, since the early

The decline of the South African economy

Table 6.4   *Average annual rates of growth of South Africa's exports and imports of goods, 1950-2000*

	Merchandise export %	Net gold exports %	Total exports %	Merchandise imports %
In constant (1995) US dollars				
1950–1955	9.34	3 00	6.98	8.11
1955–1960	2.22	6.04	3.55	1.38
1960–1965	3.43	7.51	5.03	9.50
1965–1970	4.65	−1.12	2.39	4.79
1970–1975	9.42	13.09	10.77	9.61
1975–1980	9.56	19.78	13.99	5.46
1980–1985	−8.93	−14.24	−11.43	−13.06
1985–1990	10.38	−2.11	5.77	7.46
1990–1995	5.16	−3.80	2.88	8.13
1995–2000	1.67	−9.94	−0.31	−1.34
1950–1960	5.72	4.51	5.25	4.69
1960–1970	4.04	3.10	3.70	7.12
1970–1980	9.49	16.39	12.37	7.52
1980–1990	0.26	−8.38	−3.21	−3.34
1950–1970	4.88	3.80	4.47	5.90
1970–2000	3.65	−0.90	2.65	2.73
1985–2000	5.68	−5.34	2.75	4.66
1990–2000	3.40	−6.92	1.27	3.28
In constant price trade-weighted foreign currency				
1970–1975	7.32	10.93	8.65	7.51
1975–1980	8.93	19.09	13.34	4.85
1980–1985	−2.00	−7.72	−4.69	−6.45
1985–1990	3.48	−8.23	−0.84	0.75
1990–1995	5.42	−3.56	3.14	8.40
1995–2000	6.14	−5.98	4.07	2.99
1970–1980	8.12	14.94	10.97	6.17
1980–1990	0.70	−7.97	−2.78	−2.92
1970–2000	4.82	0.24	3.78	2.89
1985–2000	5.01	−5.94	2.10	4.00
1990–2000	5.78	−4.78	3.60	5.66

Source: Calculated from the South African Reserve Bank database.

1980s. It has impacted particularly on manufacturing industry, as the most import-intensive sector of the economy, and within manufacturing, on the principal capital goods-producing sectors which, as we have seen, have been in decline since the early 1980s.

It raises questions. Why has the foreign exchange constraint persisted? Part of the answer is the persistent decline in gold exports. There is, however, a host of factors which may have impeded expansion of domestic production of other tradable goods (both importables and exportables), especially of manufactures, and hence prevented the removal of the foreign exchange constraint. One of these factors, much emphasized in South Africa today, is a shortage of skills.

6.5.3 Is an Inadequate Supply of Skills a Major Reason for the Stagnation of the Manufacturing Industry?

There is evidence of a significant increase in the demand for skilled relative to unskilled labour in South Africa. For instance, Edwards (2000: Table 1), and calculations based on his data, indicate that the number of skilled workers employed increased in all the main sectors of the economy – primary, secondary and tertiary – between 1984 and 1997, and that only in the skilled category did employment increase (with the minor exception of the number of 'elementary' workers in manufacturing). In all other categories, in all sectors, employment fell. The result was a substantial increase in the proportion of skilled workers in each sector.[37] This suggests a growing scarcity of skilled relative to unskilled labour, consistent perhaps with the idea that a scarcity of skills is a key reason for the stagnation of manufacturing industry. Yet it poses a puzzle, brought out more clearly by other evidence.

Using a different dataset, Bhorat (2001: 12) finds that in manufacturing industry, between 1993 and 1997, there was an increase of 16283 in 'highly skilled' workers, but a decline of 4589 'skilled' and 28192 'unskilled' workers, giving an overall job loss of 16478 in manufacturing. In marked contrast, in the finance, insurance, real estate and business services sector (commonly called FIRE for short), there were increases of 27302 'highly skilled' and 30487 'skilled' workers, but a decrease of 9709 'unskilled' workers, giving an overall increase of 48080 jobs. It should be noted too that according to Bhorat's (2001: 12–14) figures, the FIRE sector is a great deal more skills intensive than manufacturing as a whole.[38] Furthermore, though the total labour force in FIRE was only one-third of that of manufacturing in 1993, the increase in employment of 'highly skilled' workers in FIRE in 1993–97 (27802) was more than two-thirds greater than in manufacturing as a whole (16288).

The puzzle is this: if a shortage in the supply of skills, as such, is a binding constraint on the growth of manufacturing industry, then why was the output and employment growth performance of the FIRE sector, a far more skills-intensive sector, so vastly superior to that of manufacturing, especially in the 1990s?[39]

The relatively rapid output and employment growth rates of the FIRE sector suggest that an inadequate supply of skills as such may not be a key reason for the stagnation of manufacturing; but, rather, that various factors have resulted in huge differences in their respective demands for skilled labour and, indeed, for labour in general. The problems of manufacturing, in short, rather than lying in skills shortages, may lie more deepseatedly within South African manufacturing itself.

The FIRE sector, commonly associated with the New Economy, seems, unlike manufacturing, to have grown rapidly worldwide in the 1990s. In this context, South Africa with its well-developed financial system, good accounting standards, and a legal system conducive to such activities, has been well placed for growth in this area.[40] These factors, which have given South Africa a comparative advantage in this area, have enabled employers to use productively, and hence to attract, skilled people.[41] Supply has thus responded to demand.[42]

This clearly does not mean that the supply of skills, as distinct from the demand for them, is irrelevant. The ability of supply to respond to demand presupposes a potential supply. South Africa, as a middle-income country, had a skills endowment (as measured by average number of years of schooling) in 1990 intermediate to those of poorer and richer nations, and apparently slightly better than the average for Latin America (Wood and Meyer 1998: 17, Figure 4b). This should give South Africa a *comparative* advantage at intermediate levels of skill intensity. Indeed, Edwards (2000: 10) finds, for the 1993-97 period, a high correlation between the skill intensity of (three-digit SIC) sectors and their export growth rates, suggesting a comparative advantage recently in relatively skills-intensive sectors.

As we have seen, though, neither the exports, nor (especially) the output of manufacturing industry, has grown nearly fast enough over the past two decades. The question is whether a shortage of skills at the higher levels is now the major obstacle to the substantial increase in the output of tradable manufactured goods that is needed. The argument here is that conditions for manufacturing itself have simply not been such as to enable manufacturers to compete with the FIRE sector and other areas of skills-intensive non-manufacturing activity (including, for instance, the communications industry), for the supply, such as it is, of high-level skills.[43]

The idea that there is a shortage of skills which is a fundamental obstacle to growth, has also relied on evidence of large and possibly increasing disparities between the earnings of skilled and unskilled people in South Africa (Bhorat,

2000: 26). As is well known, however, growing skilled/unskilled earnings differentials have also been a feature of the United States over the past few decades.[44] It clearly does not follow from this that the long-term relative decline of US manufacturing industry is due to a shortage of skills.[45] The reasons for this decline, as for the decline in the growth trajectories of industrial and developing countries in general since the 1960s – and for the deterioration in the growth performance of South Africa in particular – must it seems be sought elsewhere.

6.5.4   Brenner's Falling Rate of Profit Thesis

The earlier discussion (in Sections 6.5.1 and 6.5.2) of the problems of the decline in real value added in mining since the early 1970s, and of slow export growth more recently (due largely to the decline of gold exports), suggests one possible perspective on the decline in the growth of the South African economy, and its stagnation (especially in manufacturing) since the early 1980s. It is (the rather pessimistic one) that, having seen the rise of an unusually minerals-rich economy from about 1870 to about 1970, we are now witnessing its more or less inevitable decline. It seems, however, that the problems of the South African economy, and the prospects for its recovery, cannot be seen simply in such South Africa-centred terms. Factors operating at a global level must also have contributed to the deterioration of South Africa's growth performance in the past, and will affect its growth trajectory in future.

In essence, Brenner (1998) sees the 'long downswing' in the advanced industrial countries, beginning in about 1973, as originating in intensifying competition for United States manufacturing industry from Japan and Germany in the 1965–73 period. This resulted in overproduction and excess capacity in world manufacturing industry, putting downward pressure on the price of manufactured goods, and resulting in a decline in the rate of profit (hence in the growth of output, employment and the capital stock) in manufacturing industry. Non-manufacturing (in the United States mainly services), not being subject to the same downward pressure on output prices, experienced a much smaller adverse effect on its rate of profit, and in due course achieved considerable further output and employment growth.

The main initial impact of downward pressure on manufacturing output prices, and profit rates, was on the United States, but via various mechanisms this had repercussions for all the major industrial economies, and indeed evidently on the world economy as a whole. The intense competition resulting from the emergence of excess capacity and overproduction, Brenner apparently sees as having persisted from the 1970s right through to the 1990s. Even in the early 1965–73 period, the four East Asian newly industrialized countries (NICs) were making their presence felt (p. 149) but in the 1980s 'the problems that resulted from ongoing over-capacity and over-production in manufacturing among the advanced capitalist economies were exacerbated ... by the accelerated intrusion of the four Asian NICs, and East Asia more generally, into the world market' (p. 185)

Any such downward pressure on manufacturing output prices would be expected to have affected all producers of manufactured goods, including those in South Africa.[46] It may well have contributed to the decline in growth, and, from the early 1980s, stagnation, of South African manufacturing industry. Profit rates in South Africa evidently did decline substantially (from 31.6 per cent in 1964 to 23.6 per cent in 1970, and further to 15.1 per cent in 1975) (Nattrass 1990: 107, Table 7.1), but whether this was due to downward pressure on output prices is unclear.[47] While Brenner's argument may shed light on the decline in the growth trajectory of the world economy as a whole since about 1973, however, it does not seem to account for the sharper decline in the growth rate of developing countries – including South Africa – than of developed countries, since the early 1980s.

6.5.5   Skills-biased Technical Change

Easterly (2001: 2) speculates that 'worldwide factors like the increase in world interest rates, the increased debt-burden of developing countries, the growth slowdown in the industrial world, and skill-biased technical change may have contributed to the developing countries' stagnation' since the early 1980s. The first two of these, higher real interest rates and the burden of foreign debt, would clearly have impacted on South Africa, at least during the 1980s, and made for slower growth relative to developed countries.[48] It is the fourth of these possibilities, skill-biased technical change since the early 1980s, on which attention is focused here. Easterly (2001: 21) elaborates as follows:

> The LDC growth during 1960–79 may have reflected the adoption in developing countries of undemanding technologies of mass production that did not place a premium on skill-level. Skill-biased technological advances of the 80s and 90s may have favored the countries that were already developed, leaving behind the poor countries ... as happened in previous technological revolutions.

Easterly (2001) does not develop this suggestion. No more detailed indications seem to be given of what he has in mind. Whether it accords with Easterly's thinking or not, it is striking that two manufacturing sectors which Jorgenson and Stiroh (2000) find have contributed particularly significantly to output and productivity growth in the US economy as a whole, over the 1958–96 period, and which are therefore singled out by them for special mention, are SIC 35 and SIC 36, the counterparts of which in South Africa are called machinery and equipment, and electrical machinery, respectively.[49] The first of these, as Jorgenson and Stiroh (1999: 164) point out, includes computer production, and the second semi-conductor production, which in the United States are manufacturing sectors central to the information technology (IT) revolution. Presumably, thus, the relatively rapid growth of output in these sectors is seen as reflecting increased production of these two IT-related products.

Nordhaus (2001), focusing particularly on the now widely acknowledged rebound in labour productivity growth in the US after 1995, confirms the importance of the contribution of these two sectors to accelerated productivity growth in the US in 1995–98. Mainly due to these two manufacturing sectors, which he also notes, include computers and semi-conductors, new-economy sectors directly contributed about a third of both total labour productivity growth in 1996–98, and of the percentage points increase in total labour productivity growth in this three-year period. Also due mainly to these two sectors, durable goods manufacturing was the most important contributor to overall total productivity growth in 1996–98. Of the behaviour of industries within manufacturing he says (p. 20) that the 'importance of industrial machinery (notably computers) and electronic machinery (notably semi-conductors) is striking'.

What is striking in the South African context is that these two sectors are part of the downstream durable goods group of manufacturing industries which, as emphasized above, has had particularly poor output growth since the early 1980s. Output in both machinery and equipment (SIC 35) and electrical machinery (SIC 36) declined in absolute terms between 1985 and 1998. Output in SIC 35 increased at 0.76 per cent a year in 1990–95, but fell at 9.41 per cent a year in the three years 1995–98, averaging –3.18 per cent in 1990–98 as a whole; while the respective growth rates for SIC 36 were 2.96 per cent, –1.66 per cent and 1.21 per cent (Table 6.3).

Some IT-related production may be taking place in these two manufacturing sectors in South Africa, but in sharp contrast to the US, their output growth rates – whatever has been happening to their labour productivity growth – have not yet shown signs of benefiting from the New Economy.[50] This suggests the possibility that an inability to penetrate significantly into skills-intensive, high-tech manufacturing of products central to the IT revolution (for various reasons, not just the shortage of skills) may be one reason developing countries, like South Africa, have fallen behind since the early 1980s (but especially in the 1990s).

In so far as the IT revolution has benefited South African manufacturing industry, it seems it would have had to be through the application of IT to various stages of the manufacturing process, from design to marketing, in other manufacturing sectors rather than through the manufacture of major new

IT products. Some in South Africa seem to be pinning their hopes on this. A major part of Nordhaus's argument, indeed (which distinguishes it from Gordon, 2000b for instance), is that, after stripping out the new-economy sectors, it is found that there was also an acceleration, after 1995, in non-new-economy labour productivity growth. So, it seems, 'it is clear the productivity rebound is not narrowly focused in a few new-economy sectors'. Significantly, though, the one non-new-economy part of the US economy which, according to Nordhaus (2001: 20), has been excluded from this is non-new-economy manufacturing. Nordhaus (2001: 20) thus concludes that 'up through 1998, the acceleration in manufacturing productivity was limited to the two major new-economy sectors led by computers and semi-conductors'.

Judging by US experience so far, thus, there seems to be no reason to expect that the indirect benefits of the IT revolution for South African manufacturing, through the application of IT to non-new-economy sectors, will be significant. We are thus left, so far, only with the stark contrast between the direct effects of the two major new-economy manufacturing sectors in the US, and their counterparts in South Africa. If skill-biased technical change has left developing countries behind since the early 1980s (as Easterly and our discussion suggest) the effects of 'previous technological revolutions' seem to have been very different – at least so far as South Africa is concerned.

6.5.6   Gordon's 'One Big Wave' and South Africa

As outlined in Section 6.2, South Africa experienced rapid industrialization in the 50 years or so from the First World War through to the early 1970s. This was also the experience of the United States. Gordon (2000a: 2) argues that in the United States 'there was a glorious half-century between World War I and the early 1970s during which US productivity growth was much faster than before or after'. There was thus, as he calls it, 'one big wave' in US productivity growth. The problem, as he sees it, is not to explain 'the post-1972 slowdown' – which he seems to regard as a return to some sort of normality, following the aberration represented by the 'one big wave' – but to explain the 'post-1913 speedup' which created 'the one big wave'. His 'preferred hypotheses combine several explanations', but 'most notably the concurrence of a multitude of important inventions occurring simultaneously prior to and at the beginning of the rapid growth period' (Gordon, 2000a: 42).

Whatever the effect of 'previous technological revolutions' on 'poor countries', to which Easterly (2001) alludes in the passage quoted above, it seems that they did not all leave South Africa (very far) behind. To take but one of many possible examples of Gordon's 'important inventions', the development of the internal combustion engine made itself felt in South Africa in the manufacture of major new products (as distinct from merely new ways of producing old ones) relatively quickly. Only 16 years after the appearance of the Model T, in the US, and only 11 years after the full development in Detroit of mass production, the Ford Motor Company established an assembly plant in Port Elizabeth, in 1924 – earlier it seems than the establishment of any such plant in any other of today's middle-income developing countries.

In some measure South Africa, between the First World War and the 1960s, apparently industrialized and grew in parallel with the US economy, during its 'one big wave', albeit always several lengths behind and never on its crest, but – unlike today – without showing any signs of drowning in the backwash. Even within the limitations of South Africa's technological capabilities – and the economics of the local production of sophisticated capital equipment and intermediate goods, which a minerals-rich economy with flourishing exports could well afford to import – there was enough scope to keep manufacturing industry growing rapidly decade after decade.

Whether the contrast with today is due to the ebbing of the tide of growth of the world economy in the early 1970s – due for instance to the petering out of Gordon's 'one big wave' or to Brenner's falling rate of profit and 'long downswing' – or to Easterly's 'undemanding technologies' of that earlier era, compared to his 'skill-biased technical change' since the early 1980s, is debatable. The question remains though: what counterparts of the local manufacture of major new products during the earlier technological revolution, either already exist, or are in the offing, in South African manufacturing industry during this, the IT, revolution?

6.5.7   Does Manufacturing Matter in the Information Age?

Only a few years ago it was taken for granted that an improvement in the performance of manufacturing industry was the key to the revival of economic development in South Africa. The shares of services in the GDP (Table 6A.4) and in formal employment, however, have increased considerably since the mid-1980s.[51] Furthermore, during the 1990s, the FIRE sector, discussed in Section 6.5.3, and the transport, storage and communication sector (which includes the cellular phone industry), both associated with the New Economy, were in terms of value added the fastest-growing components of the services sector.[52] In the face of the impressive performance of these sectors, a more sanguine view of the stagnation of manufacturing is now prevalent, with the shift to services apparently seen as a natural and beneficial transition from the old to the new economy.

Even in the United States, the epitome of the New Economy, however, the shift towards services is not accepted with complete equanimity. It is seen by Brenner (1998: 204–5) not as 'an expression of economic rejuvenation' but as a 'manifestation of US economic decline' – despite the fact that there 'the reverse side' of the decline of manufacturing employment has been a massive increase in the number of jobs in services.

In South Africa there has been no such compensating increase in employment in services. Between 1990 and 1998, employment fell in *both* manufacturing (by 161 827 or 10.6 per cent), and services as a whole (by 71 241 or 3.2 per cent). In South Africa, furthermore, unlike the US, the problem of the decline of manufacturing employment has been greatly compounded by the decline in employment in the primary sector.[53] The increased share of services in GDP has not been due to particularly rapid growth of value added in this sector, but to very slow growth in the rest of the economy (Table 6A.3); and its increased share in formal employment so far, is due entirely to larger proportional declines in employment in other sectors.[54]

In the case of the US, Brenner (1998: 205) sees the substantial growth of employment in services as due to 'the emergence of the low wage economy into which the US began to descend as early as the first part of the 1960s'. In South Africa, employment growth outside formal sector manufacturing has predominantly been in relatively low-income informal sector service activities, with some much less significant amount in the form of subcontracting in informal manufacturing.

As the discussion of the findings of Nordhaus (2001) in Section 6.5.5 indicated, the direct contribution of the two new-economy manufacturing, sectors SIC 35 and SIC 36, accounted for a significant proportion of the acceleration of US labour productivity growth in 1995–98. Manufacturing, thus, has evidently mattered a good deal in the US in recent years, despite the lacklustre performance of non-new-economy manufacturing.[55] Similarly as the discussion above suggests, the revival of growth in the South African economy depends to a significant extent on an improvement in the performance of the downstream durable goods-producing sectors, of which SIC 35 and SIC 36 are part. Indefinitively continuing increases in the relative importance of the services sector in South Africa are unsustainable, and are incompatible with a significant increase in the rate of growth of GDP. A revival of the growth of manufacturing output and employment, thus, is vital for the future of the South African economy, even in this, the era of the New Economy.

6.5.8 Restructuring a Natural Resource-abundant Economy: The Challenges

Manufacturing, thus, still matters a good deal. Given trends in other sectors of the economy, it is hard to see how growth rates of the sort needed not only for economic, but also for political reasons, can be achieved without a substantial acceleration of the growth of manufacturing industry.

The obstacles to significantly faster growth of South African manufacturing industry, however, are formidable in today's global conditions. The challenge facing South Africa is that of climbing the international ladder of industrial production to more high-tech, more skills-intensive, and higher value-added manufacturing activities. This is in some respects particularly difficult for a natural resource-abundant economy such as South Africa's. As Findlay and Lundahl (1999: 36) observe, there is 'the possibility that under certain circumstances pursuing a pattern of primary specialisation makes it difficult to switch at all' to a more diversified export pattern. And, as we have seen above, it can be yet more difficult sustaining a rapid rate of growth of output while transforming the export pattern, especially in unfavourable world economic conditions such as have prevailed for the past 30 years.

In these conditions, South Africa, as a country of intermediate skills endowment, faces fierce competition in activities at all levels of the skill intensity of production. Owing largely to its natural resource abundance, South Africa's transition to export-orientated industrialization was considerably delayed – indeed to the mid-1980s – by nearly 30 years, compared to natural resource-poor South Korea, for instance. Thus, having had a relatively advanced and diversified manufacturing sector at the beginning of the 1970s, as noted at the outset, South Africa in the mid-1980s found itself a relative latecomer in relation even to developing countries like Korea which had in the meantime entrenched themselves in world markets for (even quite skills-intensive) manufactures. A problem is that most developing countries have improved their skills endowments over the past few decades, and, like South Africa, are striving to raise them further. Raising levels of educational and skills attainment – while very necessary – does therefore not necessarily increase *comparative* advantage in skills-intensive activities or increase the growth rate.[56]

The important implication of the foregoing is that dependence on natural resource-based (primary and manufactured) products may today be more of a blessing and less of a curse for South Africa than it has sometimes appeared to be in the past.[57] Wood and Mayer (1998: 64) state:

> Africa's comparative advantage in primary exports, which arises basically from its abundance of natural resources, is in our view at worst neutral, and quite possibly favourable, to its long-term development prospects, as compared with those of Asia. Exporting manufactures is no longer a barometer of national prosperity. Over the past few decades the world has changed: both developed and developing countries are now exporters of manufactures on a large scale ... .[58]

Furthermore, it suggests that though this dependence may gradually diminish, as it has done in the past, South Africa is likely to remain heavily dependent on natural resource-based products for a considerable time to come.[59] This does not mean that South Africa can significantly increase its rate of economic growth, without a major increase in the MVA growth rate, and considerable diversification not only of exports, but also of output, towards more high-tech and more skills-intensive downstream manufacturing activities. It does mean, in keeping with the advice given by Wood and Mayer (1998: 65–8) to African economies in general, that South Africa should make the most of its comparative advantages in natural resource-based products, to increase its exports and output, while upgrading its skills and educational levels, and in other possible ways trying to promote the necessary further diversification of the economy.

Much, however, seems to depend on the future growth of the advanced industrial countries. South Africa's 2.45 per cent a year GDP growth rate in 1995–2000 was substantially higher than in any other five-year period since 1980 (though not as high as in any such period before 1980). Growth rates in virtually all the main sectors, excepting mining, improved in the latter half of the 1990s (Table 6A.5).

This improvement in South Africa's growth rate, however, has occurred in the context of, and is probably due to, the protracted US upswing, beginning in 1992, which saw US GDP growth accelerate to 3.9 per cent a year in 1995–2000 (DeLong, 2001: 11). Although South Africa has not yet been pulled up to these levels, a quick and sustained resumption of such growth rates in the US could well raise further the rate of growth of the South African economy, and facilitate its restructuring.

We must hope therefore that the analyses with pessimistic implications for the US economy are wrong, and that the optimists are right. That is, for instance, we must hope that it is not the case that Western capitalism is in terminal decline, as Brenner's (1998) analysis seems to imply; or that the benefits of the IT revolution in the US have been limited to one key new-economy sector (Gordon, 2000b: 12–17); or that 'the greatest benefits of the computer age', rather than 'awaiting us in the future' have already been left 'in the past' (Gordon, 2000a: 43). We must hope, too, that Nordhaus is right in finding that there has been a significant productivity growth rebound since 1995, which has not been narrowly focused on a few new-economy sectors; that DeLong's (2001: 9–16, and Abstract) confidence is not misplaced when he declares (despite the current downturn and collapse of IT stocks) that the 'boom in information technology investment' is not a flash in the pan, but will 'pay dividends in the form of accelerated labor productivity growth for at least a decade to come' – and, hence, perhaps that we have seen only the beginnings of another 'big wave'.

NOTES

*   Niki Cattaneo of Rhodes University has made an invaluable contribution to this study, from the very beginning of the project. This included more than a week's intensive work with Trevor Bell in Grahamstown in early January 2001 – assembling and processing data, downloading numerous useful studies from the Internet, and discussion of some of the issues. Thereafter, over a period of several months, she made further substantial contributions – supplying numerous additional papers and data, and giving us the benefit of her advice on various matters, on the telephone and through the e-mail, as well as at a workshop of the Trade and Industrial Policy Secretariat, in Johannesburg. Without her help and support the research might well have stalled altogether, and the study would probably have not been completed. Greg Farrell of the South African Reserve Bank, too, in his personal capacity, has, as usual, provided exceedingly valuable help in various ways. We are indeed fortunate to have had the generous, unstinting help of these two friends. Dirk van Seventer of the Trade and Industrial Policy Secretariat has also contributed on data-related issues; and both the National Accounts and Balance of Payments divisions of the South African Reserve Bank have provided statistical information used in the study. To all of the above, none of whom bears any responsibility for the views expressed in the study, we are most grateful.

1. Probably the most notable exception was the chemicals industry, which (owing to the establishment of a substantial explosives plant to meet the needs of mining) in 1916–17 was strikingly more advanced than in other countries at a comparable stage of development. See T.A. du Plessis (1965).

2. See for instance, Martin (1990) and Christie (1991).

3. The import/domestic supply ratio for manufacturing in the aggregate fell from 57.2 per cent in 1926/27 to 38.5 per cent in 1946/47, 28.7 per cent in 1956/57, and was down to 19.6 per cent by 1972 (Bell and Farrell, 1997: 596).

4. Particularly rapidly growing subsectors in the inter-war period were basic metals (owing to the establishment of ISCOR, which came into production in 1933); motor vehicles (Ford and GM having established plants in 1924 and 1926, respectively); rubber products (Firestone having begun production in 1936); machinery; paper and paper products; and fabricated metal products.

5. A major development in the 1950s was the establishment of South Africa's first oil-from-coal synthetic fuel plant, at Sasolburg. In the 1960s, various substantial plants were established in the basic metals sector (such as Highveld Steel, RMB Alloys, Southern Cross Stainless Steel, and the Alusaf aluminium smelter); and in the chemicals sector (such as the AECI-Sasol polythene plant, SA Nylon Spinners, the AECI petrochemicals plant at Sasolburg, the Karbochem synthetic rubber plant, Sentrachem-Hoechst production of polyethylene, and the Natref oil refinery).

6. Between 1926/27 and 1972, non-durable consumer goods, as a proportion of MVA, fell from 48.9 to 21.7 per cent; the major consumer durable, motor vehicles, rose from 2.0 to 5.7 per cent; intermediate goods increased from 24.8 to 45.8 per cent; and capital goods from 3.1 to 15.1 per cent (Bell and Farrell, 1997: 602, Table 2).

7. Derived from T.A. du Plessis (1965).

8. See Bell and Farrell (1997: 602, Table 2, and pp. 608–9) and World Bank (1987: 1–5) for South Korean data.

9. See Findlay and Lundahl (1999: 13–15) on resource-led growth.

10. The year 1981 is taken as the end date for this period rather than 1980, since the cycle peaked in August 1981.

11. See Table 6.4 in Section 6.5.2, below.

12. See Bell et al. (1999) for more detail, including estimation of separate real exchange rates for natural resource-based and downstream durable goods manufactures.

13. These low real interest rates, it might be noted, may also be seen as a consequence of the increase in oil prices in 1973. See Bruno and Sachs (1985: 23–6).

14. It is interesting to note that the 1974–79 period, when the decisions to construct these two plants were taken, coincides almost exactly with the period of South Korea's heavy and chemical industries (HCI) programme.

15. Gross domestic fixed capital formation grew relatively rapidly (at 7.6 per cent a year) in 1970–75, faster than in any earlier five-year period since the Second World War, except

1960–65, fell (at 3.00 per cent a year) in 1975–78, and increased rapidly again thereafter (at 9.7 per cent a year) in 1978–81, to reach the highest absolute level of investment attained in any one year, before or since, in 1981.

16. Indicative of the sensitivity of these sectors to economy-wide investment, is that their collective value added increased at rates of 8.6 per cent in 1970–75, fell at 0.7 per cent during the recession of 1975–78, and increased rapidly at 13.6 per cent a year in 1975–81 (Table 6.3).

17. The incentive to achieve this was a rebate on excise duties related to local content. The penalty for failure to meet the local content targets made non-compliance prohibitively costly, so that the stipulated requirements were in effect compulsory minimum local content levels.

18. Its import/domestic supply ratio in 1970 was 40.1 per cent, higher than for any other 3-digit SIC manufacturing subsector excepting machinery and equipment (50.9 per cent) and professional and scientific instruments (67.4 per cent). Also, in 1972, the motor vehicle industry accounted for 13.6 per cent of South Africa's total manufactured imports, lower than for machinery and equipment (19.6 per cent) and other industries (20.9 per cent), but much higher than for other manufacturing subsectors.

19. Cyclical movements in the South African economy, it seems, followed the OECD cycle but with a lag of a year or so. South African cyclical peaks, for instance, occur in August 1974 and August 1981, whereas OECD cyclical downturns occur more immediately following the 1973 and 1979 oil crises. In the case of South Africa, and perhaps also of other natural resource-abundant oil-importing, developing countries, the adverse impact of higher oil prices was probably delayed due to continued increases in the world prices of their primary commodity exports.

20. For more detailed description of developments in trade policy, see Bell (1993: 83–90).

21. These values have been derived by multiplying exports in rands by the nominal effective exchange rates, such as those for 1978–2000 in South African Reserve Bank (2001: B-217), and using an estimated trade-weighted index of the price level of South Africa's major trading partners as a deflator.

22. As noted earlier, Bell et al. (1999) estimate real exchange rates for exporters of natural resource-based and downstream durable goods manufacture separately. These indicate a significant increase in the price competitiveness of exporters of durable goods manufactures, relative to foreign products, and relative to exporters of natural resource-based manufactures, after 1985.

23. Exports of the durable goods group of industries as a proportion of total manufactured exports, increased substantially from 9.6 per cent in 1985 to 18.82 per cent in 1998, somewhat higher than the 15.7 per cent level reached by 1970 (Table 6A.3).

24. The export/gross output ratio of this category of sectors increased from 4.9 per cent in 1985 to 21.4 per cent in 1998, proportionally much more than the increase from 19.9 per cent to 34.8 per cent in the case of the natural resource-based sector, and from 10 per cent to 21.3 per cent in the case of the group of labour-intensive industries.

25. There are three reasons for this: a significantly larger proportion of the sales of the natural resource-based sectors is in foreign markets, so that they are less dependent on the state of the domestic economy, their exports have grown at a reasonably good rate; and they are not as directly dependent on the level of investment, which has fallen sharply as a proportion of gross domestic expenditure since the early 1980s.

26. The average annual rate of growth of mining value added as a whole was 5.15 per cent in 1950–55, 6.47 per cent in 1955–60, and 5.7 per cent in 1960–65, but fell to 2.23 per cent in 1965–70, and then in 1970–75 was *minus* 4.51 per cent (Table 6A.5).

27. In 1970, mining accounted for 15 per cent of GDP (at constant 1995 prices). The *direct effects alone* of the absolute decline in mining value added (which involved a 6.75 percentage points swing from a positive 2.23 per cent growth rate in 1965–70 to a negative 4.51 per cent in 1970–75), thus, would, it seems, account for about 0.67 of a percentage point of the 1.50 percentage point decline in the GDP growth rate between 1965–70 and 1970–75.

28. While, as noted above, mining value added declined at 4.51 per cent in 1990–95, it fell at

3.16 per cent a year in 1970–73 and more rapidly at 6.50 per cent a year in 1973–75. It increased at an average annual rate of 2.26 per cent in 1960–73 but fell at 0.41 per cent a year in 1973–82.

29. Bell et al. (1999) estimate that the ratio of imported capital goods to gross domestic fixed investment in South Africa in 1975–90 averaged about 20 per cent.

30. See the prescient analysis of J.C. du Plessis (1965).

31. Unlike the 1985–90 period, during 1995–2000 the US dollar appreciated significantly against other key currencies, so that export growth rates in constant US dollars in 1995–2000 are much lower than in trade-weighted foreign currency units, as Table 6.4 shows.

32. It should also be noted that these improvements in export growth rates, in the 1990s, occurred during a period which has included the long US upswing, which began in 1992, and which continued, with relatively minor corrections, through to 2000. There are thus doubts about their sustainability.

33. The following two paragraphs draw heavily on Bell et al. (1999).

34. As noted earlier, the exceptions in the 1970s, were the motor vehicle industry, and the natural resource-based chemicals and iron and steel industries.

35. See Krugman (1992: 49) on the possible beneficial effects of growth which is biased towards import-competing industries.

36. Bell et al. (1999) estimate that the ratio of imported capital goods to gross domestic fixed investment in 1975–90 averaged about 20 per cent.

37. As a percentage, it increased from 2.1 to 6.9 in mining; 9.6 to 20.2 in manufacturing; and 15.1 to 25.7 in services.

38. In FIRE and manufacturing, 23.0 per cent and 10.2 per cent, respectively, were 'highly skilled', and 'highly skilled' and 'skilled' workers together comprised 97.9 and 38.2 per cent of employees respectively.

39. By contrast with the stagnation of manufacturing, described earlier, the average annual growth of value added in FIRE was 2.0 per cent in 1985–90, 1.92 per cent in 1990–95, and rose sharply to 5.6 per cent in 1995–98 (Table 6A.5). And, whereas the average annual percentage rates of employment growth in manufacturing were 1.09, –1.25 and –1.66, in 1985–90, 1990–95 and 1995–98 respectively; in FIRE they were 2.96, 1.38 and 2.69, respectively.

40. See Bell et al. (1999) on aspects of this.

41. Another advantage of this sector in the context of a foreign exchange constraint is that it is less dependent on imported inputs.

42. The fact that, unlike manufacturing, there is a worldwide demand for skilled people in this sector, has also given people the incentive to position themselves for work in it.

43. On emigration as a problem, see Bhorat (2001: 17–20).

44. Indeed, Bhorat (2000: 24, Table 17) shows both higher 50–10 and 90–10 percentile wage differentials for the US than for South Africa. South Africa has a higher 90–10 percentile wage differential than the other developed countries. This is to be expected given their much higher levels of educational attainment. But none of this on its own tells us that skills scarcity is an effective constraint on South African growth.

45. Contrary to Bhorat (2000: 26), it also does not follow from relatively high skilled/unskilled wage differentials that measures such as South Africa's Skills Development Policy are warranted on economic grounds: this depends on entirely different considerations. See, for instance, Archer (1997).

46. It has been argued that the geographical dispersal of manufacturing industry, which was a feature of industry in South Africa from the 1960s on, was a result of such intensified international competition, for example, Bell (1987).

47. Crucial to Brenner's argument is that profit rates fell sharply in manufacturing relative to services. He rejects the idea that this is explicable in terms of differences between the two sectors in the rate of growth of real wages relative to labour productivity growth. In South Africa, in keeping with Brenner's argument for the US, it seems that real wage growth in manufacturing fell progressively from the late 1950s to the end of the 1970s, while labour productivity growth rose or at least did not fall significantly. Comparable information for services, necessary to test Brenner's argument, however, is not as yet available to us.

48. So far as the OECD slowdown is concerned, it is not clear to us why this should have made for larger declines in developing countries, except perhaps by causing a long decline in the relative prices of natural resource-based products.

49. They differ thus in name from their US counterparts, industrial machinery and equipment, and electronic and electrical equipment.

50. Two possible, minor exceptions to this are the television, radio and communications (SIC 371-373) and professional and scientific equipment (SIC 374-376), manufacturing sectors, which do perhaps increasingly manufacture information and communication technology products, and which have done relatively well in terms of output and export growth. The TV etc. sector has had positive output growth in every subperiod since 1980, excepting 1990-95, and was the second fastest growing manufacturing subsector (at 9.82 per cent a year) in 1995-98. The professional etc. subsector had positive output growth in all periods from 1975-80, excepting 1995-98 (Table 6.3). They have probably been the fastest growing manufacturing subsectors in the past two decades, though off very small bases. Of manufacturing subsectors, TV etc. had the second fastest export growth rate (18.6 per cent a year) in 1990-98, and the export growth of professional etc. (10.4 per cent a year) was tenth fastest (Table 6.2).

51. The shares of services in formal employment at these dates were 37.9 per cent, 38.7 per cent and 43.25 per cent.

52. The transport, storage and communications sector indeed had a higher rate of output growth (4.47 per cent a year) in 1990-98 than any other main sector (Table 6A.5), or any manufactur-ing subsector, but for one (non-ferrous basic metals).

53. Employment in mining has fallen virtually without interruption since 1980. It fell at 5.23 per cent a year in 1990-95, and by 4.68 per cent a year in 1995-98, involving a loss of 347 308 jobs or 45 per cent of the 1990 mining labour force, between 1990 and 1998.

54. It should be noted too that despite FIRE and the communication sector, the great bulk of employment in services in South Africa, as in the US, is relatively unskilled.

55. Nordhaus (2001: 20) finds that the two non-manufacturing sectors retail and wholesale trade also made significant contributions to overall productivity growth in the US in 1995-98, but he seems to regard these findings as anomalous. They are, he says, 'more surprising' than in the case of durable manufacturing; and 'the data in these sectors are somewhat of a mystery'.

56. See Wood and Mayer (1998: 17, Figure 4b) and Easterly (2001: 9). Easterly (p.20) also remarks on the analagous problem that 'all countries reforming [their economic policies] together', in an attempt to attract 'worldwide financial (and other kinds of) capital' ... 'will not increase their average growth rate'.

57. It is indeed noteworthy that natural resource-based manufacturing has been the sheet-anchor of manufacturing value added since 1980 (Table 6.3).

58. It is perhaps significant that the 'Asian tigers', heavily dependent on the US market, and on IT-related exports, were predicted by the International Monetary Fund to be worst affected by the current global downturn, whereas natural resource abundant Africa and Latin America were expected to be much less affected by its adverse effects (*The Economist*, 28 April 2001, p.88).

59. The combined share in South Africa's exports of goods and non-factor services, of primary products and the four sectors treated above as representing natural resource-based manufactures, has fallen from its 76 per cent level in 1985, but was still substantial, at 60 per cent, in 1998 (Tables 6A.2 and 6A.6).

REFERENCES

Archer, S. (1997), 'The Finance and Organisation of Training: Theoretical Issues: A South African Perspective', South African Network for Economic Research, Working Paper 3.

Bell, T. (1987), 'International Competition and Industrial Decentralization in South

Africa', *World Economy*, vol. 15, no. 10/11, October/November, pp. 1291-307.

Bell, T. (1993), 'Should South Africa Further Liberalise its Foreign Trade?', in M. Lipton and C. Simkins (eds), *State and Market in Post Apartheid South Africa*, Johannesburg: Witwatersrand University Press; and Boulder CO: Westview Press, pp. 81-127.

Bell, T. and Farrell, G. (1997), 'The Minerals-energy Complex and South African Industrialisation', *Development Southern Africa*, vol. 14, no. 4, December, pp. 591-613.

Bell, T., Farrell, G. and Cassim, R. (1999), 'Competitiveness, International Trade and Finance in a Minerals-rich Economy: The Case of South Africa', Contribution to an International Development Research Centre project. Forthcoming in Rohinton Medhora (ed.), *Finance and Competitiveness in Developing Countries*, Routledge Studies in Development Economics.

Bhorat, H. (2000), 'Wage Premia and Wage Differentials in the South African Labour Market', Paper presented at the 2000 Annual Forum of the Trade and Industrial Policy Secretariat, held in Johannesburg, 18-20 September.

Bhorat, H. (2001), 'Employment Trends in South Africa', Occasional Paper no. 2, March, Johannesburg: Friedrich Ebert Stiftung.

Brenner, R. (1998), 'The Economics of Global Turbulence: A Special Report on the World Economy', *New Left Review*, no. 229, May/June.

Bruno, M. and Sachs, J. (1985), *Economics of Worldwide Stagflation*, Cambridge, MA: Harvard University Press.

Christie, R. (1991), 'Antiquated Industrialisation: A Comment on William Martin's "The Making of an Industrial South Africa"', *International Journal of African Historical Studies*, vol. 24, no. 3, pp. 589-608.

De Kock, M.H. (1936), *The Economic Development of South Africa*, London: P.S. King & Son Ltd.

DeLong, B. (2001), 'Do we have a "New" Macroeconomy?', http//www.j-bradford-delong.net/.

Du Plessis, J.C. (1965), 'Investment and the Balance of Payments in South Africa', *South African Journal of Economics*, vol. 33, pp. 311-40.

Du Plessis, T.A. (1965), 'The Industrial Growth Pattern and the Real Forces of Economic Expansion of South Africa, 1916/17-1956/57', Unpublished D.Comm. thesis, University of South Africa, Pretoria, pp. 311-38.

Easterly, W. (2001), *The Lost Decades: Developing Countries' Stagnation in Spite of Policy Reform 1980-1998*, Washington DC: World Bank.

Edwards, L. (2000), 'Globalisation and the Skill Bias of Occupational Employment in South Africa', Paper presented at a conference of Economic Research Southern Africa, University of the Witwatersrand, Johannesburg.

Findlay, R. and Lundahl, M. (1999), 'Resource-led Growth - A Long Term Perspective: The Relevance of the 1870-1914 Experience for Today's Developing Economies', United Nations University: World Institute for Development Economic Research, Working Paper no. 162, July.

Frankel, S.H. (1967), *Investment and the Return to Equity Capital in the South African Gold Mining Industry 1887-1965: An International Comparison*, Oxford: Basil Blackwell.

Gerschenkron, A. (1952), 'Economic Backwardness in Historical Perspective', in B.F. Hoselitz (ed.), *The Progress of Underdeveloped Areas*, Chicago: Chicago University Press, pp. 3-29.

Gordon, R.J. (2000a), 'Interpreting the "One Big Wave" in US Long-term Productivity

Growth', National Bureau of Economic Research, Cambridge, MA, Working Paper no. 7752.

Gordon, R.J. (2000b), 'Does the "New Economy" Measure Up to the Great Inventions of the Past?', National Bureau of Economic Research, Cambridge, MA, Working Paper no. 7833.

Jorgenson, D.W. and Stiroh, K.J. (1999), 'Information technology and growth', *American Economic Review*, vol. 89, no. 2, pp. 109–15.

Jorgenson, D.W. and Stiroh, K.J. (2000), 'US Economic Growth at the Industry Level', *American Economic Review*, vol. 90, no. 2, May, pp. 161–7.

Krugman, P.R. (1992), *Currencies and Crises*, Cambridge, MA and London: MIT Press, Chapter 3, 'Differences in Income Elasticities and Trends in Real Exchange Rates', pp. 41–57, originally published in *European Economic Review* (1989), vol. 33, pp. 1031–54.

Martin, W. (1990), 'The Making of an Industrial South Africa: Trade and Tariffs in Interwar South Africa', *International Journal of African Historical Studies*, vol. 23, no. 2, pp. 59–85.

McCarthy, C. (1999), 'The Manufacturing Sector during the 1970s', *South African Journal of Economic History*, vol. 14, September, pp. 143–61.

Nattrass, N. (1990), 'Economic Power and Profits in Post-war Manufacturing', in N. Nattrass and E. Ardington (eds), *The Political Economy of South Africa*, Cape Town: Oxford University Press, pp. 107–128

Nordhaus, W.D. (2001), 'Productivity Growth and the New Economy', National Bureau of Economic Research, Cambridge, MA, Working Paper no. 8096.

Pritchett, L. (2000), 'Understanding Patterns of Economic Growth: Searching for Hills among Plateaus, Mountains and Plains', *Word Bank Economic Review*, vol. 14, no. 2, pp. 221–50.

Reynders Commission (1972), *Report of the Commission of Inquiry into the Export Trade of the Republic of South Africa*, R.P. 69/1972, Pretoria: Government Printer.

Ros, J. (1995), 'Trade Liberalization with Real Appreciation and Slow Growth: Sustainability Issues in Mexico's Trade Policy Reform', in G.K. Helleiner (ed.), *Manufacturing for Export in the Developing World: Problems and Possibilities*, London and New York: Routledge, pp. 99–130.

South African Reserve Bank (2001), 'South Africa's Balance of Payments 1946–2000', Supplement to the South African Reserve Bank *Quarterly Bulletin*, June.

Van Eck, H.J. (1961), 'Over 50 Years of Economic Development in South Africa', *The South African Exporter*, February/March, pp. 98–105.

Wood, A. and Mayer, J. (1998), 'African Development in a Comparative Perspective', United Nations Conference on Trade and Development, Geneva, Study no. 4.

World Bank (1987), *Korea: Managing the Industrial Transition. Vol. II: Selected Topics and Core Studies*, March, Washington, DC: World Bank.

APPENDIX

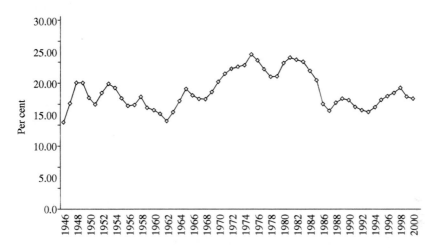

Source: Calculated from South African Reserve Bank data. The numerator is 6009Y and the denominator is 6006Y in the database.

Figure 6A.1   The ratio of gross domestic fixed capital formation to GDP in South Africa (%)

Table 6A.1 Average annual rates of growth of South Africa's total exports of goods and non-factor services by main sector (%)

	1970–75	1975–80	1970–80	1980–85	1985–90	1980–90	1990–95	1995–98	1990–98
Exports in Constant (1995) US Dollars									
Agriculture, forestry and fishing	9.94	3.00	6.41	–20.45	8.58	–7.06	3.08	4.10	3.46
Mining excluding gold	13.00	17.63	15.29	–7.80	5.53	–1.36	2.74	0.91	2.05
Manufacturing	7.55	6.94	7.24	–7.26	14.19	2.91	8.42	–0.38	5.03
Exports of goods excluding gold	9.35	10.11	9.73	–8.52	10.51	0.54	6.38	0.18	4.01
Gold	13.06	19.88	16.42	–14.36	–2.14	–8.45	–3.82	–8.91	–5.76
Total exports of goods including gold	10.80	14.57	12.67	–11.36	5.69	–3.21	3.74	–1.54	1.73
Wholesale and retail trade, catering etc.	4.38	–1.49	1.40	–8.28	15.59	2.97	2.60	5.17	3.55
Transport, storage and communication	10.66	6.07	8.34	–12.77	8.01	–2.93	2.71	2.02	2.45
Finance, insurance, real estate & business services	14.46	–0.37	6.79	–3.80	10.08	2.91	2.11	9.31	4.75
Community, social and personal services	34.88	–9.99	10.19	–0.34	13.97	6.58	3.79	2.56	3.32
Total	10.54	12.90	11.71	–11.19	6.31	–2.83	3.59	–0.70	1.96
Exports in Constant-Price Trade-Weighted Foreign Currency									
Agriculture, forestry and fishing	7.83	2.4	5.08	–14.4	1.79	–6.65	3.34	9.48	5.6
Mining excluding gold	10.82	16.96	13.85	–0.78	–1.07	–0.93	3	6.13	4.16
Manufacturing	5.46	6.3	5.88	–0.21	7.05	3.36	8.69	4.77	7.21
Exports of goods excluding gold	7.23	9.46	8.34	–1.56	3.6	0.99	6.64	5.36	6.16
Gold	10.89	19.19	14.96	–7.84	–8.26	–8.05	–3.58	–4.2	–3.81
Total exports of goods including gold	8.66	13.9	11.25	–4.62	–0.91	–2.78	4	3.55	3.83
Wholesale and retail trade, catering etc.	2.39	–2.08	0.13	–1.3	8.36	3.42	2.85	10.61	5.69
Transport, storage and communication	8.52	5.49	6.99	–6.14	1.26	–2.51	2.97	7.29	4.57
Finance, insurance, real estate & business services	12.26	–0.89	5.48	3.48	3.21	3.34	2.37	14.96	6.92
Community, social and personal services	28.78	–10.28	7.49	6.99	6.84	6.92	4.04	7.88	5.46
Total	8.43	12.24	10.32	–4.45	–0.33	–2.41	3.84	4.44	4.06

Source: Calculated from the DRI-WEFA and SA Reserve Bank databases.

Table 6A.2 Shares of sectors and industry groups in South Africa's total manufactured exports (%)

	1970	1975	1980	1985	1990	1995	1998
Chemicals	11.01	10.76	14.56	15.80	13.44	14.88	14.2
Iron and steel	7.50	8.07	13.62	18.21	19.82	20.06	21.21
Non-ferrous basic metals	2.73	4.28	6.36	12.07	7.52	5.77	8.11
Pulp and paper	3.01	2.33	2.53	4.52	4.59	5.75	3.99
Total natural resource-based group	24.25	25.44	37.07	50.60	45.37	46.48	47.51
Fabricated metal products	2.39	2.05	1.84	1.66	3.27	3.53	4.00
Machinery and equipment	8.63	5.41	4.36	4.35	5.65	7.09	6.66
Electrical machinery	1.57	1.09	1.01	0.80	1.24	1.67	1.71
Motor vehicles	2.13	1.77	1.71	2.20	3.28	4.22	4.99
Other transport equipment	1.01	0.86	0.68	0.58	0.72	0.78	0.86
Total durable goods group	15.73	11.18	9.60	9.59	14.16	17.29	18.22
Textiles	5.28	3.54	3.38	4.03	3.77	3.36	3.18
Wood and wood-based products	0.19	0.28	1.01	0.98	1.11	0.95	0.90
Leather products	0.55	0.35	0.51	0.81	0.57	0.92	0.86
Furniture	0.11	0.09	0.35	0.29	0.70	1.73	2.03
Footwear	0.14	0.12	0.28	0.22	0.23	0.27	0.19
Clothing	1.34	1.19	1.74	1.93	1.65	1.48	1.31
Total labour-intensive group	7.61	5.57	7.26	8.27	8.04	8.71	8.47
TV, radio & communication equipment	0.47	0.29	0.21	0.34	0.46	0.78	1.02
Professional & scientific equipment	0.71	0.39	0.30	0.35	0.45	0.53	0.57
Other manufacturing sectors	51.23	57.12	45.55	30.84	31.53	26.21	24.22
Total manufactured exports	100.00	100.00	100.00	100.00	100.00	100.00	100.00

Source: Calculated from the DRI-WEFA database.

Table 6A.3 Shares of sectors and industry groups in South African manufacturing value added in constant (1995) prices (%)

	1970	1975	1980	1985	1990	1995	1998
Chemicals	10.11	9.46	11.98	15.86	14.14	14.30	15.82
Iron and steel	7.66	8.25	7.23	6.25	5.89	7.10	7.60
Non-ferrous basic metals	1.09	1.78	1.49	1.75	1.73	2.35	3.84
Pulp and paper	4.05	4.18	3.99	4.91	4.85	5.32	4.82
Total natural resource-based group	22.90	23.67	24.70	28.77	26.61	29.07	32.08
Fabricated metal products	8.77	8.57	8.28	6.98	5.13	4.90	5.41
Machinery and equipment	8.54	9.69	9.52	8.28	6.86	7.07	5.16
Electrical machinery	2.34	3.42	3.85	3.88	2.73	3.14	2.93
Motor vehicles	7.06	8.81	9.28	6.86	7.54	7.65	6.37
Other transport equipment	1.73	1.73	1.29	1.10	0.71	0.52	0.60
Total durable goods group	28.42	32.22	32.21	27.10	22.98	23.28	20.47
Textiles	3.97	3.25	3.95	3.28	2.43	2.52	2.37
Wood and wood-based products	1.85	1.68	1.81	1.79	1.49	1.67	1.64
Leather products	0.47	0.46	0.34	0.43	0.40	0.44	0.49
Furniture	1.43	1.26	1.46	1.50	1.59	1.53	1.57
Footwear	1.36	1.08	0.92	0.98	0.98	0.89	0.65
Clothing	2.68	2.36	2.71	2.77	2.84	2.81	2.51
Total labour-intensive group	11.76	10.09	11.18	10.75	9.74	9.84	9.22
TV, radio & communication equipment	0.73	0.81	0.53	0.71	1.20	1.02	1.33
Professional & scientific equipment	0.28	0.13	0.11	0.21	0.28	0.31	0.25
Other manufacturing sectors	35.91	33.09	31.26	32.46	39.19	36.48	36.67
Total MVA	100.00	100.00	100.00	100.00	100.00	100.00	100.00

Source: Calculated from the DRI-WEFA database.

Table 6A.4 Shares of main sectors in total value added in South Africa in constant (1995) rands (%)

	1970	1975	1980	1985	1990	1995	1998
Primary	19.62	14.30	14.18	13.13	12.30	10.82	11.03
Agriculture, forestry and fishing	4.70	4.69	4.96	4.49	4.95	3.86	4.53
Gold mining	11.72	6.43	4.67	3.83	3.32	2.83	2.61
Other mining	3.19	3.18	4.55	4.82	4.02	4.14	3.89
Total mining	14.91	9.61	9.22	8.65	7.34	6.96	6.50
Secondary	27.15	29.88	30.65	29.07	28.87	27.85	26.91
Manufacturing	19.97	21.62	23.32	22.03	22.00	21.22	20.18
Electricity, gas and water	1.74	2.06	2.40	2.90	3.16	3.48	3.60
Construction	5.44	6.20	4.93	4.15	3.71	3.15	3.14
Tertiary	53.23	55.82	55.17	57.80	58.83	61.33	62.05
Wholesale and retail trade, catering etc.	13.88	15.97	13.88	14.84	14.31	14.34	13.75
Transport, storage and communication	6.75	7.50	8.26	7.89	7.88	8.90	9.99
Finance, insurance, real estate & business services	14.37	14.18	14.43	15.30	15.60	16.42	17.63
Community, social and personal services	18.24	18.17	18.60	19.77	21.04	21.66	20.69
Total value added	100.00	100.00	100.00	100.00	100.00	100.00	100.00

Source: Calculated from the DRI-WEFA database.

Table 6A.5   Average annual rates of growth of value added by main sector in South Africa at constant 1995 prices: 1950-2000

	1950–55	1955–60	1960–65	1965–70	1970–75	1975–80	1975–81
Primary	4.98	5.26	4.55	2.38	−2.58	2.61	2.39
Agriculture, forestry and fishing	4.53	1.71	0.26	3.30	4.20	4.06	4.35
Total mining	5.15	6.47	5.70	2.23	−4.51	2.06	1.62
Secondary	6.58	4.09	9.72	7.54	6.28	3.90	4.43
Manufacturing	7.48	4.56	9.85	7.38	5.93	4.47	5.25
Electricity, gas and water	8.61	6.05	6.41	7.02	7.80	6.09	6.96
Construction	2.25	0.67	11.19	8.59	7.03	−1.71	−0.54
Tertiary	3.84	3.64	5.05	5.78	5.26	2.83	3.22
Wholesale and retail trade, catering etc.	3.46	4.26	7.33	7.20	7.23	0.06	1.56
Transport storage and communication	4.81	2.97	5.58	6.51	6.49	4.91	5.15
Finance, insurance, real estate & business services	4.27	4.12	5.11	6.57	4.00	3.26	3.58
Community, social and personal services	3.78	2.74	3.93	4.14	4.20	3.40	3.32
GDP	4.89	4.11	6.28	5.15	3.65	3.09	3.47

	1970–81	1980–85	1985–90	1990–95	1995–98	1990–98	1995–2000
Primary	0.10	0.59	0.15	−1.59	1.95	−0.28	1.41
Agriculture, forestry and fishing	4.28	0.07	3.66	−4.04	5.28	−0.64	4.61
Total mining	−1.22	0.80	1.65	−0.19	−0.02	0.12	−5.55
Secondary	5.26	−0.28	0.75	0.32	1.22	0.66	1.32
Manufacturing	5.56	0.95	1.59	0.15	0.71	0.36	1.11
Electricity, gas and water	7.34	6.02	3.40	2.83	3.53	3.09	3.42
Construction	2.84	−1.37	−0.61	−2.36	2.08	−0.72	0.27
Tertiary	4.15	2.86	1.98	1.61	3.04	2.15	3.20
Wholesale and retail trade, catering etc.	4.10	3.48	0.89	0.92	0.89	0.91	1.81
Transport storage and communication	5.76	1.16	1.60	3.37	6.92	4.69	6.96
Finance, insurance, real estate & business services	3.77	3.31	2.00	1.92	5.55	3.26	5.56
Community, social and personal services	3.72	3.34	2.90	1.47	0.80	1.22	0.43
GDP	3.55	1.35	1.67	0.86	2.43	1.45	2.45

	1950–60	1960–70	1970–80	1980–90	1990–2000
Primary	5.12	3.46	0.02	0.37	–0.10
Agriculture, forestry and fishing	3.11	1.63	4.13	1.85	0.19
Mining	5.81	3.95	–1.28	0.43	–0.37
Secondary	5.33	8.62	5.08	0.23	0.82
Manufacturing	6.01	8.61	5.20	1.27	0.63
Electricity, gas and water	7.32	6.72	6.94	4.70	3.13
Construction	1.46	9.88	2.57	–0.99	–1.05
Tertiary	3.74	5.42	4.04	2.41	2.40
Wholesale and retail trade, catering etc.	3.86	7.27	3.58	2.17	1.36
Transport storage and communication	3.89	6.05	5.70	1.38	5.15
Finance, insurance, real estate & business services	4.20	5.84	3.63	2.66	3.72
Community, social and personal services	3.26	4.04	3.80	3.12	0.95
GDP	4.50	5.71	3.37	1.51	1.65

Source: Calculated from the South African Reserve Bank database.

Table 6A.6 *Shares of main sectors in South Africa's exports of goods and non-factor services (%)*

	1970	1975	1980	1985	1990	1995	1998
Primary	50.85	55.85	68.69	62.79	49.12	40.26	37.62
Agriculture, forestry and fishing	7.05	6.86	4.33	2.5	2.78	2.71	3.12
Gold	30.84	34.52	46.59	38.86	25.69	17.72	13.68
Other mining	12.97	14.48	17.77	21.43	20.65	19.83	20.81
Secondary	31.52	27.39	20.91	26.03	37.15	46.66	47.1
Manufacturing	31.37	27.35	20.85	25.90	37.03	46.52	46.98
Electricity, gas and water	0.01	0.03	0.05	0.1	0.1	0.11	0.1
Construction	0.14	0.02	0.01	0.03	0.03	0.03	0.03
Tertiary	17.62	16.76	10.39	11.18	13.73	13.08	15.28
Wholesale and retail trade, catering etc.	6.6	4.96	2.51	2.95	4.48	4.27	5.07
Transport, storage and communication	8.39	8.43	6.17	5.64	6.11	5.86	6.35
Finance, insurance, real estate & business services	2.47	2.94	1.57	2.35	2.8	2.6	3.47
Community, social and personal services	0.16	0.43	0.14	0.25	0.35	0.35	0.39
Total value added	100.00	100.00	100.00	100.00	100.00	100.00	100.00

Source: Calculated from the DRI-WEFA database.

7. The freight transport sector, 1970–2000

Trevor Jones

7.1 INTRODUCTION

The role of the transport sector in any modern economy is to generate a broad infrastructure and set of associated services that integrates diverse social and economic actors within and beyond the nation. Passenger transport moves persons from areas of lower to higher utility for the purposes of work, recreation or residence; freight transport moves goods from less-productive to more-productive areas of employment, and realizes the potential gains from trade by linking national economies into a globalizing international community.

In the 1970s and 1980s, the South African transport sector limited its cohering services to a minority of the overall population, and for the most part it served that community well, sometimes remarkably well. World-class ports were constructed to funnel bulk exports to world markets, in order to finance domestic import substitution. The rail system was re-modelled to service these ports, and maintained a network of high-density and low-cost (if subsidized) passenger services to shuttle black commuters over relatively long distances between dormitory townships and urban industries. World-class national roads linked cities occupied by residents enjoying high levels of private car ownership, and generally adequate roads served commercial agriculture. Other groups were less well served. Major rural communities were excluded from the transport network, leaving numbers of low-income persons stranded; peri-urban residents distant from commuter rail services were left to the mercies of chaotically-organized taxi and bus services; and general freight-orientated industries were left with facilities that lagged far behind the assets provided for their bulk counterparts. In 1994, South Africa's new democracy therefore inherited a transport sector skewed towards selected segments of the wider society. In many respects, the sector was poorly prepared for the needs of a more inclusive political economy, to a point where the Department of Transport's influential *Moving South Africa* study identifies 'a transport system and infrastructure ... in fundamental misalignment to the new national objectives' (Department of Transport, 1998: 5).

This chapter will attempt to explore dimensions of that misalignment. Major areas of technical and policy interest emerge in the spheres of both freight and passenger transport, but this coverage will be limited to the realm of the former, and will focus exclusively on the three principal surface modes of sea, rail and road transport. In all three modes, enormous changes have been effected over the period from 1970 to 2000, by no means all of them for the better, and by no means all of them in the direction of serving better the widening needs of an increasingly inclusive and democratic South African community.

7.2   PORTS AND MARITIME TRANSPORT

Between 1970 and 2000, the port- and maritime-related landscape of the southern African region changed dramatically and irreversibly. These changes have also been distinctly lop-sided over time. The 1970s witnessed massive capital widening as bulk ports were constructed to propel the South African economy into a phase of export-led growth predicated on high volumes of low-value bulk staples, and as existing ports were re-fashioned to cope with the global 'container revolution'. The 1980s saw a substantial consolidation of bulk-handling investment, in the process creating world-class harbours and associated land-side transport connections on the east coast at Richards Bay and on the west coast at Saldanha, while general cargo facilities received scant attention. By contrast, the 1990s produced not only a slowdown in overall port expansion, but also a realization that world-beating bulk ports and mediocre general cargo facilities were seriously at odds with the development orientation of a 'new' South African economy that was attempting to re-enter the mainstream of an increasingly globalized international trading community (Department of Transport, 1998; Lawrance, 2000).

During the last quarter of the twentieth century, South Africa became a major sea-trading nation. Sea transport activity is conventionally measured in two ways: nominally, in terms of the crude tonnages of cargo carried, and in 'real' ton-mile[1] terms by considering both cargo volumes and the distance travelled between sources and destinations. Port performance is generally measured in terms of the former more simple *numéraire*. On this basis, as shown in Table 7.1, South African port traffic doubled from 40 million tons in 1969/70 to 80 million tons by 1977/78, and roughly doubled again to reach 160 million tons by the mid-1990s. By 2000, total cargo handled stood at some 186 million tons.

The first and most obvious trend to emerge from Table 7.1 is that the lion's share of traffic growth has come from Richards Bay and Saldanha, both of

Table 7.1   Cargo handled at South African ports, 1969/70 to 2000, selected years (all cargoes, including petroleum products, in million metric tons)

Year[1]	Richards Bay	Durban	East London	Port Elizabeth	Cape Town	Saldanha	Total traffic[2]
1969/70	–	24.0	1.7	6.7	7.8	–	40.2
1974/75	–	34.7	3.5	10.4	10.4	–	59.0
1976/7	6.7	34.5	3.1	9.3	9.4	5.5	68.7
1977/78	13.1	35.4	3.5	7.3	9.4	11.7	80.4
1978/79	15.7	34.0	4.0	7.3	9.7	14.1	85.0
1983/84[3]	37.9	32.8	2.6	5.9	7.9	9.7	96.8
1987	47.1	44.3	2.5	4.3	5.9	12.3	116.4
1990	52.6	38.4	2.5	5.3	7.1	25.0	130.9
1994	69.0	41.4	3.2	4.9	9.8	23.3	151.6
2000[3]	91.8	49.7	1.1	7.1	11.8	24.5	186.2

Notes:
1.   Traffic volumes are shown for financial years (1 March to 28/29 February) up to 1983/84, and thereafter for calendar years.
2.   Total traffic excludes the activities of the small port of Mossel Bay, where volumes were tiny before the Mossgas project came on stream from 1992.
3.   Traffic magnitudes for 1983/84 and 2000 include estimates for unpublished oil and petroleum traffic. All other years include more accurate measures of these previously classified commodities.

Sources: South African Railways and Harbours, *Annual Report* (various years); Charlier, (1996); Portnet (2000).

which were transformed from virgin sites into deepwater ports in the 1970s. These two projects, the largest discrete infrastructural projects ever undertaken in the South African economy, provided the export maingates for two key bulk commodities – coal in the case of Richards Bay and iron ore in the case of Saldanha – to be transported to foreign markets in the largest Cape-sized bulk carriers[2] in international service. Since they opened for business in 1976, the roles the two bulk ports have played in the wider economy have diverged. To a large degree, Saldanha has remained a one-commodity industrial port, based on iron ore and some limited downstream steel products. In the case of Richards Bay, although coal has remained the central prop of port traffic, major diversification into various mineral products, neo-bulk cargoes[3] such as steel and forest products and general cargo has widened the port's traffic base to a point where it competes with other eastern seaboard ports over a broad front. Richards Bay's competitive strengths rest on a combination of deep water, suitable for large bulk carriers offering the most competitive freight rates; ample space in the immediate quayside hinterland, suitable for pre-assembly and efficient handling of neo-bulk cargoes; and proximity to the industrial heartland of Gauteng (Jones and Cawood, 1974). It is therefore no surprise that considerable traffic diversion from Durban, and to a lesser extent from Maputo, has taken place.

The second observation that can be made from the information in Table 7.1 is that, despite increased inter-port competition on the eastern seaboard, the centre of gravity of Southern African seaborne commerce has shifted firmly eastward over time, and is now entrenched in KwaZulu-Natal. In 1970, some 59 per cent of total port traffic was handled in Durban. By the mid-1980s, the combined traffic share of Durban and Richards Bay had risen to 73 per cent, and by 2000 to 76 per cent. In terms of value as opposed to volume, Durban cargo alone accounts for a little more than two-thirds of national imports and exports carried by sea (Pearson, 1995; Jones, 1997). The losers in this process have been the Cape ports, whose hinterlands, with few exceptions, have shrunk to their immediate geographic regions, and Maputo, which once commanded a guaranteed share of Witwatersrand traffic and rivalled Durban in terms of facilities and port activity.[4]

The dominant characteristics of late twentieth-century South African sea transport development remain its strong growth and overall size. Indeed, seatrade broadly associated with the South African economy and ports is substantial by global standards: the 186 million tons of traffic handled in 2000 represents approximately 3.5 per cent of world seatrade in tonnage terms. In terms of 'real' sea transport activity, traffic passing through local ports generates some 12 200 million ton-miles of maritime freight activity, or about 6 per cent of global activity – a performance that places South Africa within the top 12 nations on the international maritime-trading league table. This country's share of global maritime activity consequently exceeds its share of global GDP by more than 20 to one. These indicators confirm that a high proportion of South African trade comprises low-value bulk staples that are handled efficiently in relatively sophisticated ports.

The relative status of the South African ports is indicated in Table 7.2, which summarizes the performance of a representative selection of leading African and southern hemisphere ports on the bases of total traffic handled and containerized traffic. A consideration of the latter is vital, as different types of traffic obviously have different economic impacts. In terms of economic linkages and value adding, handling a ton of crude oil is not the same as handling a ton of refined sugar, while both of these differ markedly from the handling of a ton of containerized machinery parts. It is the broad category of general cargoes, now almost universally moved in standard freight containers, that confer the richest economic linkages on the local economies of the ports

Table 7.2   African and southern hemisphere port traffic 1996–1997 (selected ports[1])

Port	Total port traffic (m tons)	Rank traffic (TEUs 000s)	Container	Rank
Richards Bay	79.0	1	11	14
Newcastle	66.9	2	9	15
Durban	46.8	3	984	1
Santos	36.3	4	772	3
Sydney	21.3	5	730	4
Melbourne	18.6	6	923	2
Casablanca	16.0	7	195	10
Abidjan	11.9	8	213	9
Auckland	11.3	9	464	6
Lagos	9.8	10	178	11
Mombasa	8.6	11	217	8
Cape Town	6.6	12	318	7
Buenos Aires	6.6	13	526	5
Dakar	6.0	14	99	13
Port Louis	3.7	15	106	12

Note
1. Most prominent multi-purpose ports are included. What are not are basically one-commodity 'industrial' ports, such as the Nigerian oil terminals, and the Australian coal export terminals.

Source: ISL (1997).

where they are worked, and on the wider national economies where they originate or are absorbed.[5]

In terms of indicators of both total port traffic and container traffic, the South African ports emerge as colossal by African standards and as dominant within the broad trading community of the southern hemisphere. Richards Bay is first past the post in the regional tonnage derby (followed by the rather similar coal-orientated Australian port of Newcastle), while Durban takes the bronze medal on the basis of total traffic but wins gold with first spot on the container league, followed by Melbourne, Sydney and Santos. On this basis, it is difficult to avoid the conclusion that South Africa (and indeed the province of KwaZulu-Natal) possesses both the leading multi-purpose general cargo port and the most active diversified bulk port on the continent of Africa and in the southern hemisphere (Fair and Jones, 1991).

All of this appears to signify a vibrant, growing and sophisticated ports sector appropriate for the needs of a middle-income developing economy. Appearance and reality may well not coincide in this regard; there is growing evidence that the facilities and services provided by the ports are seriously out of line with the development needs of the economy. For the 'old' South Africa, growth through penetration of relatively anonymous bulk markets made considerable sense. Consequently, the creation of world-class bulk transport facilities also made eminent sense. They make a great deal less sense in the context of a 'new' economy, whose principal development drivers are growth of manufacturing output and expansion of manufactured exports, energized by the ability to acquire imports at minimum cost (Department of Transport, 1998). What this development path requires from the nation's ports are *general* cargo-handling facilities of the requisite quantity and the highest quality, at the lowest price. Sadly, in terms of all three of these *desiderata*, the performance record of the South African ports is well below the world-class benchmarks achieved in the bulk arena.

The transport and handling of general cargoes is now dominated to an overwhelming degree by containerization and unitization, so the efficiency of general cargo-handling facilities is essentially determined by the existence and maintenance of suitable container terminals and distribution systems. Containerization impacted seriously on international liner shipping from the late 1960s, but it was only in 1977 that South African maritime transport joined the 'container revolution' as a somewhat reluctant fellow traveller, whereafter the ineluctable box has appropriated an increasing share of the subcontinent's general cargo cake. Mainstream container facilities were established in the three principal general cargo ports of Durban, Cape Town and Port Elizabeth, and capacity well beyond the traffic parameters of the late 1970s was installed in all three. This capacity (both in terms of the basic marine infrastructure of the various port terminals and the equipment and logistic networks required to move boxes between the terminals and their hinterlands), proved to be adequate for roughly the first 15 years of operations. Container traffic passed the 300 000 TEU[6] threshold in 1979, doubled to reach some 600 000 TEUs by 1981, and then languished at this level until the late 1980s, when an upward growth trajectory resumed.

By 1993, supply (in the form of inherent and still largely original terminal capacity) was still suffficient to cope with seatrade demand on the part of cargo owners, but thereafter the container-handling problems of the South African ports have escalated. This problem has several dimensions, affecting both the demand and the supply sides of the transport market mechanism. On the demand side, the re-entry of the economy into the mainstream of the international trading community following the first democratic elections in 1994, precipitated a surge in seaborne container volumes as the leading liner carriers returned to the South African trades, and as container penetration rates rose from levels that had been low by international standards. In the leading container port, Durban, container trafffic rose by 23 per cent over the 1993–94 period, by 14 per cent in 1994–95, and by a further 10 per cent in 1995–96. These booming volumes threatened to overwhelm terminal capacity, and produced the inevitable consequences of berth delays, cargo distribution hold-ups and vessel queues outside the ports. On the domestic supply side, reactions were *ad hoc* and limited: additional areas for container stacking were fashioned, and additional cargo-handling *super*structure (in the form of additional and more capable gantry cranes and straddle carriers) was installed on essentially fixed *infra*structure. The breakneck pace of demand growth slowed somewhat in the late 1990s, but by 2000 the South African ports handled a total of 1.80 million TEUs (of which Durban alone accounted for 1.13 million TEUs), with the same basic container quays that had been constructed in 1977.

At the same time as these demand–supply pressures were building, a series of exogenous supply-side changes were unfolding in the international liner shipping industry. When container operations first superseded conventional breakbulk shipping services, the routes over which vessels operated changed relatively little; many liner vessels continued to ply north–south, region-to-region routes. From 1990, this pattern has changed significantly, with most high-density liner routes now organized around skeins of round-the-world or long-swing pendulum services,[7] operated by collaborative consortia of shipping lines, and connecting at a limited number of 'hub' ports, from which radiating 'spoke' services feed cargoes to secondary ports. Two powerful concomitants of these arrangements are the deployment of larger, deeper-drafted post-Panamax[8] container vessels, and a reduction in the number of port calls in any discrete geographic region. This new *modus operandi* first took root on the highest-density northern hemisphere trade routes, but many southern hemisphere services have followed suit, albeit with smaller vessels more suited to lower levels of seatrade demand. The consequences for ports are substantial, as the container 'majors' attempt to concentrate their activities at a single regional 'hub', that acts as both a sink for national cargoes and as a distribution centre for transshipment traffic. Successful 'hub' ports therefore have to provide capacity beyond the dictates of national demand, hence attainment of 'hub' port status becomes inordinately difficult in a capacity-constrained situation. That is exactly the situation in which the South African ports in general, and the dominant port of Durban in particular, have found themselves since the early 1990s. Durban is the only South African port with any pretensions to hub status, and it has been favoured as the principal, or in some cases as the sole, South African port of call by many liner operators (Lloyd's List Africa Weekly, 1999) for several years. Preference for Durban has arisen from its proximity to the economic powerhouse of Gauteng, ample spare capacity on inland rail and road arteries,[9] and an excellent network of port ancillary industries serving the needs of vessels and their cargoes (Jones, 1997).

From the 1990s, these strengths have been threatened by capacity constraints that have been exacerbated by a reluctance on the part of shipowners to shift to less-preferred ports, such as Port Elizabeth, despite the blandishments of (uneconomic) rail-rate equalization to bring rail costs on the longer Cape–Gauteng routes in line with the shorter route from Durban. The overall picture to emerge from this account is of container facilities that have lurched from capacity crisis to capacity crisis since 1993, with investment spending well below long-term capital requirements (Department of Transport, 1998: 50). The response of the port authorities (who also happened to be the terminal operators) has been muted to a point of near-catatonia. In Durban, a reconfiguration of the port to permit container expansion into a port segment hitherto dedicated to neo-bulk activities was given the green light in October 2000, and will create additional capacity sufficient to give cargo owners a breathing space of five to seven years. However, if container seatrade continues to grow at the annual average 7 per cent rate recorded from 1992 to 2000, major new infrastructure will have to be created, preferably on the eastern seaboard, before the end of the first decade of the twenty-first century.

The final dimension of the South African ports sector to give cause for concern is the cost of port functions to users. The *Moving South Africa* study demonstrated that waterfront charges in this country's ports are high by international standards when measured against comparable ports in both developed and developing countries (ibid.: 46). This blanket comparison also masks some major intra-port price-cost skewness. Historically, marine charges (such as port dues and tug charges) have been low relative to both foreign harbour tariffs and underlying costs. This under-recovery has been more than made up by cargo charges that have been grossly in excess of cost (Jones, 1985). The principal culprit in this regard is the single item of *ad valorem* wharfage, which is levied differentially on imports and exports, and which is, as the name suggests, driven by commodity value rather than by considerations of cost. This economically inefficient pricing mechanism is intended to finance the cargo-working infrastructure of the ports, and throughout the second half of the twentieth century it has been the principal source of harbour revenues and substantial overall port profits. In overall tariff terms, the South African ports have therefore been cheap for ships but expensive for their cargoes. This unfortunate asymmetry militates against marginal parcels of cargoes, most notably the categories of higher-valued general cargoes that top the agenda in the state's manufacturing-led development strategy. These tariff anomalies are unlikely to survive port privatization, which is set to commence early in the new century (a pre-condition to which has been the separation of landlord and operating functions effected by Portnet in 2000), but they have dominated the port pricing landscape for the last 50 years.

In overall terms, the South African ports sector has developed a distinct split personality: a top-quality bulk infrastructure offers first-world services to bulk exporters and importers at competitive prices, while container and general cargo terminals, operating at their elastic limits, offer a poor service at high cost. Sadly, the opposite strengths and weaknesses would better serve the development needs of the economy.

7.3 RAIL TRANSPORT

The performance of rail transport[10] between 1970 and 2000 mirrors the overall behaviour of the transport sector over the same period. An exuberant phase of expansion in the 1970s was followed by something very close to a stationary state during the 1980s, and by a decline in the substance if not necessarily in the arithmetic of rail performance during the 1990s. By the end of the century, rail had developed the same chronic bipolar disorder as the ports, with a bulk export infrastructure of genuine world class co-existing with a general cargo-handling network of increasing fragility. Once again, the overarching development imperatives of the South African economy would have been better served by a reversal of the manic and the depressive dimensions of this disorder.

During the 1970s, the expansion of rail was inextricably bound up with the economy's leap into the premier international bulk-export league, through the Richards Bay and Saldanha projects, and by the large-scale containerization of imports and exports of general cargo. During the 1980s, bulk-related activities continued to deepen, most notably those associated with the Coallink connection to Richards Bay, but the position of rail as the dominant domestic mode of transport for higher-rated general cargoes was to come under increasing pressure from road carriers, despite the regulatory strictures that hamstrung the latter. After these shackles fell away from 1989, rail has lost further market share in the broad general-cargo arena, has contracted its services to areas of low-density demand, and maintains a traffic base heavily skewed towards low-valued bulk staples.

The crude arithmetic of rail transport's performance since 1970 does not conjure up an image of a transport mode in either crisis or irreversible decline. The basic rail infrastructure of the South African economy, massive by African standards, has changed relatively little over the last three decades of the twentieth century. Total route kilometres of track under the control of

Spoornet (and its predecessor, South African Railways), the rail division of
Transnet, rose from some 19 800 kilometres in the early 1970s to 21 217
kilometres by 1987, largely as a result of the completion of lines to the bulk
export ports of Richards Bay and Saldanha (SAR&H *Annual Report,*
1973–74; S A Transport Services *Annual Report,* 1986–87). Thereafter, the
public rail infrastructure has shrunk somewhat to approximately 20 400
kilometres by the end of the 1990s, as certain low-density branch lines have
been closed.

In qualitative terms, the proportion of the entire rail network that was
electrified rose from 26 per cent in 1970 to 43 per cent by the end of the
century, while improvements not only in the permanent way itself, but also in
rolling stock, signalling capacity and tractive power have raised potential
carrying capacity. In terms of tractive power, the centre of gravity has also
shifted strongly towards electric units, as shown in Figure 7.1, which depicts
the shape of the locomotive stock in 1970 and 1998. In 1970, South African
Railways initiated a coherent policy of steam replacement, whereby steam
locomotives would be successively phased out in favour of electric traction on
high-demand routes and by diesel power on less-patronized lines.[11] Electric
traction is associated with high fixed capital costs (of the catenaries and power
grid) but low variable costs, while diesel incurs lower fixed costs but higher
operating costs. The association of the former with high-density routes and the
latter with low-density services, branch lines and shunting is thus obvious.

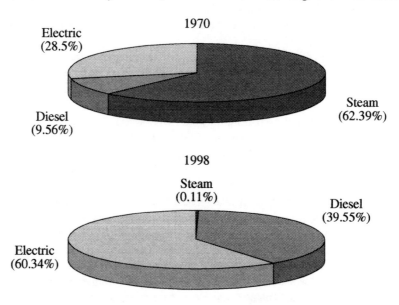

Figure 7.1   Profile of tractive power in South African rail, 1970 and 1998

A pivotal determinant of tractive power choice is fuel cost, hence the oil 'crises' of the 1970s accelerated the process of electrification, slowed the rate of acquisition of diesels, and even gave steam a temporary reprieve. Falling real oil prices from the early 1980s to the late 1990s put the original power plan back on track, to a point where electric power provides 60 per cent of the locomotive stock, but generates over 85 per cent of the real output of that stock, as electric units dominate high-density, long-haul routes.

In terms of crude tonnages of freight conveyed, freight activity increased from 111 million tons in 1970 to a peak of 188 million tons by 1981, or by some 62 per cent. Thereafter, no monotonic growth trend is discernible, with volumes fluctuating between a low of 159 million tons in 1983 and highs of 186 million tons in 1989 and 1998. Crude tonnage data provide a poor basis for measuring changes in real transport activity, for they ignore the crucial dimension of length of haul. It is clearly both the volume of cargo and the distance over which it is carried that more accurately captures transport activity. In real output terms, rail's performance is very similar over the expansionary period, rising from 53 300 million freight ton-kilometres in 1970 to 87 100 million by 1979, or by 63 per cent. Thereafter, real activity continued to grow but at a decreasing rate to reach some 99 000 million ton-kilometres by 1999 (SAR&H *Annual Report*, 1969–70 and 1978–79 and Railroad Association of South Africa, 2001). This indicates that rail volumes have stabilized after the early 1980s, but that average lengths of haul have risen somewhat, from approximately 475 kilometres in 1980 to some 550 kilometres by 1999.

If South Africa's public rail network, rolling stock and output levels are compared with those of other significant economies in Africa or elsewhere in the southern hemisphere, as shown in Table 7.3, South Africa shows up strongly. This country's basic rail backbone, measured in route-kilometres, stands well below that of Argentina's rail network and somewhat below that of Brazil, but exceeds those of other South American, African and Australasian economies. In terms of locomotives, freight wagons, freight tons carried and freight ton-kilometres of 'real' activity, South Africa eclipses all other countries enumerated, in most cases by a wide margin. By contrast, staff numbers employed by the national rail carrier, Spoornet, are well below railway employee levels in Argentina, Brazil and Egypt, despite the generally lower levels of output generated in all three of these countries. This broadly favourable comparative international performance of South African rail largely mirrors the dominance of the ports sector, and suggests that this country is generally well equipped, if measured alongside other middle-income developing economies, in terms of hard-core transport infrastructure.

The data in Table 7.3 can also be used to generate various measures of rail productivity. In terms of freight ton-kilometres per employee, South African

Table 7.3   Rail transport size and scale indicators, selected African and
southem hemisphere countries, mid-1990s[1]

Country	Network route-kms	Staff	Loco-motives	Freight wagons	Freight tons×10⁶	Freight ton-kms×10⁶
Argentina	34 059	67 000	992	32 823	No data	7 860
Brazil	26 648	61 645	1 805	52 039	105.03	45 664
Chile	2 472	2 237	132	347	4.53	967
South Africa	20 441	47 140	3 547	133 645	180.13	95 591
Nigeria	3 054	11 346	200	no data	0.16	No data
Egypt	4 810	91 065	835	3 102	52.41	No data
Algeria	4 290	15 847	231	572	1.80	No data
Australia[4]	16 492	28 765	2 007	12 807	76.10	40 000

Notes
1. Years of enumeration vary across countries, but are generally drawn from the 1990–95 period. The South African staff level is based on 1998 data.
2. Over 10 000 kilometres of the Argentinian rail infrastructure comprise narrow-gauge lines.
3. Excluding private lines operated by various mines and industries; 1998 data.
4. The Australian information represents an amalgam of the activities of the Australian National Railways (ANR) and State operations in South Australia and New South Wales. Ton-kilometre calculations were furnished only by the ANR, but have been aggregated heroically for the whole country.

Sources: Business Rail Report (1998); RailRoad Association of South Africa (2001).

rail outperforms Australia by some 70 per cent, Brazil by a factor of three, and others by larger margins. In terms of freight ton-kilometres per wagon, this country's rail productivity stands at 54 per cent of the level produced by the Australian National Railways (an Australia-wide calculation cannot be made), and at a little over 80 per cent of the Brazilian level. Other useful performance indicators may be constructed around rail rate levels as measures of the cost of rail services to users. On the basis of 1998 traffic levels, price per ton-kilometre weighted across the aggregate South African rail traffic base emerged as some R0.22. This compares unfavourably with the United States (R0.11 per ton-kilometre) and Sweden (R0.13), but favourably alongside many other developed economies such as France (R0.37), the United Kingdom (R0.48) and New Zealand (R0.51) (Railway Gazette International, 1998 and Portnet, 2000). Comparative data for other middle-level developing economies are not available. In user cost terms, South African rail services are moderately priced by international norms across the full gamut of traffic, while the specialist Coallink 'produces the lowest-cost inland coal transport in the world at a high level of efficiency' (Department of Transport, 1998: 36).

The above account generates a picture of South African rail that is substantially positive: this country possesses a larger and more productive rail network than those of many other comparable nations, and offers its services to users at costs in line with or below those associated with many economies. These broad indicators may, however, convey a seriously distorted image of a mode of transport that this chapter will argue is far from healthy, and far from fulfilling the role it should play out in the South African economy. The overall fortunes of rail may perhaps better be represented not by examining aggregate levels of nominal or real output, but rather by considering the changing composition of that traffic base. Figure 7.2, shows both the growth of total rail freight traffic (and reveals readily the turnaround from steady growth in the 1970s to stasis thereafter), and the performance of the principal contributors to that total.

What Figure7.2 indicates is that traffic growth has been driven by two dominant and relatively limited activities – the transport of iron ore from the Sishen area in the Northern Province to Saldanha on the Orex line, and more powerfully by the carriage of coal from mining areas in Mpumulanga to Richards Bay. As noted above, these two niche activities are of world class, both technically and in user-cost terms. What is seriously less than world class is virtually everything else in the rail arena. The category of general freight (a congealed aggregate of activities on routes other than the Coallink and Orex operations) has fallen from over 130 million tons in 1976 to 95 million tons in 1999, or by some 27 per cent. Although the broad category of general freight includes a number of low-value primary products, its secular decline is part of

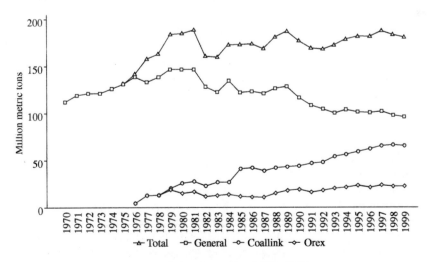

Figure 7.2   Evolution of rail freight traffic, 1970-1999

a longer-term phenomenon, whereby rail has lost command over higher-value, and consequently higher-rated, goods (van der Veer, 1982: 6). This also has some serious implications for pricing and sustainability.

In terms of legislation,[12] public rail has historically been recognized as the national domestic carrier, and as such has been required to act as a common carrier and to operate several uneconomic freight (and, particularly in the past, passenger) services. Moreover, the same legislation required the national transport services to operate in terms of business principles, and to balance their books. The latter was always interpreted very broadly, and was applied to the public transport sector, not to individual modes, and certainly not to discrete services within modes. The result was a complex web of cross-subsidization, with generally profitable ports and pipelines bailing out loss-making rail activities.

Within rail, the tariff philosophy adopted was that followed by most common carriers (in all transport modes) who face a diverse traffic base covering a broad spectrum of commodity types and values. That standard practice is to raise rates on higher-value cargo, in respect of which demand is relatively price inelastic, in the process charging 'what the market will bear', while low-value cargo, for which demand is conventionally believed to be more price elastic, attracts lower rates.[13] This type of 'Ramsay' pricing was indeed the norm in South African rail for much of the twentieth century, but after the mid-1970s, it has become increasingly difficult to pursue, for four principal reasons. The first was the increase in low-rated bulk traffic associated with the new bulk-export ports. The second was the 'container revolution' that transformed heterogeneous general cargo into standard freight containers, for which unitary tariff rates became the only sensible pricing mechanism. The third emanated from the recommendations of a series of public commissions of inquiry and multi-disciplinary studies that were tasked to investigate domestic transport policy.[14] Common to all of these was the advocacy of a more competitive domestic transport market, characterized by freer competition between road and rail, with both modes charging the 'right' (cost-related) prices for their services, but with rail relieved of the financial burden of providing uneconomic services, most notably the transport of commuters from distant Black dormitory suburbs to industrial areas. The fourth and most powerful reason has been the emergence of a road freight transport industry based on prices that are emphatically 'wrong', in so far as heavy freight vehicles systematically underpay for the use of the road infrastructure. The result of these influences is a set of rail prices that more closely approximates underlying cost, albeit based on capital cost levels that are below long-term capital replacement needs, but which none the less fails to undercut road rates (Department of Transport, 1998: 51), and which therefore also fails to stem a migration of general cargoes from rail to road.

There is ample evidence that these institutional factors have been aided and abetted by rank bad service to general users on the part of rail itself. *Moving South Africa* reports widespread dissatisfaction with general freight services (ibid.: 46) and unreliability in the case of breakbulk freight. From many comments made to the author over time, this problem does not appear to be limited to the higher-value end of the cargo spectrum; complainants range from bulk terminal operators in the port of Durban to users of branch lines in southern KwaZulu-Natal. Wagon availability and inflexibility in respect of 'just-in-time' articulation of supply to match fluctuating demand were advanced as particular problems (Jorgensen, 1999).

In sum, the combination of indifferent service quality and an inability to set prices at levels that are both competitive and sufficient to cover long-term capital replacement needs, bodes ill for the sustainability of the general freight services of rail in South Africa. The oft-expressed view of public spokes-persons (from the Minister of Transport downwards) and transport economists is that rail should be fulfilling a larger role in the long-distance carriage of commodities other than bulk mineral exports. Without a fundamental revision of modal costs and general quality of service delivery, it is hard to see how these fine sentiments can be transformed into changed behaviour on the part of transport users and rail transport providers.

7.4 ROAD TRANSPORT AND INTERMODAL COMPETITION

In the last 30 years of the twentieth century, road freight transport in South Africa has been utterly transformed. In 1970, commercial road haulage operators were regulated virtually out of existence by a permit system that systematically favoured rail on long-haul inter-city routes. Some significant road haulage was effected by private companies transporting their own products, often over short distances, but public carriers were responsible for a minuscule market share (van der Veer, 1982). By 2000, road had entrenched itself as the dominant land mode in both nominal tonnage terms and in terms of 'real' transport activity. At the same time, the regulatory and policy framework within which road transport functions has lurched from draconian *dirigisme* in the 1970s to virtually untrammelled *laissez-faire* by the 1990s. There is very little positive that can be said about either arrangement, and much that the recent (non-)policy environment has done to destroy equitable intermodal competition, and to threaten the survival of the economy's road infrastructure. The story of South African road freight transport since 1970 is consequently largely a story of regulation, its relaxation and its mismanage-ment. The road hauliers themselves are almost incidental actors in the drama.

In 1970, the commercial road freight industry was a puny creature, denied natural growth by the legacy of the 1929 Road Motor Competition Commission, whose recommendations to control road transport in order to eliminate 'wasteful and destructive competition' were embodied in the 1930 Motor Carrier Transportation Act (Freeman, 1982: 27). This piece of legislation had an enduring impact on the road transport industry, for it provided the blueprint for the controversial permit system, whereby certificates for prescribed journeys were granted to operators by various transportation boards and later by the National Transport Commission, under the auspices of the Department of Transport. For roughly the next four decades, this massive market imperfection effectively shut road hauliers out of the long-distance land transport market. By the late 1960s, policy sentiment was changing in favour of a more open and competitive transport market, in which road would play a more significant role, and as Freeman notes, 'it was clear that some relaxation of the control of road transport was coming if not imminent' (ibid.: 34).

Imminent the changes were certainly not. The provisions of the 1977 Road Transport Act and its subsequent regulations extended the gamut of permit-exempt goods, increased the radius of unrestricted carriage, and lifted permit restrictions in certain areas. This did not signal the end of the road permit system, and it did not immediately fashion a competitive land transport market in South Africa, but it did usher in a period of somewhat greater competition between road and rail. Formal deregulation of road transport was only to come in 1989 with the abandonment of the permit system, but thereafter liberalization of the environment in which road freight transport operates proceeded at breakneck pace. The principal changes from 1978 onwards are:

- From January 1978, motor carriers were permitted up to 80 kilometres without permits. The maximum permissible length of vehicles was increased from 13 to 17 metres; gross combination mass (GCM) rose from 38 to 41 metric tons, thereby increasing the maximum payload from 24 to 28 tons.
- In 1987, a Govemment White Paper stipulated that a comprehensive road transport quality system (RTQS) should be in place before transport deregulation took place. Maximum permissible vehicle lengths were increased to 20 metres, increasing GCM to 47 tons and maximum payload to 33 tons.
- In 1989, the road permit system was abandoned, signalling de facto deregulation of road transport, but without the RTQS being implemented.
- In 1990, maximum permissible vehicle lengths were increased to 22

metres. Interlink multi-trailer combinations come into regular use for long-haul freight traffic.

- In 1991, GCM was increased to 56 tons, permitting a maximum (legal) payload of 37 tons.
- In 1994, overloading tolerance of 5 per cent was allowed on GCM, increasing effective payloads to 39 tons for lightweight trailer combinations.
- In 1996, axle load limits of 8.2 tons, for which most South African bridges and roads are designed, were replaced by a limit of 9 tons, with a 5 per cent tolerance. Legal payloads of up to 45 tons could be achieved (RailRoad Association, 2001; Kempen, 2001).

From the end of the permit system in 1989, in the space of a single decade, the South African road freight transport industry has moved from the periphery of the market to a position where it operates with some of the largest heavy vehicles in the world that are not restricted to designated routes.[15] Under these circumstances, it is not surprising that road's freight market share has risen markedly, largely at the expense of rail. Precise estimation of modal shares is bedevilled by a paucity of accurate data relating to road freight activity, most notably activities of private carriers transporting their own products. Van der Veer attempted to compute the shares of rail, private road and public (commercial) carriers in 1971/72 and 1980/81. His data show private 'in house' carriers maintaining a relatively stable share of 35–37 per cent of total land transport tonnages over this period, while public carriers increased their share from 4 to 12 per cent in a still heavily regulated environment (van der Veer, 1982). This contrasts strongly with 1999 estimates produced by Spoornet and the RailRoad Association, which put total land-based transport volumes at some 820 million tons, of which rail controls 180 million tons (or 22 per cent of the total), and commercial hauliers 140 million tons (17 per cent), leaving 500 million tons (or 61 per cent) in the hands of private carriers of their own products. All of these exercises suffer from the common weakness of a nominal tonnage rather a real ton-kilometre basis. This has the effect of overstating road's share in general and the share of generally short-haul private road in particular.[16] Rail transport generates some 99 000 million ton-kilometres of 'true' transport activity, while a very rough and ready estimate would put road's output at approximately 113 000 million ton-kilometres (Railroad Association of South Africa, 2001). This suggests that road is now the senior partner in the South African land transport market, with a modal share of about 55 per cent of aggregate transport activity, while rail commands the remaining 45 per cent, albeit with a traffic base heavily skewed towards basic bulk commodities.

This represents a startling transformation in the fortunes of road transport, and one that would be both welcome and unremarkable if it came about as a consequence of freer-working and more-efficient transport markets, driven by the right price signals. Sadly, the overwhelming weight of evidence points to a market mechanism so distorted by externalities that the resultant pattern of resource allocation threatens the sustainability of both the road infrastructure and the rail system.

South Africa's road infrastructure is substantial – comprising a little under 60 000 kilometres of paved roads – but by no means all of this is in good condition. *Moving South Africa* reports only 18 per cent of national roads to be in 'very good condition' (Department of Transport, 1998: 79). Inter-city trunk roads are generally in the best condition, and long-distance secondary and rural roads in the worst. The biggest problem is the long-term financial sustainability of the road network, with a backlog of R40–57 billion 'just to maintain the current-sized network – already deteriorated – in a steady state' (ibid.: 80). At the heart of this problem is the absence of clear user charges for the country's roads: users pay through the fuel levy, through licence fees and through charges on toll roads, but with the exception of the last there is no direct link to specific road expenditure. In many areas, but particularly in the case of heavy road freight, the 'prices' that are in place are the wrong prices, thereby 'distorting the true economies of road freight with effects on modal choice and the balance of modal competition' (ibid.: 49). Many studies have explored the extent to which various users pay for the damage they inflict on the road infrastructure, and although the precise results generated are open to interpretation, most reveal a strongly positive correlation between vehicle mass and the extent of underpayment. A study commissioned by the Automobile Association in the mid-1990s indicated that light vehicles overpay by some 7 cents per vehicle-kilometre, or by R3.02 billion annually (in 1994 prices) in aggregate terms. All categories of heavy vehicles underpay, with the extent of under-recovery of pavement damage rising from 15 cents per vehicle-kilometre in the case of 2-axle heavy vehicles, to R1.49 for 6-axle heavies, and to a peak of R2.04 per vehicle-kilometre in respect of the heaviest 7-axle rigs. Total under-recovery from the heavy road freight industry was estimated at R3.87 billion in 1994 (Automobile Association, 1995). These estimates are based on legal maximum payloads, and would rise more than proportionately in the case of overloading. The obvious conclusion to draw from these exercises is that licence fees and road levies faced by light road users are too high, but this overpayment is more than offset by an array of 'prices' for heavy road users that are manifestly too low. These wrong prices are passed on to cargo owners in the form of freight rates that do not capture full economic costs, and consequently distort patterns of demand.

What this analysis suggests is that too much freight transport activity in South Africa is conducted by road, in vehicles that are too heavy, and which in the process inflict significant net damage costs on the roadway. This does not imply that heavy road hauliers are villains (other than those that systematically overload), but that operators and users alike respond to the wrong price signals. The immediate task of road-freight policy makers is to get prices right.

7.5 CONCLUSION

The overall picture of the South African freight transport sector that has taken shape in this account, is of a system that is large and sophisticated by regional standards, but which is coping poorly with several fundamental requirements of the new nation.

The South African ports are the maritime giants of the southern hemisphere, and produce certain products – notably bulk services – to the highest world standards. Unfortunately, these are not the port services that stand highest on the economy's agenda. More important is enhanced capacity and lowered user cost in respect of general cargoes to power manufacturing output and exports. A realignment of port priorities will consequently be needed as a matter of some urgency. There is, however, reason for confidence. Basically profitable ports are good candidates for privatization, and future private port entrepreneurs are likely to be responsive to the rents offered by growing general traffic.

The outlook for rail and road–rail competition is more complex and less sanguine. Rail currently has the same asymmetry as the ports, with strength in bulk operations and weakness in general freight. There is spare capacity on arterial routes, which better-quality management could exploit, but rail capillaries serving lower-density areas face a cloudier future. These are poor candidates for concessioning to private operators, unless the latter can be relieved of financial responsibility to maintain the rail infrastructure. More ambitious models of infrastructure/operating separation, along the lines already initiated by the ports, may be a possibility, but a rail renaissance cannot realistically be fashioned without a simultaneous reconsideration of the entire regulatory and pricing environment within which land transport functions. *Moving South Africa* calls for a 'restoration of value-based competition between rail and road', with a larger stake for rail in the long-haul transport of a wide array of products (Department of Transport, 1998: 112). Such an outcome would be excellent news for the South African economy, but it would require a firm commitment on the part of policy makers to re-establish the right price signals in transport markets. Without such commitment, a better alignment between transport performance and national objectives may prove elusive.

NOTES

1. Sea transport has not followed its land-based counterparts into metrication of distances and data. The miles referred to are nautical miles, equivalent to approximately 1.8 kilometres.
2. Cape-sized bulk carriers, commonly referred to as 'Capes', are vessels that exceed the maximum dimensions of the lock systems on the Panama Canal, and consequently have to sail on long-haul routes around Cape Horn and the Cape of Good Hope. They are generally vessels in excess of 110 000 deadweight tons.
3. Seaborne traffic is most broadly disaggregated into homogeneous bulk cargo, such as coal, grain or sugar, where individual units of cargo cannot be identified on the basis of individual mark or number; and heterogeneous general cargo, with individual mark or number. Neo-bulks are cargoes that have some characteristics of bulk cargo, but are partially differentiable. Examples would include steel rolls, coils and I-beams, reels of paper or blocks of granite.
4. In the early 1970s, Maputo (then Lourenço Marques) handled up to 15 million tons of cargo annually, much of it entrepôt cargo to South Africa in line with the provisions of the now-defunct Mozambique Treaty, which required that 47.5 per cent of traffic to the 'Witwatersrand Competitive Area' be directed through Maputo. The largest contributor to this traffic was always oil cargo. In the 1980s and 1990s, annual Maputo port traffic had fallen to 2–3 million tons,
5. Containerized import–export traffic per capita is used as one of many indicators of economic development. On this basis, South Africa still lags behind the performance of other comparable middle-level developing economies, suggesting that container traffic growth may well continue to outpace overall GDP growth.
6. Container traffic levels are conventionally measured in terms of twenty-foot-equivalent-units or TEUs. One TEU represents a standard 20-foot (or 6-metre) freight container. Since 40-foot boxes are increasingly supplanting 20-foot containers, the number of physical box moves through a port is lower than the number of TEUs.
7. Many of these are de facto round-the-world services. Container vessels may run from the east coast of the United States, across the Atlantic to a single port of call in the north-west Continent, through the Mediterranean and the Suez Canal to Singapore, thence onward to Japan and finally to a single port on the west coast of North America, before reversing direction.
8. Post-Panamax container vessels, as the name suggests, are vessels with dimensions too large to transit the Panama Canal.
9. On the Durban–Gauteng rail line, the highest utilization (of approximately 50 per cent) is experienced on the Durban–Pietermaritzburg segment and in the environs of Johannesburg. Elsewhere, utilization levels of 28–30 per cent were the order of the day in the mid-1990s.
10. Coverage of rail transport is limited to the network and activities of Spoornet, the rail division of Transnet Ltd. The few privatized lines, as well as rail transport effected 'in house' by various mining and industrial organizations, are ignored.
11. Apart from their poorer thermal efficiency, steam locomotives were unsuitable for longer, heavier trains requiring multiple locomotives. A multi-unit electric tractive set required manning only in the lead locomotive; all other units could run unmanned. For steam, all locomotives required both drivers and stokers. In other respects, the poor productivity of steam is more illusory, and has elements of a Catch 22 situation, for as steam was increasingly relegated to shunting and branch services, so its performance in terms of freight ton-kilometres dropped, and so the apparent case for steam elimination was strengthened.
12. Republic of South Africa Constitution Act (Act No. 32 of 1961), section 103(1).
13. In the case of high-value goods, freight charges represent a small fraction of total distribution costs, hence cargo owners are relatively unresponsive to tariff changes, and are consequently vulnerable to price mark-ups. For low-value staples, the opposite argument applies.
14. The most influential included the Schumann (1964), Marais (1969) and Van Breda (1973) commissions, and the broadly-directed National Transport Policy Study (NTPS) group,

orchestrated by the Department of Transport in the mid-1980s.
15. Maximum permissible GCM per vehicle in South Africa of 56 tons (or 58.8 tons with the 5 per cent overload tolerance) exceeds that in other South African Development Community (SADC) countries except Zambia, and stands well above levels in developed economies. In the United States the federal limit is 36.7 tons, although higher loads are permitted in some states, in most European countries it is 40 tons, and Japan and the United Kingdom permit a GCM of 38 tons.
16. Average rail haul is approximately 550 kilometres, perhaps comparable to long-haul road. Private road movements are much shorter, generally of the order of 100 kilometres or less.

REFERENCES

Automobile Association of South Africa (1995), *Heavy Vehicle Overloading in South Africa*, Durban: Automobile Association of South Africa.

Business Rail Report (1998), *International Data Bases*, Sutton: Railway Gazette International.

Charlier, Jaques (1996), *Le système portuaire sud-africain à l'aube du 21ème siècle*, Brussels: Académie Royale de Marine de Belgique.

Department of Transport (1998), *Moving South Africa (Draft for discussion)*, Pretoria: Government printer.

Fair, Dennis and Jones, Trevor (1991), *The Ports of Sub-Saharan Africa and Their Hinterlands*, Pretoria: Africa Institute of South Africa.

Freeman, Peter (1982), *The Recovery of Cost from Road Users in South Africa - Part 1: Background and Theory*, Pretoria: National Institute for Transport and Road Research.

Institut für Schiffahrtswirtschaft und Logistik (ISL) (1997) *Shipping Statistics Yearbook - 1997*, Bremen: ISL.

Jones, Robert and Cawood, Carey (1974), *Planning of the New Deepwater Harbour at Richards Bay*, Amsterdam: International Havencongres.

Jones, Trevor (1985), *Coastal Sea Transport and Intermodal Competition*, Pretoria: National Institute for Transport and Road Research.

Jones, Trevor (1997), *The Port of Durban and the Durban Metropolitan Economy*, Durban: Economic Research Unit, University of Natal.

Jorgensen, Allen (1999), 'Rail network in desperate need of reform', *Sunday Tribune Business Report*, Durban, 5 December.

Kempen, Willem (2001), 'The road to ruin', *Financial Mail*, Johannesburg, 19 January.

Lawrance, Derek (2000), 'Ports and transport logistics in Southern Africa: performance and prospects', *Maritime Africa 2000 Conference Proceedings*, Durban: Butterworths.

Lloyd's List Africa Weekly (Various years), *Liner schedules*, Johannesburg: Lloyds of London Press.

Pearson, Anthony (1995), *African Keyport*, Rossburgh: Accucut Books.

Portnet (2000), *Port of Durban Statistics*, Durban: Portnet.

Railroad Association of South Africa (2001), Website www.rra.co.za.

Railway Gazette International (1998), *International Databases*, Sutton: Reed Business Publishing.

South African Railways and Harbours (SAR&H) (Various years), *Annual Reports 1969-70 to 1979-80*, Johannesburg: South African Railways and Harbours.

South African Transport Services (Various years), *Annual Report, 1980-81 to 1988-89*, Johannesburg: South African Transport Services.

Van der Veer, G.D. (1982), 'The role of rail transport in the total transport scene: freight transport', *Annual Transportation Conference Proceedings*, Pretoria: Council for Scientific and Industrial Research.

Webster, J. (1982), 'The role of road transport in the total transport scene', *Annual Transportation Conference Proceedings*, Pretoria: Council for Scientific and Industrial Research.

Wiese, Berndt (1981), *Seaports and Port Cities of Southern Africa*, Wiesbaden: Bruno Verlag.

8. The financial sector, 1970–2000

Stuart Jones

8.1   INTRODUCTION

In the last third of the twentieth century major developments occured in the financial sector, when both the functions and ownership of traditional institutions were transformed. Market forces were the driving force behind these changes, technology the instrument that made them possible and determined their timing. These 30 years may accordingly be divided into two periods, the years of comparatively little change from 1970 to 1990 and the years of more rapid change from 1990 to 2000.

In the first period, banks, building societies and insurance companies continued along their traditional paths. In the face of declining real per capita incomes there was little pressure to innovate, though the growth of the previous decade made possible a functioning money market and an increase in the number of merchant banks. The commercial banks were also impinging more and more upon the traditional business of the building societies, and these changes in their functions, accentuated by the development of wholly-owned merchant banking and hire purchase subsidiaries led to changes in their structure. Bank holding companies became the norm. Life insurance companies were also increasingly making loans to their policy holders and looking for new ways to employ their assets, the most spectacular of which was the development of shopping centres and the most far-reaching, the ownership of the commercial banks. Tight exchange controls were responsible for many of these developments at a time of sustained poor monetary management. Yet, overall, the muted performance of the Johannesburg Stock Exchange in these years reinforced the impression of stability in the financial sector.

Indeed, in the 1970s, in real terms the financial sector which included property companies declined at the rate of 2.6 per cent a year and was holding back the growth of the economy. In the 1980s this situation was reversed and the financial sector grew at a faster rate than GDP. As a result, over the 20 years from 1970 to 1990, the growth rate of the financial sector in current prices was only marginally less than that of GDP – 16.2 versus 16.6 per cent. The banking sector, by contrast, grew at a rate of 18.1 per cent and was contributing to the growth of GDP.

Media attention was directed to political issues such as the disinvestment campaigns against the two leading banks, the Standard Bank and Barclays National, which forced their British parents to disinvest and withdraw from South Africa. Both the British banks incurred considerable loss as a result of misguided political sentiment and the economy, already dominated by a handful of giant corporations, suffered a further reduction in competition. Nor could disinvestment campaigns guarantee that the assets of overseas companies would not pass into the hands of supporters of the existing political dispensation. However, the two leading banks ended up in the hands of Anglo American and Liberty Life, both of which were highly critical of the National Party government. Competition may have been reduced within South Africa, but mere changes in ownership did not lead to any significant changes in functions or alter the shape of the financial structure.

Radical changes in the financial structure had to wait until the last decade of the century. Superficially the timing suggests that this was the result of the new political dispensation. This was not the case. The changes that occurred were the result of market forces making themselves felt after the collapse of the Soviet Union and the universal discrediting of communism. Market forces in the capitalist economies of the West led to the development of the new technologies that were the driving force behind the changes sweeping across the globe. Computers made possible number crunching on a hitherto unimaginable scale at a time when economic theory was transforming risk management into a more exact science. The explosive growth in information technology and telecommunications had the effect of binding the South African economy more closely into the international economy and bringing South Africa into line with her main trading partners.

The pace of change was accelerating. First, the building societies began to undertake other functions than lending to prospective home buyers. Then they demutualized and quickly lost their independence, passing into the hands of the existing commercial banks. Volkskas, the most politically correct bank in the apartheid era, acquired the loss-making Trust Bank and then added to it by buying the United Bank, formerly the country's biggest building society, and the Allied Bank, formerly the country's third largest building society. The other building societies followed their example, the Permanent Building Society jumping into bed with Nedbank and the Natal Building Society amalgamating with the Boland Bank and then both joining up with the Board of Executors in a cumbersome structure designed to enable a few shareholders to control the whole group. The demutualization of the building societies was followed by that of the life insurance companies. Southern Life had led the way in 1985. A decade later Norwich Life followed their example and at the end of the decade the country's two largest life companies, Old Mutual and Sanlam, converted to public quoted joint-stock companies. This enabled them to raise additional capital more easily and to begin the transformation from being non-profit-making institutions into modern profit-orientated business corporations. 'Financial socialism' was giving way to market capitalism.

In the 1990s, too, bank assurance made its entry onto the scene, as a result of initiatives by the life assurance companies. First, in 1998, Rand Merchant Bank Holdings, the company which controlled Momentum, a rapidly growing insurance company, engineered the amalgamation of its banking and assurance interests with Southern Life and First National Bank into the First Rand Corporation. This was the first large bank assurance development in South Africa and was made possible by Rand Merchant Bank Holdings increasing its capital and coming to an agreement with the Anglo American Corporation, the controlling shareholder of both Southern Life and First National Bank. Rand Merchant Bank benefited from having the merchant banking business of First National transferred to it and, in time, the amalgamation of Southern Life and Momentum should lead to substantial cost savings, but whether the amalgamation of large life assurance companies with a large commercial bank will lead to gains for shareholders and policy holders is not yet clear, though Lloyds Bank in England, the country's most profitable bank, is in favour of this approach. By contrast, Old Mutual, South Africa's largest life assurance company, has come out against bank assurance. This became clear when Old Mutual orchestrated the bid by Nedcor for the Standard Bank in 1999. The market pressures for this move were exogenous, originating in Old Mutual's desire to reduced its ownership of Nedcor from over 50 per cent to around 30 per cent in order to meet the preferences of the City of London, which dislikes financial institutions owning over half the equity of other financial institutions and not making an offer for the entire shareholding. This, apparently, Old Mutual has decided not to do. Two options are open to them. They could sell Nedcor shares on the market, thereby driving the prices down, or manoeuvre an amalgamation with the Standard Bank which would reduce their holding in the combined bank. This was made possible by the way in which Liberty Life unbundled its holding in the Standard Bank, which was acquired as a result of the forced disinvestment of Standard Chartered in 1987 and the founder's decision to withdraw from the South African market.

Unfocused financial institutions fell out of fashion at the end of the 1990s and this hit the Board of Executors. BOE had mushroomed from being a small niche bank into a mini-conglomerate attempting to combine the functions of an industrial bank, an investment bank, a merchant bank, a trust company, a private bank, a building society and a stock brokerage. Not surprisingly it failed. Its directors never explained why they had bought 20 per cent of the country's biggest retail disaster, OK Bazaars, or 20 per cent of a Black empowerment firm noted for its directors' fondness for stock options, but such actions certainly hit the share price and at the beginning of 2000 the company announced the resignation of its executive chairman and managing director and its intention of returning to its original business.

Accompanying these developments in banking and assurance was the formation of a host of new Black empowerment firms, specialising in asset management and merchant banking, some of which enjoyed spectacularly short lives. Political correctness was the order of the day in the financial sector, perhaps most visibly displayed in First National Bank's attachment to Bank City in central Johannesburg, a development that has cost the bank's shareholders dearly, and a variety of micro-lending projects, not normally associated with the business of the commercial banks, but which frequently entail loans to persons without collateral, business experience or business skills. Whether such institutions will add to the wealth of the country was still uncertain in 2000, for the motives behind their creation were political rather than economic. Finally, we might note that in the 1990s the Johannesburg Stock Exchange was virtually transformed, as screen-based trading replaced the old floor trading system and daily turnover rose to astronomical new heights. Accompanying this was an equally impressive expansion in the market for unit trusts.

8.2   THE YEARS 1970–1990

8.2.1   The Commercial Banks

In 1970 the two imperial banks still dominated banking in South Africa and they maintained their position throughout the decade, though market forces were weakening their grip. Foremost among these was the decline in the economic position of the United Kingdom and the beginnings of disinvestment by British firms, a trend which was aggravated by the UK's entry into the European Economic Community. This brought an end to imperial preference and introduced the Common Agricultural Policy to Britain. Temporarily the rise in the price of gold strengthened traditional forces within the South African economy. This benefited the imperial banks. They may also have benefited from the collapse of Trust Bank, the brash Afrikaner bank that had been pioneering new markets and competing at the lower end of the market, although Trust Bank seems to have been more successful in taking customers from Volkskas than from Standard and Barclays.

In the 1980s this situation changed. Nedbank was growing faster than the two British banks, but then almost went under in 1985, when its rapidly growing domestic bad debts coincided with its inability to pay depositors at its New York branch. Nedbank's branch network was much smaller than those of the British banks and it had been financing its rapid growth by borrowing in the wholesale market. Needing to pay interest on these borrowings led Nedbank to undertake riskier business – hence their growing volume of bad debts. It also led them to embark upon the extraordinary policy of borrowing in New York and then investing the proceeds in South Africa, without apparently thinking about the foreign exchange implications of such a course of action. When Chase Manhattan refused to renew their loans, after P.W. Botha's Rubicon speech, Nedbank was driven to default and this then triggered the collapse of the rand. Nedbank's actions were made possible by the high inflation in South Africa, where interest rates were quadruple those of New York. They led to a run on the rand that cost South Africa billions of rands and forced financial policy into a straitjacket that was to last until after the election in 1994. More immediately it led directly to the disinvestment by the two British banks, Standard Chartered and Barclays. As the former had been one of the world's best-managed banks for over a century, this politically-inspired action benefited neither South Africa nor Britain. It did, however, allow the former British subsidiaries in South Africa to increase their capital, the growth of which had been held back by their British parents' reluctance to invest in South Africa.

In line with worldwide developments, the number of banking institutions operating in South Africa declined in the 20 years after 1970. In that year there were 58 made up of nine commercial banks, 29 general banks, seven merchant banks, two discount houses, two hire purchase banks and eight savings banks. Ten years later this number had fallen to 50, though the number of commercial banks and merchant banks was still increasing as a result in the decline in the number of savings banks and general banks. By 1990 the 58 of 1970 had been reduced to 45, of which four were discount houses and the rest all put into one category, deposit-taking institutions, as a result of the authorities' decision to define banks by function rather than type of institution.

At a time when boundaries between the traditional functions of the various financial institutions were becoming blurred, this decision in Pretoria reflected economic realities. It was in this period, when Standard and Barclays converted into South African companies and marketed a portion of their shares in South Africa, that bank holding companies became normal. Twenty years earlier, in 1950, such moves would have been unthinkable, but following the lead set by New York banks the traditional high street banks converted into holding companies that allowed them to own a variety of specialist financial institutions without interfering with their regular business. Details of how the banks changed their organization structures in the 1970s are given in the special issue of the *South African Journal of Economic History* devoted to that decade (Jones, 1999). Clearly changes in strategy required changes in structure.

Government policy towards banking also began to change in the 1970s. The basic legislative framework was still that provided by the 1965 Banks Act, but towards the end of the 1970s free market principles began to influence a government long dominated by mercantilist ideas that were popular in the rural–clerical background of the National Party of 1948 and continued to influence its thinking throughout this period. Nevertheless, winds of change could be detected in the appointment of the De Kock Commission in 1977. An interim report was published in 1979 and the final one in 1984. These paved the way for more market-orientated methods of implementing monetary policy replacing the direct controls that had placed limits on interest rates and ceilings on lending (Gidlow, 1999 and Goedhuys, 1994). For a brief moment at the beginning of the 1980s exchange controls were relaxed and a number of South Africa's leading entrepreneurs were able to move money out of the country. Anton Rupert began the growth of Richemont and Gordon Liberty Life's insurance and property investments in London. However, the final report of the De Kock Commission was more ambivalent on the question of abolishing exchange controls and favoured monetary targeting as a means of controlling inflation rather than the use of interest rates. In other words, throughout this period, the authorities in Pretoria could not fully abandon their penchant for controls and accept wholeheartedly the role of the market in determining the value of the currency or the rate of interest. The siege economy that developed after 1985 reinforced these backward leaning tendencies in policy and delayed the wholesale acceptance of the market as the vehicle and engine of growth.

8.2.2   Assets

Asset growth was impressive in the 1970s and 1980s, but much of it was the result of inflation. In the 1970s Barclays National grew rapidly, because of its strength in the mining industry, Nedbank too, was experiencing rapid asset growth, but the Standard Bank was falling behind. More importantly, in the 1970s the commercial banks, clearing banks in English terminology, were, as a group, falling behind their main competitors, the general banks, the merchant banks and the hire purchase banks. In the 1980s, this decline was reversed, when the more difficult trading conditions hit the newer and more risk-exposed banks harder than the well-established commercial banks. Table 8.1 gives the details of the banking sector's performance from 1970 to 1989 and Table 8.2 its growth rates.

The merchant banks were a good barometer of business confidence. At the beginning of the 1970s they were still benefiting from the boom of the late 1960s, but after the Soweto riots in 1976, confidence evaporated rapidly and with it went their days of easy growth. Eventually most of them passed into

Table 8.1   Assets of the banking sector, 1970–1989

Type of bank	1970	1975	1980	1985	1989
Commercial	3 802	8 118	15 782	47 927	111 131
General	1 585	2 863	7 999	16 064	33 331
Merchant	541	1 397	2 340	3 568	7 734
Discount	362	751	1 089	1 859	1 429
Hire purchase*	76	319	798	–	–
Savings*	125	262	86	–	–
Total	6 491	1 370	28 094	69 418	153 625

Note: * From 1980 hire purchase banks and savings banks were classified as general banks. In 1990 the new Deposit Taking Institutions Act put them all together as deposit taking institutions

Sources: South African Reserve Bank, *Quarterly Bulletin*, various issues and *Supplement*, June 1991; Registrar of Banks, *Annual Reports*, various years.

Table 8.2   Rate of growth of assets in the banking sector (in constant prices), 1970–1989

Type of bank	1970-75 %	1975-80 %	1980-85 %	1985-89 %	1970-89 %
Commercial	5.9	1.5	9.2	7.3	5.9
General	2.4	9.2	0.5	4.4	3.4*
Merchant	9.9	–1.4	4.9	5.5	2.0
Discount	5.3	–4.2	–2.7	–18.6	–4.7
Hire purchase*	21.1	6.8	–	–	–
Savings*	5.5	–28.9	–	–	–
GDP	3.5	3.1	1.4	1.9	2.5

Note: * Includes the assets of the hire purchase and savings banks in 1970.

Sources: South African Reserve Bank, *Quarterly Bulletin*, various issues and CPI figures provided by the Economics Department of the Standard Bank.

the hands of the established commercial banks.

The other banks experienced varied fortunes, either as a result of government reclassification (in the 1970s, Trust Bank was still classified as a general bank) or of a change in functions, as when the Reserve Bank opened its discount window and took that business away from the discount houses. Also, in the later 1970s, Afrikaner banking interests were coming together in groupings organized by Volkskas and Sanlam, moves that were expedited by the collapse of Trust Bank in 1977 and the need to bolster some of the new Afrikaner banks that had emerged during the growth of the 1960s (Verhoef, 1992). Galloping inflation spelled the doom of the savings banks. Between 1970 and 1980 the consumer price index (CPI) almost trebled, while the recession triggered by the stock market crash of 1969 and the tightening of the local content requirement in the automobile industry hit the hire purchase banks hard. Wesbank, the industry leader, was quickly sold to Barclays in 1975, and its losses brought under control by 1977 (Jones and Scott, 1992).

8.2.3   Liabilities

The principal liabilities of the banks were their deposits and paid-up capital. Both grew rapidly, the former benefiting from the economic expansion of the 1960s, the latter from the South Africanization of the imperial banks. In 1970 the traditional way of assessing the strength of a bank still was considered to lie in the size of its deposits and these were to a great extent provided by the holders of current accounts, on which the banks paid no interest. In other words, in 1970, competition for deposits was still weak and the bank cartel still strong.

This situation began to change in the 1970s, as competition from newer financial institutions, such as Trust Bank and the life assurance companies, compounded by double-digit inflation, put pressure on the banks' ability to draw in deposits. Competition for a limited supply of funds was beginning to shake the somewhat sleepy banking establishment. Inflation also tended to increase the attractiveness of equities over fixed deposits, but the education of the public in this regard was a slow process. Memories of the stock market crash of 1969 lingered on and only gold shares captured the imagination of investors. The poor performance of the Johannesburg Stock Exchange in the 1970s retarded the growth of the unit trust industry, while sanctions and disinvestment campaigns further held back change in the 1980s. The notion of capital–asset ratios providing a better tool than capital–deposit ratios for assessing the security and performance of banks took root only slowly. Government interference also continued to exert an impact upon the financial sector, with its panoply of exchange controls, interest rate ceilings and credit ceilings. Private enterprise had pioneered the development of the South African economy, but in the neo-mercantilist National Party era it could only operate with one arm tied behind its back. This situation was beginning to change before the stirrings of globalization, but the full effects of the impending changes had to await the collapse of the Soviet Union and the communist system which it supported.

The pattern of deposits, given in Table 8.3, shows the growth of deposits in

Table 8.3   Liabilities of the banking sector, 1970-1989 (Rm)

Type of liability	1970	1975	1980	1985	1989
Bank notes	457	949	1724	3333	7474
Demand deposits	1749	3264	6562	19190	20984
Near money	1722	4302	7861	19244	23999
Long-term deposits	755	2248	4629	5513	18181
Government deposits	501	1067	2722	1949	12999
Capital & reserves	415	809	1428	2938	9837

Source: South African Reserve Bank, *Quarterly Bulletin*, various issues.

current prices and the beginning of the long decline in the economy. In constant prices demand deposits grew slowly until 1985 when they collapsed, with the result that in 1990, in 1970 prices, they were only marginally higher than in 1970, R1 845.7 million as opposed to R1 749.0 million. Banknotes grew at a slightly faster rate, reflecting the underdeveloped nature of much of the economy. Long-term deposits, on which higher interest was paid, were the most dynamic component of the banks' liabilities. They more than trebled in real terms, but in general the picture is one of sluggish growth. Both demand deposits and near money grew at a slower rate than GDP in these 20 years, capital and reserves only marginally faster (see Table 8.4).

Table 8.4   Growth rate of liabilities in the banking sector (in constant prices), 1970-1990

Type of liability	1970–75 %	1975–80 %	1980–85 %	1985–90 %	1970–90 %
Banknotes	5.3	0.2	-0.2	2.2	1.8
Demand deposits	3.0	2.2	8.4	-11.4	0.3
Near money	9.2	0.3	4.6	-9.1	1.0
Long-term deposits	13.1	2.7	-9.5	20.5	6.1
Government deposits	5.8	7.2	-18.2	27.1	4.2
Capital & reserves	3.9	-0.4	1.0	10.8	3.7
Total liabilities	7.9	3.3	3.0	10.4	6.1

Source: South African Reserve Bank, *Quarterly Bulletins*, various issues.

The banks were having difficulty adjusting to double-digit inflation and competition from other savings-seeking institutions. Competition from merchant banks and hire purchase banks was met by the traditional commercial banks developing their own specialized subsidiaries or by purchasing dangerous competitors. Barclays National, which was the country's leading bank in the 1970s, lost ground in the 1980s, while the Standard Bank, which had been slipping behind in the 1970s had a revival in the 1980s. Overall the two imperial banks were facing growing competition. Their proportion of banking assets declined, before revival of Nedbank and the amalgamation of Volkskas, Trust and the United Building Society into the Amalgamated Banks of South Africa.

8.2.4   The Merchant Banks

Union Acceptances pioneered the development of merchant banking in South Africa in the 1950s at a time when their traditional business of 'accepting' bills was considered their main function. To this was added in the 1960s mergers and acquisitions and corporate finance. The industrial expansion of the 1960s not only brought about the formation of new merchant banks but tempted overseas firms, such as Slater Walker and Oliver Jessel, to make a brief entry into the South African market. The stock market crash of 1969 and the three-year depression in prices that followed discouraged further initiatives and led to the withdrawal of a number of the new entrants. In the 1970s the rise in the price of gold provided the government with the means to engage in a number of large infrastructure projects at a time when real per capita national income was beginning its long decline. This undoubtedly acted as a brake upon industrialization and the growth of potential merchant banking business.

The seven merchant banks of 1970 had grown to ten by 1973 and that number had not changed in 1980. Senbank and Union Acceptances were the two leading houses. In the following decade, when the economy was no longer dominated by the gold price rise, two new merchant banks appeared, which were to become major players in the last decade of the century. These were: Investec, founded in 1985, and Rand Merchant Bank in 1987. Their entrepreneurial founders were able to achieve the rapid economic growth that enabled them, not merely to stay independent, but to be counted among the major players in the 1990s.

Some idea of the slow growth of the merchant banks may be gathered from the growth of their deposits by the public and of their acceptances. The former rose from R290.9 million in 1970 to R1 195.4 million in 1985, the latter from R1 94.2 million to R1 381.8 million. In constant prices deposits by the public had declined, while acceptances grew only moderately, confirming the picture presented in Table 8.2, which shows the assets of the merchant banks declining between 1975 and 1985 after vigorous growth in the early 1970s. This was then restored in the sanctions era of the late 1980s. Financial sanctions would appear to have benefited specialized financial institutions by removing some of their competition.

8.2.5   The Building Societies

By 1970 the great era of the building societies was over. Technology was not yet threatening their independent existence, but sustained economic growth was inexorably pushing the commercial banks in the direction of expanding their functions by moving into the territory of merchant banks, building societies and hire purchase banks. The onset of double-digit inflation further hit the traditional building societies by retarding the inflow of funds into the societies at a time when their expenses were increasing.

Building societies, it was argued, were fundamentally uneconomic propositions, because they operated chains of branches that took in interest-paying deposits without generating any income. The granting of mortgages was centralized in regional head offices, an administrative practice that enabled the centre to retain tight control of assets at the expense of dynamism in the branches.

In the 1970s, too, they received assistance from the government in two ways. They were able to offer tax-free interest on certain deposits at the same time when the government was interfering with the market mechanism by enforcing interest rate ceilings and credit ceilings on the financial sector. It is easy to forget in AD 2000 that the Vorster government was not very sympathetic to free enterprise and market capitalism. Fears of nationalization had died down, but Vorster was constantly threatening the banks that were controlled overseas. Such populist attitudes encouraged the policy of helping the building societies and probably enabled them to continue in business along traditional lines longer than would otherwise have been the case (Jones, 1992, 238).

The growth of the building societies ultimately depends upon the growth of the economy that produces both the savings class and the growth of the class of home buyers. In South Africa the decline in real per capita GDP after 1975 was particularly harmful to the building societies. Negative interest rates made a bad situation worse. Personal savings declined rapidly. As a proportion of personal disposable income, personal savings fell from 6.2 per cent in 1970 to 1.5 per cent in 1989, as a proportion of gross domestic savings from 19.8 per cent to 3.9 per cent (Jones, 1992, 241). In real terms, personal savings in 1989 had fallen to less than two-fifths of their 1970 level. By 1990 the economic underpinnings of the building societies were crumbling rapidly.

This occurred at the time when the worldwide moves to de-regulation and privatization were sweeping all before them. The reports of the De Kock Commission reflected these developments. Its second report, issued in 1982, focused on the building societies and paved the way for their conversion into banks, and its final report in 1985, led to their demutualization. These moves towards a more liberal regulatory climate occurred at a time when the Pretoria government's attention was concentrating on the balance of payments and its domestic budgetary problems. In the new dispensation the building societies/ banks had to meet the same liquid asset requirement and to maintain the same cash reserves as the commercial banks. With their competitive advantages gone, the independence of the building societies soon followed. Within a decade of the final report of the De Kock Commission all the leading building societies had disappeared. The United Building Society, the largest, had amalgamated with Volkskas and Trust Bank and then taken over the Allied after a short but bitter battle with First National Bank. The second largest, the Permanent Building Society, which for years trumpeted its determination to keep its mutual status, engaged in politically trendy operations that led directly to a liquidity crisis, the resignation of its managing director and its final absorption into the Nedbank in 1988. The Natal Building Society became a bank and fell into the arms of the Board of Executors. Today the building society movement, which played such an important role in the provision of houses for urbanizing South Africa, is now a mere memory.

8.2.6   Hire Purchase Banks

These banks were primarily concerned with vehicle finance. They had grown rapidly in the prosperous 1960s, when real per capita incomes were rising, and this growth continued until the middle of the 1970s. Real asset growth, for example, grew at the rate of 21.1 per cent between 1970 and 1975. Even in the difficult later 1970s real annual growth of 6.8 per cent was achieved. Thereafter the statistics of the hire purchase banks are merged with those of the general banks. As these were growing less rapidly than the population in the early 1980s (Table 8.2), it is likely that the hire purchase banks were sharing in this decline.

Wesbank was the leading vehicle finance bank in these years. It was formed in 1968 by the Schlesinger Organisation, when the original Schlesinger bank, the Colonial Banking and Trust Company was amalgamated with Western Credit, a vehicle finance company the Schlesinger Organisation had acquired in 1964. Restrictions on hire purchase by the Vorster government led to Western Credit pioneering leasing in South Africa and this business further expanded under the influence of the Schlesinger Organisation. Between 1969 and 1974 profits trebled. Wesbank introduced the modern credit card into South Africa in 1970. When credit restrictions were lifted in 1972 business boomed. Advances more than doubled to R195 million in the financial year ending 30 June 1973 (Jones and Scott, 1992, 218–19). Profits peaked in the financial year ending 30 June 1974, encouraging John Schlesinger to disinvest, which he duly did at the height of the boom in March. Anglo American bought the group in order to gain control of Schlesinger's property and insurance interests. When the profits turned into losses in the second half of 1974, Anglo American sold Wesbank to Barclays National which was weak in the new fringe banking activities such as instalment finance. Barclays management then decided that Wesbank should concentrate solely on vehicle finance and discontinue all operations that were in competition with its parent. The Wesbank credit card was replaced by the Barclay card and, after 1975, the fortunes of Wesbank mirrored those of the motor industry.

With interest rates high, well over 20 per cent, the market for vehicles of all types was severely squeezed throughout the 1980s. All the hire purchase arms of the big four banking groups complained about the difficult trading conditions. The Nedbank hire purchase bank was hit by the loss of confidence in Nedbank, but Stannic, the vehicle arm of the Standard Bank, went from strength to strength in the second half of the 1980s, when Wesbank's assets as a proportion of vehicle sales fell from 88 per cent in 1985 to 34 per cent in 1988. It would seem that the experience of the hire purchase banks reflected the decline in per capita GDP.

8.2.7 Life Insurance

The life insurance companies were the stars of the financial scene in the 1970s and they maintained this reputation in the 1980s. They benefited from the inflation and the higher pension payments that went along with it, from their ability to invest in equities that was denied to the building societies, and from a tax system that favoured the life insurance companies. As a result, their assets grew at a faster rate than those of the commercial banks and they were able to take control of the traditional commercial banks. By 1990 Standard Bank was effectively controlled by Liberty Life, Nedbank by Old Mutual, Volkskas, Trust Bank and the former United Building Society by Sanlam and Anton Rupert and Barclays National, now First National, by Southern Life. All the big banks had passed into the hands of insurance companies.

This growth of the local insurance companies coincided with the disinvestment of the British insurance companies that had been long-term players in the South African market. Federated Employers, SA Eagle and Commercial Union had all moved out of life insurance in South Africa by 1980, though the last mentioned remained active in the short-term market. The move of the British companies out of South Africa began before the Soweto riots of 1976 and reflected the pull of Europe and the diminishing attractiveness of former colonial markets.

The consequence of the large cash flows generated by the life insurance sector and the continued baleful effect of exchange controls enabled the life insurance companies to dominate large swathes of the economy and almost to challenge the might of the Anglo American colossus, which, by the 1980s, was said to control between 65 and 85 per cent of the capital quoted on the Johannesburg Stock Exchange. Exchange controls, together with the continued expansion of the historic mining finance houses, brought about skewed growth and wealth distribution. Yet the life insurance company controlled by Anglo American was the poorest performer among the big four or five life insurance companies. Size, it seems, did not equate with profitability and Anglo American's dominance of the economy could not ensure the dominance of its insurance arm.

Judged by asset growth the insurance sector did better in the 1980s than in the 1970s, despite the decline in the real per capita GDP in that decade. In the aggregate their assets remained smaller than those of the commercial banks, but they were not hampered by credit ceilings or interest rate limits and they were led by a very dynamic company. Liberty Life pioneered the development of massive out-of-town shopping centres in the 1970s and it easily outperformed its older rivals, growing its assets at the rate of 26.8 per cent a year in constant prices. Its nearest rival, Sanlam, notwithstanding the advantage of government patronage and the burgeoning growth of an Afrikaner middle class, grew its assets at the rate of 6.8 per cent. Southern trailed at 1.4 per cent. In the next decade Liberty Life's meteoric growth slowed down and that of its competitors accelerated. There is little evidence that sanctions hurt the financial sector in the 1980s. The assets of the commercial banks were growing, in constant prices, at 8.4 per cent a year and those of life insurance companies at 9.7 per cent.

South Africa's financial sector, well managed and experienced, was able to achieve very creditable results, notwithstanding a declining real per capita GDP and a variety of embargoes and sanctions aimed at damaging the economy. Tables 8.5 and 8.6 provide the details.

Table 8.5   Domestic assets of life insurance companies and the total income of life companies, 1970–1990

	Assets of life companies Rm	Assets of short-term companies Rm	Income of life companies Rm
1970	2 501.2	384.7	392.9
1980	14 235.2	1 240.8	3 274.9
1990	141 541.1	11 090.9	38 827.1

Source: Registrar of Insurance Companies, *Annual Reports*, various years.

Table 8.6   Real growth rate of life insurance companies' assets and of the total income of life companies, 1970-1990

	1970–80	1980–90	1970–90
Life insurance companies	7.0	9.7	8.4
Short-term insurance companies	1.1	8.6	4.8
Total income of life companies	11.2	11.7	11.4

Source: Registrar of Insurance Companies, *Annual Reports*, various years.

8.2.8   The Johannesburg Stock Exchange

Structure and functions
In these years of economic decline the Johannesburg Stock Exchange reflected the prevailing mood. The difficult trading conditions were accentuated by the effects of the 1969 stock market crash. Not until 1979 did the prices on the Johannesburg Stock Exchange surpass their levels of 1969. Meanwhile continued exchange controls locked capital within South Africa, further encouraging the skewed distribution of share ownership. Economic and political conditions favoured the growth of a handful of very large corporations. Typical of these were Anglo American, Rembrandt, Old Mutual and Sanlam. An increasing proportion of the shares quoted on the Exchange were owned or controlled by these very large groups, with the result that trading volume did not keep pace with the growth of market capitalization.

The functions of the Exchange did not significantly change in the 1970s. They continued to be (Jones et al., 1999, 249):

1.   The provision of a market, where securities could be freely traded.
2.   The provision of investment liquidity.
3.   The evaluation of securities and of management.
4.   The channelling of savings into investments.

A regulated environment in which securities can be freely traded is an essential feature of a modern market economy. The discovery of gold had provided the stimulus for the formation of the Johannesburg Stock Exchange in 1887 and the rise of the gold price in the 1970s further stimulated it. At the same time the Vorster government was pressuring foreign companies to place a proportion of the shares of their South African subsidiaries on the Johannesburg Stock Exchange and the beginning of disinvestment campaigns was encouraging foreign firms to sell out and withdraw from South Africa. In these circumstances the 1970s saw an increase in the number and variety of counters listed without any increase in either market capitalization or turnover.

As a means of channelling savings into investment the Johannesburg Stock Exchange was increasing its importance. Attitudes towards equity investment had changed considerably in the 1960s before the impact of sustained industrialization and the beginnings of inflation. The chief executive of Northern Trust, who had condemned investment in equities as speculation in the late 1950s, could not have made such a remark in the 1970s. The boom in gold shares after 1974 reinforced the popularity of equities, which was further underlined by the profitability of this form of investment. Between 1972 and 1982 dividends paid by companies on the Johannesburg Stock Exchange rose at an annual rate of 19.6 per cent, giving a real return to investors of 7.2 per cent a year (Jones et al. 1999, 250–51).

The Growth of Business on the Johannesburg Stock Exchange (JSE)

By the standards of the year 2000 the volume of business on the Johannesburg Securities Exchange was small in these years. The number of members of the Exchange grew from 265 in March 1970 to 357 in 1987 at the height of the boom, but the number of companies listed and the number of securities listed both declined, the former from 737 to 51, the latter from 981 to 794. The number of securities listed declined almost continuously. Table 8.7 gives the details. The year 1985, the year of the financial crisis, was the turning point. From 659 securities listed in December of that year the number had risen to 1 054 five years later. One of the byproducts of the sanctions and disinvestment campaign was a flurry of new listings on the Johannesburg Stock Exchange.

Inflation made the rise in the market capitalization of equities on the Johannesburg Stock Exchange seem enormous, a rise from R13.2 billion in 1970 to R495.1 billion in 1990. Even in constant prices the growth was impressive, from R13.2 billion to R43.5 billion. Only some of this growth in market capitalization reflected growth in the economy as for example the listing of Iscor and Sasol, the country's leading steel and oil from coal producers. Other growth reflected the repatriation into South African ownership of existing assets, such as banks and insurance companies, and car assembly plants. Between 1970 and 1990 the market capitalization of industrial securities rose from R3.174 million to R158.071 a rate of growth well in excess of the rate of inflation. At a time when consumer prices had risen by 1 036.9 per cent, the market capitalization of industrial securities had risen by 5 607.8 per cent.

The number of equity securities listed, however, did not keep pace with the growth in market capitalization until after 1985. From 964 in 1974 the number fell to 847 in 1975 and then stabilized at close to that level until 1980, when

Table 8.7   Number of equities listed and the market capitalization of the Johannesburg Stock Exchange, 1970-2000

Year Dec.	Equities listed No.	Market capitalization (current prices) Rm	Market capitalization (constant 1970 prices) Rm
1970	964	13 195	13 195
1975	847	20 760	12 918
1980	843	74 700	25 803
1985	659	187 340	33 087
1990	1 054	495 050	43 544
1995	839	1 022 656	52 452
2000	914	1 551 488	53 936

Sources: JSE Library and the Market Research Department of the JSE.

another decline set in that took the number of securities listed down to 659 in 1985. Then, growth was renewed and by 1990 there were 1 054 securities listed. By contrast the number of loan capital securities listed rose rapidly before 1985 and then declined.

Not surprisingly new capital raised on the JSE rose substantially. This increased from R1 254.3 million in 1970 to R6 572.7 million in 1980 and R20 614.3 million in 1990, with public sector borrowing increasing at a faster rate than that of the private sector. Interest rates remained high and the public sector was tending to make this situation worse as a result of the relentless succession of unbalanced budgets that characterized the Botha era in South Africa. Public sector borrowing accounted for 56.6 per cent of new capital raised in 1970 and 60.9 per cent in 1990. The public sector was beginning to crowd out the private sector in the competition for capital resources at a time when the savings rate was declining.

Turnover did not keep pace with market capitalization. This was the result of the skewed distribution of capital ownership in South Africa, which went back to the emergence of large mining finance companies in the 1890s and was accentuated in the second half of the twentieth century by the excessive pyramiding in the control structures of equities on the Johannesburg Securities Exchange. With the majority of shares tightly held by the cartels, only a small minority of shares were available for trading. Turnover was low in relation to market capitalization. The number of shares traded did not get back to the level of 1969 until 1980 in the aftermath of the 1979–80 gold boom, but the real growth in the volume of shares traded only took off only in 1985 with the collapse of the rand and the fear of the currency becoming worthless. Between 1984 and 1990 the number of shares traded quadrupled.

The value of the shares traded on the JSE followed the same pattern, with growth accelerating in the later 1970s and again in the later 1980s. Table 8.8 gives the details. By 1990 the value of shares traded had increased more than 32-fold from a mere R727.7 million in 1970 to R223 676.9 million in 1990.

Table 8.8   Turnover on the JSE (in current and constant prices), 1970–2000

Year Rm Rm	Current prices prices	Constant 1970
1970	727.7	727.7
1975	775.0	482.3
1980	4 036.4	1 394.3
1985	6 372.0	1 125.4
1990	23 676.9	2 082.6
1995	63 247.0	3 243.9
2000	536 877.0	18 664.2

Source: JSE Library.

Turnover on the JSE increased only after 1975, when the rise in the gold price was tending to conceal the real decline in the economy. Another decline in turnover occurred in the first half of the 1980s, when the second gold-induced boom faded and the Botha government was pursuing its total onslaught strategy and devising a new constitution. Ironically, values traded rose as the political situation deteriorated. The conclusion to these movements is clear. The gold price rise that accompanied the rise in the price of oil, was not good for the financial sector of the South African economy, which perversely seems to have benefited from the adverse political climate induced by the Soweto riots of 1976 and the 'necklacing' of the later 1980s.

8.3   THE 1990s

The 1990s has been the decade of private enterprise and free markets. South Africa could not stand apart from a global phenomena, triggered by the collapse of the brutal Soviet system and its supporting communist ideology. As a result, the African National Congress, hardline Stalinists to a man only a decade ago, have modified their views and claim to have moved towards a free market approach to policy. Such a radical transformation in what was once one of the world's most Stalinist parties has inevitably exerted a significant impact upon the financial sector. Instead of outright nationalization and destruction, as practised in Mozambique, the new government claims to favour market forces and the creation of Black-owned financial corporations! Some cynics might say that Black empowerment – the fashion of the 1990s – comes perilously close to equating with Black enrichment, but either way it represents an enormous volte-face on the part of the ruling party and, with it, the prospect of normal economic growth.

Globalization in the 1990s is popularly associated with the emergence of worldwide financial institutions of a mega-variety – mega-banks, mega-insurance companies and mega-stock exchanges dominated by mega-asset managers. South Africa has not seen the emergence of mega-banks, though Old Mutual's orchestration of a bid by Nedcor for the Standard Bank may be seen as attempting to create such an institution. Old Mutual's control of Nedcor represents the coming together of banking and insurance in only a half-hearted way. The demutualization of Old Mutual and Sanlam, the two largest life insurers, was the most dramatic change in the financial sector, but instead of giving a clear boost to 'bank assurance', it has been followed by Old Mutual expanding into asset management and Sanlam refocusing on its core business, life insurance, with plans to reabsorb Metropolitan Life, a Black controlled company that was formerly part of Sanlam. Old Mutual's move into asset management in Britain and America was influenced by the cost of attempting to buy control of an established European life insurer in the wake of Gordon and Liberty Life's failure to take full control of Guardian Royal Exchange.

The jury is still out on whether bank assurance is the road to future success. The top management at Rand Merchant Bank still proclaim their faith in it as do three-quarters of South African banks (PriceWaterhouseCoopers, 2000) but the amalgamation of Rand Merchant Bank, First National Bank, Southern Life and Momentum Life into First Rand in 1998 has not yet led to a marked increase in earnings. Indeed, *The Financial Mail*, in its 'Top Companies 2000' edition, suggests that the difficulties in integrating the Cape-based Southern Life with Johannesburg-based Momentum were underestimated (*The Financial Mail*) 30 June 2000). Nor has Sanlam's influence over ABSA, the amalgamation of two former building societies with two commercial banks, yielded noticeable results in the field of bank assurance. According to *The Financial Mail* it is the Standard Bank/Liberty Life relationship that has been the most successful. This has occurred despite the well-known difficulties in the working relationship between the bank and the insurance company. In practice the Standard Bank let Liberty Life 'consultants' have access to the details of the personal accounts of customers, who were then contacted by life assurance salesmen. Now that the bank controls the insurance company, rather than the insurance company the bank, these practices may cease.

Foreign investment in the financial sector in the 1990s has not occurred on a large scale, but foreign developments in the financial services sector are affecting South Africa. In a brilliant article in *The Economist*, Peter Drucker (1999) has analysed the revolutionary changes that have taken place in financial services in the second half of the twentieth century. He was focusing on the renaissance of the City of London and 'globalisation'of banking that has been at the heart of it. This change has been accompanied by a relative decline in the importance of interest earnings and a relative increase in the importance of fee earnings. At the same time banks have begun to trade on their own account more extensively than in the past (Barings) and this has increased the risks involved. More significantly there has been no single major innovation for 30 years, which is why, Drucker argues, the financial services industry is in trouble. The eurodollar, the eurobond, the first modern pension fund by General Motors in 1950, the first modern institutional investor, Donaldson, Lufkin & Jenrette, the new role for the private banker as initiator of mergers and acquisitions by Felix Rohatyn, and the invention of the credit card, all occurred before 1970 and brought great profits to the pioneers, just as software developments brought great 'Schumpeterian' profits to Microsoft and Oracle in the later 1990s. All these developments entered South Africa later than Europe or America, and have been restricted by exchange controls. Nevertheless, the Drucker arguments that existing financial services have become 'commoditised' and therefore less profitable applies equally to South Africa.

The road to future success lies in innovation, either by existing firms or by outsiders moving into financial services. The great opportunities at the end of the twentieth century lie in the middle-class investment market. In the nineteenth century the first mass market for financial services was built around the provision of life insurance, because of the rising middle class's fear of death; at the end of the twentieth century this has been replaced by the fear of living too long and is creating a mass market in asset management for the expanding middle class.

In the last decade of the century, with the fear of Soviet communism removed and innovation accelerating in information technology, tele-communications and bio-technology, economic growth has led to 'Schumpeterian' profits for those firms first in the field. Wealth accumulation has been accelerating. This wealth needs to be managed and, not surprisingly, it is in this area of the financial services that the most dynamic changes are occurring. The boom in asset management companies and in unit trusts has been phenomenal. From 31 unit trusts with assets of R6.6 billion in 1990 the number has mushroomed to 260 trusts with assets of R112.2 billion. Originally designed as a savings mechanism for monthly payments by debit order, they have evolved into investment outlets for the beneficiaries of lump-sum payments by insurance companies and pension funds. Life insurance companies followed this route, because of the change from policies with prescribed benefits to ones with prescribed payments. These were more suitable in an inflationary environment and could meet the needs of wealth creation in a better-educated and better-informed market. 'Banking', as Walter Wriston noted 30 years ago, 'is not about money, it is about information' (quoted in Drucker, 1999, 31).

In this global environment wealth creation and capital accumulation are now praised, capital gains are no longer seen as the result of exploitation, save in the minds of a few South African politicians and trade unionists. In South Africa, too, globalization is forcing change upon the dinosaurs in the labour movement, though more slowly than in the ranks of the government. As a result, the 'pension fund socialism' of the 1970s and 1980s has given way to the unit trust capitalism of the 1990s. This extraordinary transformation has been accompanied by the incorporation of brokerage houses and the disappearance of the old partnerships. Most stock brokerage firms are now owned by banks or asset managers, with overseas banks prominent in the process. The Hong Kong and Shanghai Bank, Société Génerale, Deutsche Bank and, for a time, National Westminster, all bought into local Johannesburg brokerages in order to compete for the limited supply of savings in the South African market.

No foreign bank, however, has been willing to invest in one of the local commercial banks with their costly branch networks. Yet by 2000 there were 16 foreign banks operating in South Africa. Five of them were American and 11 European, and it is arguable that foreign direct investment in the financial sector may have had a greater impact than in any of the other sectors. It has forced South African banks to be more competitive and to become more efficient.

8.3.1   The Commercial Banks

The 1990s have seen the relative decline of the two former imperial banks, Standard and First National. In 1990, the Standard Bank with assets of R50 759 million was way ahead of its nearest rival, First National with R35 326 million. They also dominated the net income after tax table, though, in terms of capital employed, Nedcor and United had moved ahead of First National. The financial press has been critical of the Standard Bank. After the Standard Bank had bungled its credit card deal with Woolworths, *The Financial Mail* quoted an HSBC–Simpson McKie research report entitled: 'Stanbic: A Bridge Too Far' as follows (*The Financial Mail*, 25 June 1999, 376), 'The track record of Stanbic's management has been tarnished in recent years by large individual debt write offs such as Soda Ash, New Age Beverages and more recently the write off resulting from the exposure to Russia'. Continuing along this line of argument that the core operation of the Standard Bank was not healthy, the report's assessment of the bank's ability to adapt to the changing environment argues (*The Financial Mail*, 25 June 1999, 376), 'Also important will be the group's determination to change its management culture from risk adverse to calculated risk taking (a shift it is obviously struggling with), from followers to leaders, and from status conscious to performance conscious managers'.

A similar comment could be made about the other commercial banks with the possible exception of Nedcor, which has been markedly more competitive than the other banks, culminating in the attempted takeover of the Standard Bank. This, however, has been blocked, not by an aggressive new competitive bank, but by the old influence-peddling bank that persuaded the Minister of Finance to veto it.

This view of Nedcor as the most efficient of the commercial banks is derived from its cost to income ratio, which fell from 61.4 per cent in 1996 to 56.2 per cent in 1998, compared with Standard's reduction from 65.2 to 62.3 per cent. Nedcor's returns on assets and equity were also way ahead of those of the Standard Bank by 1996. According to James Slabbert, the Merrill Lynch financial analyst (*The Financial Mail*, 25 June 1999, 376), 'Its leadership status in banking technology, its efficiency levels, its focus and its strong management make Nedcor our core holding in the bank sector'.

Echoing the earlier comments on the City of London in *The Economist*, *The Financial Mail* quotes Russel Laubscher, Managing Director of Nedcor, as saying: 'The global information age forces businesses to re-invent themselves' (*The Financial Mail*, 25 June 1999, 376). Certainly Nedcor has been more focused than its competitors. While the Standard Bank has mixed commercial banking with merchant banking, Nedcor has floated off its merchant and industrial banking arms into a separate listed company – Nedcor Industrial Bank. Asset management has been added to this new company, thereby leaving the commercial banks with a clearer focus. Laubscher, moreover, has made it clear that he is not in favour of bank assurance; he favours bank mergers. First National, by contrast, is now pressed into bank assurance, while ABSA is opposed to it and the Standard Bank is moving in that direction. (See Table 8.9.)

The decade of the 1990s has presented a more competitive environment than those of the 1970s and 1980s, and this new situation is leading to improved efficiency in the banking sector. Heavy investment in technology is the driving force behind the greater efficiency in banking operations. Pressure on margins has forced management to invest heavily in technology at the same time that the difference between financial products has led to greater emphasis

Table 8.9   Statistics of the four major banking groups, 1989 and 1999

Year	ABSA	Standard Bank Investment Corporation	First National Bank	Nedcor
		Total assets (R billion)		
1989	50.0*	43.9	36.2	29.2
1999	168.7	184.3	143.9	129.8
		Total advances		
1989	31.2*	29.6	23.1	19.9
1999	139.9	134.2	100.5	103.8
		Total deposits		
1989	37.3*	33.1	26.9	23.2
1999	153.9	172.7	129.2	118.2
		Net attributable income		
1989	0.10*	0.34	0.27	0.13
1999	1.9	2.4	1.9	2.4
		Return on assets		
1999	1.2	1.4	1.3	1.9
		Return on equity		
1999	18.5	20.6	22.5	25.3
		Expenses to income ratio		
1999	63.3	61.9	61.1	51.7

Notes: * Figures include Bankorp and Volkskas.
Dates are as follows:
    1989:   ABSA   31 March & 30 June
              SBIC   31 December
              FNB   30 September
              Nedcor   30 September
    1999:   ABSA   31 March
              SBIC   31 December
              FNB   30 June
              Nedcor   31 December

Source: *The Financial Mail*, 'Top Companies', 1990 and 2000.

being placed upon building long-term relationships with business customers. Ordinary current account holders, by contrast, have experienced deteriorating service and rising bank charges, up to 2 per cent of the value of a cheque.

8.3.2   Functions and Changing Financial Services

At the beginning of the decade the merchant banks remained a distinct group led by Senbank, Standard Merchant Bank and UAL. Rand Merchant Bank and Investec were a long way behind the leaders and few contemporaries could have foreseen that Rand Merchant Bank's management would take the lead in forming the country's largest financial institution in 1998. The traditional business of accepting bills had long since given way to financing industry and financing mergers and acquisitions and in 1990 the merchant banks were just beginning to expand into privatization. By the end of the decade banking functions that had once been associated with specialist institutions were being performed by all the main banks. The Registrar of Banks no longer required separate returns from merchant banks and general banks, but grouped the banks' quarterly returns into seven categories, six of which are reproduced in the Top Companies survey of *The Financial Mail*.

These returns for February 2000 show that there were 57 reporting financial institutions, whose functions were: instalment sales, leases, credit cards, overdrafts, public overdrafts and investments. The first three of these were not traditional commercial banking functions. Nor were the financing of industry and the granting of home loans. In February 2000, First National Bank was leading the pack in instalment sales, leases and overdrafts, Nedcor in credit cards, ABSA in public overdrafts and Investec in investments. In this last-mentioned category, Standard Bank had been overtaken by the three commercial banking groups and the brash new merchant/industrial bank.

BOE, sixth largest in terms of both capital and assets, came a long way behind, though at one time it had been the country's most profitable bank. For example, CFC, one of the partners in the controlling consortium of BOE, paid R36.7 million for their 44.6 million shares in 1994, which by 1998 had risen in value to almost R900 million. Fifteen managers led by the chairman had paid R23.7 million for a block of shares in BOE that had risen to almost R600 million before the stock market crash of August 1998 (*Finance week*, 1998, 11). BOE's rise to prominence among the financial institutions of South Africa was one of the features of the 1990s. Another was the move into asset management, led by BOE and Investec, and the importance attached to private banking, both of which were global phenomena.

8.3.3   Competition and the New Smaller Financial Institutions

The 1990s also saw the appearance of a number of new players in the financial markets, driven partly by the arrival of foreign banks, partly by niche players and partly by a flurry of affirmative action initiatives. Their number included Gensec, PSG Investment Bank, Corpcapital Bank, Brait Merchant Bank, FBC Fidelity Bank, Decillion, the Business Bank, TA Bank, Real Africa Durolink and Peregrine. The market crash of 1998 hit them hard. When the deals stopped and asset values fell, profits evaporated and a number of them collapsed. One of them, the Business Bank, set up by a former managing director of Nedbank with entrepreneurial ambitions, failed as a result of placing over 10 per cent of its assets in one company. At the end of 2000 it is not clear that the rash of new banking ventures has added wealth to the South African economy.

A further threat to banking profitability is the pressure emanating from government to lend to small businesses. In effect the government is trying to push the commercial banks to take on the functions performed by the money lender in countries such as India, but lending other people's money to individuals without business experience and without collateral is a very high risk type of business and it is debatable whether it should be carried out by the commercial banks. If they charge interest comparable to the risks involved, as in the informal sector, or in India, they will be heavily criticized. If they do not charge accordingly, their profits will be hit. This applies particularly to the Standard Bank, which has been adding 2 500 low income customers a month to its client base. Political imperatives may well alter the face of banking in South Africa.

Finally, we might note how the functions of the banks have changed in the past 30 or so years. In 1970 they were still very traditional, deposit taking and retail lending dominating. By the year 2000 PriceWaterhouseCoopers, in their analysis of strategic issues in banking were able to identify 19 different functions. These are presented in Table 8.10 and show not only how the banks responded to the challenge of increased competition, but how, in 2000, in one area, retail brokerage, a South African firm had succeeded in pushing a foreign firm out of the top place. More important, though, are the functions themselves, which are so different from those of 1970.

8.3.4 The Life Assurance Companies

During the 1990s the life assurance companies changed their names and image from firms providing life cover and annuities to financial services companies. Asset management was now emphasized and cost structures examined. Competition and technology together are driving down costs in what has traditionally been an inefficient industry. Single premiums are now growing faster than recurring ones. Old Mutual and Sanlam still account for 60 per cent of the market, with the embedded value of Old Mutual more than twice that of Sanlam and almost four times that of the Liberty Group, the third largest life assurer. Liberty is the only one of the top three whose share price is greater than its embedded value and this has been achieved as a result of the decision to dispose of their investments in Libsil, FIT, Stanbic and Bevcom, in order to employ their funds more efficiently. The total assets of the life companies are large. Those of the Old Mutual are larger than those of any individual bank

The decline of the South African economy

Table 8.10   Top banks ranked by function, 1999 and 2000

Function	2000	1999
Corporate lending	Standard	Standard
Corporate finance – listing	First Rand	First Rand
Corporate finance – mergers and acquisitions	First Rand	First Rand
Capital markets – foreign exchange	Standard	Standard
Capital markets – bonds	JP Morgan	JP Morgan
Capital markets – money markets	Standard	Standard
Structures finance	First Rand	First Rand – tax standard project
Institutional brokerage	Merrill Lynch	Deutsche Morgan
Asset management	Investec	Investec
Retail brokerage	Sasfin	HSBC
Internet banking	Standard	n/a
Retail lending	Standard	n/a
Credit cards	Nedcor	n/a
Retail deposit taking	ABSA & Standard	n/a
Mortgages	ABSA	n/a
Vehicle finance	First Rand	n/a
Unit trusts	Coronation & Investec	n/a
Private banking	Investec	n/a
Private equity investment	First Rand	n/a

Source: Price Waterhouse Coopers (2000, p. 11).

and only the Standard Bank Investment Corporation has larger assets than Sanlam. In the 1970s the assets of the life insurance companies had been growing faster than those of the banks, and this was still the case in the 1990s. Yet in 1999 the assets of the four largest banking groups at R626.7 billion were still ahead of the R511 billion of the four biggest assurers. This may not last much longer for assets of the life assurance companies have been growing faster than those of the banks by 4 per cent a year, 18.7 per cent versus 14.7 per cent.

8.3.5   Capital Markets

The ending of the political isolation of South Africa in 1994 had a dramatic effect upon the Johannesburg Securities Exchange. Turnover which had reached R727.7 million in 1970, R4.036 million in 1980 and R23 676.9 million in 1990 rose to R34.127 million in 1993 before taking off in 1994. In that year the increase was greater than total turnover in 1990 and by 2000 it had reached R536.877 million, almost 23 times the level of ten years earlier. In constant prices it had risen almost ninefold. A significant proportion of this turnover was derived from London which has long been the centre for the purchase of South African equities. Foreign purchases rose from R22.427 million in 1994 to R157.797 million in 2000. After 1994 they exceeded foreign sales of South African equities every year. Globalization was more in evidence on the JSE than in the figures of external trade, those of foreign direct investment, or in those of labour movements. In 2000 foreign purchases and sales accounted for 55 per cent of turnover.

Market capitalization more than trebled, rising from R495,1 billion in 1990 to R1 551.5 billion in December 2000. Even new capital raised on the JSE began to increase, rising from R20 614.4 to R79.475 million in 1998 though by 2000 this had fallen to R71.297 million. All of the increase has occurred after 1996.

By world standards the Johannesburg Securities Exchange has been known to have a fairly high market capitalization but a small turnover. Yet placed in perspective, the Johannesburg market is small. Just as the South African economy is small, less than half the size of that of Belgium, so too is the market capitalization of JSE small, less than that of South Korea or Taiwan. By turnover it is smaller than the stock markets of Greece and Brazil, less than a twelfth that of South Korea and barely a fourteenth of that of Taiwan. Much progress had been made in reintegrating the South African economy into the world markets, but the legacy of four decades of mercantilist policies is a burden that cannot be rectified overnight.

8.3.6 Unit Trusts

The explosive growth of the unit trust industry is part of the second mass market for financial products referred to earlier. In 1990 there 31 unit trusts, of which 19 had been launched in the previous ten years. At the beginning of 1990 their total assets amounted to R6 642.7 million and their three biggest investment portfolios were industrials (R2 396.2m), mining finance (R978.7m) and other mining (R561.8m). At a time of high inflation the growth of the unit trust industry offered investors a way of maintaining the value of their capital (*The Financial Mail*, 'Top Companies 2000', 236). In this situation it is not surprising the rand hedge funds should dominate, with 67.4 per cent of the equity business.

Ten years later the amount invested in unit trusts had grown to R112.2 billion in 260 funds supporting a host of asset managers. *The Financial Mail* considers the years from 1993 to 1997 were the golden age of the unit trusts. In the 1990s, too, money market funds became popular and, with assets of R33.1 billion in March 2000, they accounted for over a third of the assets of domestic unit trusts (*The Financial Mail*, 'Top Companies 2000', 323). Rand-dominated funds invested in foreign markets were also very popular by 2000, but their growth was restricted by the Reserve Bank's limit on the amount that could be invested outside the country. This was 15 per cent of assets, until the February 2000 budget, when it was raised to 20 per cent. Unit trusts are expensive. Annual charges of 1.25 per cent of the capital value plus a 5 per cent initial charge suggest that there is opportunity for further competition in this area and index funds have already reduced their charges considerably. While the market in South Africa has been subject to sharp corrections and many of the blue-chip companies have prices lower in 2000 than in 1995, the middle-class fear of inflation and currency mismanagement is likely to maintain a vigorous unit trust market, despite the long-term decline in real per capital GDP.

8.3.7 Derivatives

Derivatives trading on a large scale is new to South Africa. The South African Futures Exchange offered foreign investors liquidity during financial crises. Business was brisk in the year after the election, but then dipped in the year ending March 1996, only to grow vigorously the following year. Merchant banks and Johannesburg Stock Exchange brokers dominate the business. Both futures and options have proved popular with the market, while on the JSE a thriving market in warrants has developed, led by Deutsche Bank and the Standard Bank. An attempt to amalgamate the three exchanges, the Futures Exchange, the Bond Exchange and the Johannesburg Stock Exchange, collapsed in 1999. In that year the South African Futures Exchange ranked sixteenth in the world, with about 5 per cent of the business of the leader, the Eurex Exchange.

8.4   CONCLUSION

In the last three decades of the twentieth century the financial sector of the South African economy has indeed been transformed. Market forces and the invigorating breeze of private enterprise have been responsible for the far-reaching changes that have swept through the sector, especially in the last decade of the century. In 1970 the sector was still dominated by two very traditional imperial banks, by two somewhat sleepy mutual insurance companies and by the great mining finance houses. The onset of double-digit inflation triggered a variety of changes in the way businesses operated while appearing to maintain the status quo. In the 1980s these were becoming clearer. The traditional banking business was changing, as competition from the life assurers threatened to divert funds away from the commercial banks. The building societies were hit hard by inflation, as both the banks and life insurance companies moved into their territory. The old distinctions between commercial banking and merchant banking were blurring and the old apprenticeship way of training financial services managers gave way to a more professional approach. The impact of technology and its cost made this essential.

By the last decade of the century the increasing volume of wealth available, as a result of the aggregate growth of the economy, despite the declining real per capita incomes, gave the expanding middle class the confidence to move wholeheartedly into the market for unit trusts. This, together with an inflow of portfolio investment after 1994, led to the Johannesburg Stock Exchange experiencing unparalleled growth in the second half of the decade. The failure of the ANC/Communist government to undertake any serious privatization in the 1990s, or to abolish exchange control, while indulging in the luxury of extraordinarily inappropriate First World-type labour legislation and ignoring the major long-term threat, the population explosion that has been relentlessly driving down per capita incomes, casts a cloud upon an otherwise buoyant sector. Nevertheless, the power of private enterprise, most visibly displayed in the host of new financial institutions, in the popularity of unit trusts and in the dynamism of the stock exchange points the way to the future in an economy still struggling to achieve satisfactory growth.

REFERENCES

Drucker, Peter (1999), 'Peter Drucker on financial services', *The Economist*, 25 September.
Finance Week (1998), 18 December.
The Financial Mail (1999), 25 June.
The Financial Mail (2000), 'Top Companies 2000', 30 June.
Gidlow, R.M. (1999), 'South African monetary policies during the 1970s', in Stuart Jones and Jon Inggs (eds), *The South African Economy in the 1970s*, Special Issue, *South African Journal of Economic History*, **14**, 37–54.
Goedhuys, Diederik (1994), 'South African monetary policy in the 1980s', in Stuart Jones and Jon Inggs (eds), *The South African Economy in the 1980s*, Special Issue, *South African Journal of Economic History*, **9**, 145–64.
Jones, Stuart (1992), 'From building society to bank: the Allied, 1970-1989', in Stuart Jones (ed.), *Financial Enterprise in South Africa since 1950*, London: Macmillan, 236–62.
Jones, Stuart (1999), 'Banking in the 1970s', in Stuart Jones and Jon Inggs (eds), *The*

South African Economy in the 1970s, Special Issue, *South African Journal of Economic History*, **14**, 195–231.

Jones, Stuart, André Liebenberg and Robert Vivian (1999), 'Asset and risk management in the 1970s', in Stuart Jones and Jon Inggs (eds), *The South African Economy in the 1970s*, Special Issue, *South African Journal of Economic History*, **14**, 232–59.

Jones, Stuart and G.W. Scott (1992), 'Wesbank: South Africa's leading hire purchase bank', in Stuart Jones (ed.), *Financial Enterprise in South Africa since 1950*, London: Macmillan, 213–35.

PriceWaterhouseCoopers (2000), *Strategic and Emerging Issues in South African Banking*, Millennium Issue, Johannesburg.

Registrar of Banks, *Annual Report*, various years.

Registrar of Insurance Companies, *Annual Report*, various years.

South African Reserve Bank, *Quarterly Bulletin*, various issues.

South African Reserve Bank, *Supplement to the Quarterly Bulletin*, June 1991.

Verhoef, Grietjie (1992), 'Afrikaner Nationalism in South African banking: the cases of Volkskas and Trust Bank', in Stuart Jones (ed.), *Financial Enterprise in South Africa since 1950, London*, Macmillan, 115–53.

9. External trade, 1970–2000

Stuart Jones

9.1 INTRODUCTION

Since the 1880s gold has been the main driving force behind the expansion of South Africa's external trade. Gold provided the export surplus that enabled larger volumes of imports to be maintained than would otherwise have been possible in a developing economy. By the 1960s producer goods had overtaken consumer goods in the volume of imports pouring into South Africa and this pattern was reinforced by the rise in the gold price in the 1970s and the government's commitment to a number of capital-intensive infrastructure projects. In the 1980s, when the gold price declined, the economy experienced a severe adjustment that was made worse by the deteriorating political situation both at home and overseas. In these circumstances, the trade-led growth of the 1970s gave way to external trade acting as a break upon the economy in both the 1980s and the 1990s. The main reason for this dramatic change was the decline in both the volume and value of gold exports.

Moreover, despite all the 'media hype' about globalization, the South African economy has been disengaging itself from the world economy in the last 20 years of the century. Nor has the arrival of an ANC/Communist government reversed this situation to any extent. Trade as a proportion of GDP has fallen dramatically. As Table 9.1 indicates, this fell from 61 per cent in 1980, the year the gold price peaked, to 38.1 per cent in 1990. Five years later, after the ending of sanctions and the arrival of streams of aid, the ratio had not changed significantly. The figures reflect, not just the long-term decline in the value of gold exports, but also the decline in the South African economy, when expressed in terms of real per capita income. Another way of interpreting the figures is to see them as representing a return to more normal trading conditions once the stimulus of soaring gold exports was removed. Nevertheless it is clear that, in the years of 'total onslaught' and sanctions, South Africa continued to maintain a very open economy when compared with either the United States or other semi-industrialized countries.

Not only did the weighting of trade in the South African economy decline after 1980, but in real terms it experienced an absolute decline (see Table 9.2) By 1994 the real value of external trade had fallen to 59.3 per cent of that of

Table 9.1　Trade as a percentage of GDP, 1970–1999

Year	Pecentage	Year	Percentage
1970	42.3	1990	38.1
1980	61.0	1999	38.7

Source:　Foreign Trade Statistics

1980. The ending of sanctions and the arrival of aid then produced a temporary bounce back in the year 1996 that took total trade to R10 800.4 million in 1970 prices. Since then growth has been slow. The growth of trade after the election was no faster than before it. In constant prices trade grew at 4.4 per cent between 1990 and 1994 and 4.4 per cent between 1994 and 1999. In 1999 the value of total trade was still below that of 1980 and per capita trade in constant prices had fallen from R418 in 1979 to R269 in 1999. This once again draws our attention to the decline that has been taking place in the South African economy. Twenty years or more of potential growth had been lost.

Table 9.2　External trade of South Africa (in constant 1970 prices), 1970–1999

Year	External trade (Rm)
1970	4 920.8
1975	8 056.8
1980	11 874.1
1985	10 504.6
1990	9 240.3
1994	7 046.8
1999	11 586.9

Sources:　As Table 9.1 and the South African Reserve Bank, Quarterly Bulletin, various issues.

A breakdown of the trade into imports and exports by decade shows how the economic fortunes of the country fluctuated (see Table 9.3). Imports rose markedly in the 1970s in response to the expansion of basic industries and the large infrastructure projects initiated by the Vorster government and then fell away in the sanctions era of the 1980s when it was necessary to maintain a positive balance of trade. In the 1990s, notwithstanding the ending of sanctions and the arrival of aid, imports have not been able to regain the position they held in the 1970s. This of course reflects the poor performance of the economy in these years, and particularly of manufacturing.

Table 9.3   *Imports and exports of South Africa and as a percentage of GDP, 1970–1999*

Year	Imports (Rm)	%	Exports (Rm)	%
1970	2 547.2	20.3	2 373.6	19.0
1980	14 414.8	24.9	19 957.8	34.4
1990	44 125.0	16.0	60 928.5	22.1
1999	146 076.2	18.2	163 966.5	20.5

Source: As Table 9.2.

Exports, also, boomed in the years of the high gold price and then slumped in the 1980s and 1990s. Yet in the 1980s a positive balance of trade was maintained by depreciating the currency and in the 1990s by the sluggish nature of the economy that held down imports at a time when exports were being boosted by further currency depreciation. Table 9.4 shows how these changes affected the economy. In the 1970s South Africa experienced both import-led and export-led growth in current prices, but in the following decade this gave way to the GDP growing faster than both imports and exports. In the 1990s exports continued to act as a break upon growth, but renewed borrowing, rather than foreign direct investment, allowed imports to grow slightly faster than GDP. As a result, in the economically depressed 1990s, the South African economy found itself experiencing import-led growth. Over the 29-year period as a whole GDP grew slightly faster than imports and slightly slower than exports. In the latter case it was the experience of the 1970s that skewed the figures for the whole period in favour of export-led growth. If there is a break in the growth pattern of South Africa's external trade, it occurred in 1980, when the gold price peaked, and not in the 1990s, when there was a change in government.

The sluggishness in the growth of South Africa's external trade has deep

Table 9.4   *Growth rate of imports, exports and GDP, 1970–1999*

	Imports (%)	Exports (%)	GDP (%)
1970–80	18.9	23.7	16.6
1980–90	11.8	11.8	15.6
1990–99	14.2	11.6	14.0
1970–99	15.0	15.7	15.4

Source: As Table 9.2.

roots that reach back to the years before Union in 1910, when the gold discoveries pushed up local prices and removed balance of payments constraints. Export promotion was never given wholehearted support by Union governments. As early as 1925, the Economic and Wages Commission noted that the introduction of tariffs did not help industries that did not compete with imports and that it would hurt export-orientated industries such as agriculture and mining. Not deterred by these economic arguments the Nationalists, then as now, supported import-substitution policies that already by 1934 were having a weakening effect upon initiative and risk taking (Botha, 1973, 345).

By the 1960s the government was actively supporting export promotion policies, but, as Zarenda pointed out, these conflicted with import-substitution policies, a conflict which was ignored by the 1977 Reynders Commission into the export trade (Reynders, 1975, 123, 131). Indeed Reynders himself would not accept the existence of a conflict and continued to support import-substitution policies while arguing that export incentives had introduced a structural change in the country's export environment (Reynders, 1975, 123, 131; Zarenda, 1975).

Such confusion in government thinking has continued to this day, with the old simple import-substitution policies built on tariffs giving way to First World minimum wages and labour laws in an economy that does not enjoy First World productivity. The lament of the Holloway Commission in 1936 that 'wages were kept high by industrial legislation and prices by protective measures' (Botha, 1973, 351), could equally apply to the situation in the year 2000.

9.2 THE GEOGRAPHICAL DISTRIBUTION OF SOUTH AFRICAN TRADE

The geographical distribution of South Africa's external trade had broadened considerably in the 1960s and this trend continued in the last 30 years of the century. Trade with Europe excluding gold bullion accounted for half of South Africa's external trade until the last decade of the century. Its proportion then declined in the face of the more rapid growth of trade with Asia that was boosted by petroleum imports from the Persian Gulf, the reopening of trading contacts with India and a vigorous new trade with China.

Imports from the developed economies of Europe, America and Japan almost always formed a larger proportion of total imports than did South African exports to these regions. South Africa imported capital goods and exported raw materials. Imports from Africa remained relatively insignificant, whereas exports to the lands north of the Limpopo rose rapidly in the 1990s and by the end of the decade had recovered the ground they had lost since 1970. The relative decline in imports from the Americas occurred in the 1980s, that from Europe in the 1990s. The sharp decline in exports to the Americas that occurred in the 1980s was a return to more normal trading conditions, following the boom of the 1970s, at a time when Japan was rapidly expanding its imports of raw materials from South Africa. Exports to Africa are unlikely to increase much beyond their present 17.9 per cent of specified exports, because of the limited purchasing power of countries north of the Limpopo, while their share of imports is still below the level of 1970. In other words South Africa's external trade is likely to remain focused on the developed economies of the world for the foreseeable future.

In current prices, as Table 9.5 indicates, the absolute growth of trade was very considerable. Imports from Asia rose from less than half a billion rands

Table 9.5   Geographical distribution of South African trade, 1970-1999

	Imports R million							
	1970	%	1980	%	1990	%	1999	%
Europe	1 322.0	54.1	5 711.9	56.3	21 631.6	56.5	67 600.9	46.3
Africa	131.2	5.4	288.1	2.8	789.8	2.1	4 628.8	3.2
Asia	409.8	16.8	1 807.5	17.8	8 988.7	23.5	45 897.3	31.4
Americas	516.2	21.1	2 233.1	22.0	6 422.6	16.8	24 435.5	16.7
Oceania	65.3	2.7	107.7	1.0	430.6	1.1	3,499.3	2.4
Total								
specified	2 444.5		10 148.3		38 263.4		146 061.8	
Unspecified	2.6		4 224.4		5 892.9		141.4	

	Exports R million							
	1970	%	1980	%	1990	%	1999	%
Europe	793.5	54.0	5 151.4	49.1	22 921.4	55.2	52 980.9	42.2
Africa	263.9	18.0	1 098.0	10.5	4 010.5	9.7	22 425.6	17.9
Asia	219.3	14.9	1 992.9	19.0	10 899.8	26.3	31 406.8	25.0
Americas	176.5	12.0	2 146.8	20.5	3 341.5	8.0	15 764.0	12.6
Oceania	15.2	1.0	96.2	0.9	349.4	0.8	2 866.9	2.3
Total								
specified	1 4684		10 484.6		41 522.6		125 444.2	
Unspecified	2.3		9 348.7		18 458.0		37 213.9	

Source: *Monthly Abstract of Trade Statistics*, December 1970, 1980 and 1999 and 1990 figures provided by the Department of Customs and Excise.

in 1970 to almost 46 billion in 1999, an increase of 11 thousand per cent. In
current prices even imports from Africa rose by over 3 thousand per cent.
Exports to Asia rose even more dramatically by over 14 thousand per cent and
to Oceania by 19 thousand per cent. Such figures give the impression of a
dynamic economy expanding its role in the global economy. This is incorrect.
Inflation distorts the picture.

A more accurate view is presented in Table 9.6, which gives the regional
growth of imports and exports in constant prices. This shows that imports from
Europe declined in the period from 1980 to 1990 by 0.4 per cent a year, from
the Americas by 12.8 per cent a year and from Africa by 3.4 per cent a year.
In this same period, too, exports to both Europe and America declined. From
growing by 15.4 per cent a year in the 1970s, exports to America declined by
8.8 per cent a year in the 1980s. In the 1990s exports to all the regions save
Europe increased led by those to Oceania which rose by 14.9 per cent
annually. Imports expanded from all five regions in the 1990s, though not as
dramatically as exports.

Table 9.6   Real growth of trade to specified regions, 1970-1999

Region		1970–80 %	1980–90 %	1990–99 %	1970–99 %
Europe	Imports	4.1	–0.4	3.2	2.3
	Exports	8.4	1.2	–0.2	3.2
Africa	Imports	–2.7	–3.4	10.7	1.0
	Exports	3.7	–0.7	10.1	4.1
Asia	Imports	4.3	2.4	8.9	5.1
	Exports	12.1	3.4	2.3	6.0
Americas	Imports	5.5	–12.8	5.5	2.0
	Exports	15.4	–8.8	8.0	4.2
Oceania	Imports	–5.5	0.2	14.8	2.4
	Exports	8.1	–0.8	14.9	7.0

Source: As Table 9.5.

These percentages probably give a fairly accurate picture of the changes
taking place, though from 1976 onwards the increasingly hostile international
environment led the authorities to encourage both importers and exporters to
omit the source of imports or the destination of exports, so much so that by
1980 the unspecified destination of exports amounted to almost half the total
and even in 1999, exports going to unspecified destinations amounted to
almost 30 per cent of the total. From 1985 to 1992, detailed breakdowns of

figures have not been published. In these circumstances the buoyancy of the African figures in the 1990s suggest that trade, hitherto unrecorded as African, was now being correctly classified.

The figures for the decade of the 1980s provide some evidence of the impact of the sanctions campaigns against South Africa. Only imports and exports to Asia grew, fuelled by the booming Japanese economy. Imports from the Americas fell dramatically, as American firms disinvested, but exports held up better, driven by American imports of raw materials. In retrospect the decade of the 1980s was a disaster for South Africa. However, one should beware of attributing all, or even most, of the trade decline to sanctions. South Africa's own economic decline was depressing the demand for imports at a time when the falling gold price strengthened the lack of confidence in the business community.

Neither the inflated current price figures, nor the broadening geographical distribution of South African trade can conceal the fact that the economy was experiencing a long-term decline and that there were few years when external trade in real terms was growing at a faster rate than the population.

Nor should one exaggerate the extent of the broadening geographical range of the country's trade, for in 1999 the four leading trading partners were the same ones that had dominated trade in 1970, namely the UK, Germany, the USA and Japan. They were the biggest export markets and the biggest suppliers of producer goods. Below the top four, however, some significant changes had taken place.

In imports the most dramatic changes occurred, because of the publication of trade with oil producers and the emergence of China as a major trading partner. In 1999, 33 countries provided imports of over R1 000 million, two in Africa, 12 in Europe, 14 in Asia and one in Oceania. The two African countries were Zimbabwe and Nigeria. Table 9.7 gives the ten largest sources of imports and shows that the five European countries, the USA and Japan had been joined by Saudi Arabia, China and Iran. Trade had also grown more unbalanced. The UK had become South Africa's largest trading partner again in 1997 and trade with the former colonial ruler was more balanced than that with the other leading trading partners. With Germany, the USA, Japan, Saudi Arabia, Italy, France and China, imports considerably exceeded exports, thereby creating the need for capital imports that were making South Africa more vulnerable to fluctuations in the international economy. The deficit with the top ten sources of imports amounted to R37.133 million in 1999.

Twenty-nine years earlier, in 1970, the top ten sources of imports had included only one Asian country, Japan, six were in Europe, with imports from the UK way ahead of those from Germany and the USA. Imperial preference was still in existence and both Canada and Australia ranked among the top ten sources of imports. South Africa's trade was much more Western orientated

Table 9.7   *Major sources of South African imports in 1970, 1980, 1990 and 1999 and their growth rate (in constant prices), 1970-1980, 1980-1990 and 1990-1999*

1970	Rm	1980	Rm	1970-80 %
United Kingdom	561.2	United States	1 949.2	4.7
United States	423.4	Germany	1 853.4	5.6
Germany	374.0	United Kingdom	1 738.4	0.7
Japan	220.8	Japan	1 287.0	7.2
Italy	104.3	France	541.6	7.8
France	88.1	Italy	438.4	3.8
Canada	70.5	Switzerland	237.1	5.1
Australia	60.4	Netherlands	196.6	1.5
Netherlands	58.4	Belgium	171.2	5.7
Switzerland	49.6	Sweden	144.0	1.0

1990	Rm	1980-90 %	1999	Rm	1990-99 %
Germany	8 687.7	1.8	Germany	21 565.9	0.6
United Kingdom	5 191.9	-2.7	United States	19 997.5	6.0
United States	5 048.8	4.1	United Kingdom	13 967.4	1.5
Japan	4 341.1	-1.5	Japan	11 434.4	1.3
Italy	1 940.4	1.2	Saudi Arabia	6 026.3	n/a
Taiwan	1 475.2	n/a	France	5 815.8	6.2
France	1 435.7	-3.9	Italy	5 739.9	2.6
Switzerland	1 191.0	2.5	China	5 003.5	n/a
Belgium	1 051.2	4.6	Iran	4 063.8	n/a
Netherlands	931.7	1.9	Switzerland	3 808.1	3.5

Source: *Monthly Abstract of Trade Statistics*, 1970, 1980 and 1990. Figures for 1990 provided by the Department of Customs and Excise.

30 years ago. Table 9.7 gives the figures of imports from these leading suppliers in 1970 in current prices and in 1999 prices so that one can form some idea of the extent of trade expansion in the last third of the twentieth century.

The real value of the imports from the ten leading suppliers almost doubled between 1970 and 1999. In 1970 the top ten suppliers had accounted for 79.3 per cent of imports, in 1999 this had fallen to 66.6 per cent of all imports. In real terms imports from Britain had fallen, while those from Germany, Italy,

France and Switzerland had more than doubled and those from the United States and Japan had almost doubled. The decline in the relative importance of Britain as a source of imports, which was a conspicuous feature of the 1960s and 1970s, was halted in the 1990s. Nevertheless, over the 29 years the most striking change in the geographical pattern of imports has been the decline in the proportion of imports coming from the United Kingdom, which fell from over 22 per cent in 1970 to below 9 per cent in 1999.

Other dramatic changes reflect the increasing importance of petroleum to modern economies and the political realignment of 1994 that led to trade opening up with China and India and the publication of the figures of trade with countries north of the Limpopo. Imports from Saudi Arabia now place that country fifth in the list of suppliers of goods to South Africa, with Iran ninth. Three of the ten leading suppliers are consequently major new trading partners, though earlier, before the revolution in Iran, that country had been a major supplier of oil to South Africa and even earlier still, before 1947. India had also been an important trading partner.

A breakdown by decade shows how this happened. In 1970 Europe provided six of the ten leading suppliers, the Commonwealth countries of Australia and Canada a further two, and the United States and Japan the balance. It was predominantly Western orientated. Ten years later in 1980, Australia and Canada had been replaced by Belgium and Sweden and the pattern of imports was even more eurocentric than in 1970. Ten years later still, in 1990, this had only marginally changed. The growth in imports from Taiwan had overtaken those from France, Switzerland, Belgium and the Netherlands and pushed Sweden out of the list, but Britain had overtaken America and moved into second place. By 1999, when petroleum imports are included, Saudi Arabia and Iran had joined the top ten and China had replaced Taiwan. The appearance of China among the ten leading suppliers is the odd man out, for the others provided producer goods, whereas China provided consumer goods. Imports from China were replacing those from other Asian countries. The negative growth of imports from so many of South Africa's leading trading partners reflects the severity of the recession at home and trade boycott campaigns in the United States and France. When these ended in the 1990s, trade bounced back and imports from those two countries rose dramatically.

In the next tier of suppliers to South Africa, Taiwan and South Korea stand out with real annual growth rates of 14.5 and 17.4 per cent in the 1990s. India, Malaysia, Singapore and Nigeria are new entrants, their imports being too small to itemize in earlier years. Together these new trading partners, mainly in Asia, have helped broaden the base of South Africa's external trade considerably. However one should bear in mind that the imports from Thailand, India, Singapore, Brazil and Nigeria together are a mere third of those from Germany and imports from the second ten largest suppliers together are only a little larger than those from Germany at a time when the Germany economy has been in a recession.

Exports enjoyed a broader geographical range than imports, because of African markets for both consumer goods and transport equipment and the Asian market for raw materials. In 1970 two of the ten major markets were in Africa, namely Rhodesia and Zambia, two were in North America, one in Asia, Japan, and five in Europe. Twenty-nine years later, Canada had dropped out of the group of major markets, and South Korea had emerged as the second Asian market of importance followed by Taiwan. China, India and Thailand were all moving up from low bases. Between 1970 and 1999 exports to South Korea were growing by 16.1 per cent a year in constant prices and those to Taiwan by 10.7 per cent. The only other important market experiencing double-digit real growth was that of Israel at 12.2 per cent. Canada was the only major market that declined.

A decennial breakdown shows how relatively little change there was until the 1990s (Table 9.8). In 1970 exports to Britain were greater than those to Japan, Germany and the United States combined. In 1980 Britain was still the major market, but Japan and the United States were not far behind, reflecting the dynamism of their economies and the sluggishness of Britain's in the 1970s. By 1990, sanctions campaigns in the United States had had an adverse impact upon sales to that country, while Switzerland had moved into first place as a result of the transfer of Kruger rand sales to that country. Political events in France also hit sales to that country.

Britain remained more important as a market than as a source of imports. In 1999, in constant prices, exports to Britain were only 22 per cent greater than in 1970, whereas exports to America had almost quintupled and to Germany they had more than quadrupled. In the 1970s exports to Britain declined, when exports to France, Germany and the United States were growing at over 10 per cent a year. The ending of imperial preference coinciding with the introduction of the European Common Agricultural Policy hit exports to Britain severely. In the next decade the United States stood out as the leading market failure, with sales to that country declining by 5 per cent a year. Conversely, when the political situation changed in the 1990s and the American economy continued to expand, exports to that country recovered and grew by 11.9 per cent a year. Even the German market, dominated by unemployment and huge payment transfers to the East, was expanding by over 6 per cent a year in the 1990s.

The broadening range in the destination of exports was highlighted by the relative decline in the importance of the four leading markets. In 1970 the top four markets took 56.1 per cent of exports, in 1980, 41.9 per cent, in 1990, 34.3 per cent and in 1999, 29.9 per cent. However, this rate of decline was slowing. In the 1970s exports to the top four declined by 2.9 per cent a year, in the 1980s by 2.0 per cent and in the 1990s by 1.5 per cent.

Table 9.8   *Major export markets of South Africa in 1970, 1980, 1990 and 1999 and their growth rate (in constant prices), 1970-1980, 1980-90 and 1990-1999*

1970			1980		1970–80
	Rm			Rm	%
United Kingdom	446.6		United Kingdom	1 226.3	–0.5
Japan	181.0		Japan	1 199.7	8.6
United States	127.9		United Kingdom	1 032.0	10.8
Germany	106.3		Switzerland	778.7	65.1*
Belgium	55.4		Germany	658.9	7.9
Italy	43.2		France	421.4	14.4
France	37.8		Italy	387.9	12.0
Netherlands	34.9		Belgium	298.9	6.4
Canada	28.2		Netherlands	247.6	9.3
Hong Kong	24.0		Hong Kong	223.0	12.3

1990		1980–90	1999		1990–99
	Rm	%		Rm	%
Switzerland	5 474.0	6.0	United States	15 764.0	11.9
United Kingdom	4 931.0	0.2	United Kingdom	14 562.0	2.6
Japan	3 889.4	–1.9	Germany	11 918.3	6.1
Netherlands	3 304.0	13.0	Japan	7 263.4	–2.5
Germany	2 982.0	1.4	Netherlands	6 190.7	–2.5
United States	2 432.9	–5.0	Belgium	5 439.8	4.7
Taiwan	1 824.7	n/a	Zimbabwe	5 120.0	n/a
Belgium	1 526.5	2.7	South Korea	4 285.4	n/a
Italy	1 526.2	0.0	Italy	4 276.6	2.0
Hong Kong	1 104.2	2.3	Mozambique	4 079.0	n/a

Notes: *Kruger rand sales transferred to Zurich from London.

Source: Same as Table 9.7.

By the end of the century, with sanctions a distant memory, the United States had overtaken Britain to assert her supremacy as a market for South African exports. Britain, however, had occupied first place in 1995, 1996 and 1997. Japan had fallen behind. Together the exports to the United States, the United Kingdom and Germany were greater than the combined total of the next seven largest markets.

The major change in the recorded statistics in the 1990s was the growth of trade with African countries. Zimbabwe once again became recognized as a major trading partner, in seventh position in 1999, while Mozambique had moved up to tenth position. This was a natural response to geographical realities, which had been held back by Portuguese mercantilist policies before 1976. Exports to Zambia, Malawi, Angola and Tanzania were all growing. Nevertheless in 1999 the seven largest African markets were smaller than that of either the United States or Britain.

9.3   THE COMMODITIES TRADE

9.3.1   Imports

In the 1960s the previous decade's policy of import substitution gave way to one of export promotion. In the 1970s both approaches to industrialization were adopted. Export promotion may be seen in the great infrastructure projects associated with Iscor and Escom and the new export-orientated railway lines to Richards Bay on the northern Natal coast and Saldanha Bay on the Cape West coast; import substitution may be seen in the expansion of the Sasol, the oil from coal undertaking, and in the tightening of the local content laws in connection with the automobile industry. Export promotion led to a significant growth in mineral and steel exports; import substitution led to a wider range of producer goods being imported. Both of these developments were somewhat overshadowed by the mushrooming value of gold exports.

Machinery and electrical equipment headed the list of imports in 1970 and also in 1999. In constant prices the value of machinery and electrical equipment imported into South Africa more than doubled. This was about in line with population growth. In real terms the value of transport equipment imported did not keep pace with population growth, reflecting the success of the local content programmes on the motor industry in South Africa. Chemical imports rocketed, led by pharmaceuticals. In 1970 pharmaceutical imports amounted to R13.6 million; by 1999 this figure had risen to R3 598.4 million. Textiles declined in importance and petroleum imports are now recorded under mineral imports at R15 516.4 million in 1999. Iron and steel imports have also continued at a high level, despite the fact that South Africa is now a major exporter with a positive balance of trade in iron and steel that amounted to R324.1 million in 1999. Categories 07 and 18, important for an industrializing country, have maintained their relative standing in the pattern of imports, somewhat more than doubling in constant prices, but only maintaining their per capita level and once again drawing our attention to relative economic decline taking place in South Africa per capital incomes in these years.

Agricultural imports reflected the vagaries of the rainfall, with poor years leading to wheat imports recorded under vegetable products. In 1999, for example, cereal imports amounted to R1 556.8 million, beverages to R845.7 million and prepared animal feedstuffs to R657.3 million. This was not new. In fact the picture presented by the pattern of imports is one of stability rather than radical transformation. Only chemical products show very significant real growth.

A breakdown into the separate decades show how these changes occurred (see Table 9.9). In the 1970s imports of producer goods boomed, led by chemical products with a real growth rate of 8.3 per cent followed by machinery and electrical equipment with 5.6 per cent, plastics with 5.2 per cent and optical, photographic and scientific instruments also with a growth rate of 5.2 per cent. Only mineral products and textiles experienced an absolute decline. A decade later only chemical products and plastic experienced positive growth. Even imports of machinery declined by 1.3 per cent. Imports figures mirrored the decline taking place in the economy. Nor was this completely arrested in the 1990s. Machinery, chemical products and plastics head the growth table, but the continued decline in motor vehicles and transport equipment provides the clue to what was happening in the economy.

9.3.2   Exports

The broadening range in the variety of products exported from South Africa is clearly indicated in Table 9.10. However, the top seven products of 1999 were the same top products in 1970, but the order had changed. Precious metals and jewellery had moved to first place, driven by platinum exports. Indeed, in 2000, the value of platinum exports overtook those of gold bullion which are excluded from the trade statistics. Platinum and jewellery exports had risen sixfold in constant prices, giving a growth rate of 6.4 per cent per annum. Both base metal and mineral exports had increased faster than prices and faster than population growth. Per capita exports of these minerals had doubled in real terms.

More significant in the long run, though, was the increase in manufactured metal products. Between 1970 and 1999, vehicles and transport equipment exports rose in real terms over 16-fold and with an annual growth rate of 10.1, ahead of plastics and rubber products at 7.9 per cent, chemical products at 6.7 per cent, platinum and jewellery at 6.4 per cent and machinery and electrical equipment at 6.2 per cent. Pulp and paper and paperboard was not far behind at 5.5 per cent and optical, photographic, musical and precision instruments at 5.6 per cent. That such growth rates could be achieved at a time of sanctions

Table 9.9 *Ten largest categories of imports into South Africa in 1970,*
1980, 1990 and 1999, and their growth rate in (constant
prices), 1970-1980, 1980-1990 and 1990-1999

1970			1980		
Category*	Rm		Category*	Rm	1970–80 %
16 Machinery, mechanical appliances & electrical equipment	706.0	16	Machinery, mechanical appliances & electrical equipment	3 528.7	5.6
17 Vehicles & transport equipment	466.4	17	Vehicles & transport equipment	1 846.5	3.2
11 Textiles	240.4	06	Chemical Products	1 026.1	8.3
15 Base metals & base metal products	200.1	15	Base metals & base metal products	698.6	1.9
06 Chemical products	160.6	11	Textiles	535.2	–2.5
05 Minerals	144.4	07	Plastics, resins & rubber products	477.4	5.2
07 Plastics, resins & rubber products	99.2	18	Optical, photographic, musical & scientific instruments	468.7	5.2
18 Optical, photographic, musical & precision instruments	97.8	10	Pulp, paper & paperboard	321.9	2.5
10 Pulp, paper & paperboard	87.1	05	Mineral products	242.2	–5.3
02 Vegetable products	61.0	02	Vegetable products	198.7	1.2

1990			1999		
Category*	Rm	1980–90 %	Category*	Rm	1990–99 %
16 Machinery, mechanical appliances & electrical equipment	12 212.5	–1.3	16 Machinery, mechanical appliances & electrical equipment	45 278.2	5.2
17 Vehicles & transport equipment	5 6926	–2.4	06 Chemical products	16 896.1	4.6
06 Chemical products	4 778.5	1.7	08 Mineral products	15 516.4	n/a
15 Base metals & base metal products	2 223.3	–2.1	23 Special classified	11 908.9	n/a
11 Textiles	2 005.7	–0.5	17 Vehicles & transport equipment	10 563.9	–2.6
07 Plastics, resins & rubber products	1 892.5	0.1	15 Base metals & base metal products	6 262.4	2.0
18 Optical, photographic, musical & precision instruments	1 819.2	–0.1	07 Plastics, resins & rubber products	6 081.2	3.5
10 Pulp paper & paperboard	1 250.4	–0.1	18 Optical, photographic, musical & scientific instruments	5 787.4	3.4
04 Prepared foodstuffs, beverages, spirits & tobacco	1 018.1	n/a	11 Textiles	5 051.1	0.8
02 Vegetable products	924.8	1.7	14 Precious stones, preciousmetals & jewellery	3 480.8	n/a

Note: *Classification according to CCC Nomenclature.

Source: Customs and Excise, *Monthly Trade Statistics*, December 1970, 1980 and 1999. 1990 figures provided by the Department of Customs and Excise.

Table 9.10   Ten largest categories of exports into South Africa in 1970,
1980, 1990 and 1999, and their growth rate (in constant
prices), 1970-1980, 1980-1990 and 1990-1999

	1970			1980		
	Category*	Rm		Category*	Rm	1970–80
15	Base metals & base metal products	261.3	14	Precious stones precious metals & jewellery	2 846.0	16.4
05	Minerals	216.3	15	Base metals & base metal products	1 580.1	7.6
14	Precious stone, precious metals & jewellery	215.3	05	Minerals	1 552.8	9.5
04	Prepared foodstuffs, beverages & tobacco	163.8	02	Vegetable products	811.8	6.6
02	Vegetable products	148.0	04	Foodstuffs, beverages & tobacco	720.6	4.3
11	Textiles	96.0	06	Chemical products	391.0	4.3
16	Machinery, mechanical appliances & electrical equipment	81.1	11	Textiles	358.9	2.6
06	Chemical products	57.3	16	Machinery, mechanical appliances & electrical equipment	263.4	1.2
08	Hides, skins etc.	39.4	01	Live animal products	185.3	n/a
10	Pulp, paper & paperboard	37.0	10	Pulp, paper & paperboard	179.8	5.3

1990				1999			
	Category*	Rm	1980–90 %		Category*	Rm	1990–99 %
15	Base metals & base metal products	9 054.9	3.9	14	Precious stones, precious metals & jewellery	41 889.7	13.4
05	Minerals	7 257.1	1.8	15	Base metals & base metal products	21 324.4	0.0
14	Precious stones, precious metals & jewellery	5 760.9	6.4	05	Minerals, chemical products	18 698.9	1.0
02	Vegetable products	1 909.4	5.0	06	Chemical products	9 011.5	8.1
06	Chemical products	1 898.3	3.9	16	Machinery, mechanical appliances & electrical equipment	8 745.51	11.8
04	Prepared foodstuffs, beverages & tobacco	1 714.1	1.1	17	Vehicles & transport equipment	6 621.6	10.5
11	Textiles	1 621.1	1.4	02	Vegetable products	5 800.8	2.9
10	Pulp, paper & paperboard	1 590.6	5.0	04	Prepared foodstuffs, beverages & tobacco	5 478.4	3.5
16	Machinery, mechanical appliances & electrical equipment	1 362.7	2.7	10	Pulp, paper& paperboard	3 552.8	–0.6
17	Vehicles & transport equipment	1 148.9	n/a	11	Textiles	3 468.4	–1.1

Note: *Classification according to CCC Nomenclature

Source: As Table 9.9.

and anti-South African campaigns was a considerable achievement. Many of these manufactured products, especially the prepared foodstuffs and beverages were going to countries north of the Limpopo that were among the loudest in calling for sanctions and trade embargoes.

Over the whole period, the changes in the structure of the South African economy may be seen in the changing pattern of exports. Negative trading balances had been converted into positive ones in a number of categories. These included vehicles and transport equipment, minerals, and pulp, paper and paperboard. Admittedly only the first and third of these were manufactured products and South Africa continued to rely very heavily upon the export of mineral products and partially processed minerals. Precious metals, base metals and minerals were the three leading exports in 1999 and accounted for 49 per cent of all exports.

A breakdown into the individual decades shows that, unlike imports, the key commodities continued to increase their exports, even in the 1980s. In the 1970s, precious stones and precious metals, excluding gold, led the way in the list of exports, growing in real terms at an annual rate of 16.4 per cent. Platinum and diamonds were the driving force behind this growth, and they continued to be the leaders in the 1980s and 1990s. By the year 2000 platinum exports had overtaken gold as the country's leading earner of foreign exchange. In the 1980s, too, pulp, paper and paperboard became a major source of foreign exchange earnings with a growth rate faster than that of precious stones and precious metals, but it could not maintain this growth in the 1990s. In the 1990s the exports of machinery in Category 16 were growing at 11.8 per cent a year and vehicles and transport equipment at 10.5 per cent a year, giving a boost to the mechanical and electrical engineering industries, which had been struggling with a sluggish home market. Mineral exports, which included coal and iron ore, were sluggish and were never able to regain the buoyancy of the 1970s.

The performance of individual industries appears to be successful, but it was achieved at the cost of massive currency depreciation. In the 1980s, when foreign investment dried up and debt payment became the major problem, a visible export surplus had to be achieved. In the 1990s, when this was no longer the case, a balance of trade deficit reappeared, despite the continued depreciation of the currency.

9.4   CONCLUSION

In this period, after the gold-induced boom of the 1970s, the external trade of South Africa ceased to be a cause of growth and trade as a proportion of GDP was lower in 1999 than in 1970. In constant prices the external trade of South

Africa was lower in 1999 than in 1980, despite the very considerable increase in the population. The main break in the pattern of growth occurred in 1980, when the gold price peaked.

Government policies encouraging import substitution counterbalanced those supporting export promotion. As a result the government's main contribution to the growth of trade was the depreciation of the currency in which the higher cost of imports neutralized the benefits of cheaper exports. In fact it may be argued that the growth of South Africa's external trade occurred despite the government rather than because of it. The market, global and domestic, was the engine of growth, not Pretoria bureaucrats.

The most far-reaching changes that have occurred in the geographical distribution of the country's trade was the relative decline in the importance of Europe, both for imports and exports, and the rise in the importance of Asia. Among individual countries the decline in the importance of Britain is the most striking. Most of this occurred in the 1970s, when imports from the United Kingdom were overtaken by those from both Germany and the United States. Exports to Britain held up better than imports and only in the later 1990s did the US market surpass that of Britain. The figures for before 1994 are skewed by the exclusion of oil imports. So important were these in 1999 that both Saudi Arabia and Iran appear in the list of top ten sources of imports. China, with which direct trade was virtually impossible before 1994, is now the eighth largest supplier of goods to South Africa. Unlike the other nine leading suppliers, who provide producer goods, imports from China are primarily consumer goods. Since neither China nor the Gulf oil exporters are major customers of South Africa, the pattern of exports shows less change than that of imports. Zimbabwe has moved into seventh place and Mozambique into tenth place in the published figures, but this might be considered a reversal to the pattern of an earlier era. The biggest single change was the inclusion of South Korea in the number of leading markets. Exports thither had been growing at the rate of 16 per cent a year in constant prices. These figures highlight the widening range of export markets. In 1970 the top four markets had accounted for 56 per cent of all exports, by 1999 this number had fallen to below 30 per cent.

The composition of trade also changed, as the new products of technology appeared in the list of imports and manufactured goods began to be numbered among exports. South Africa, however, continued to be predominantly an exporter of primary products and semi-processed goods and an importer of manufactures. Producer goods dominated the pattern of imports, led by machinery, chemical products and petroleum while imports of vehicle and transport equipment declined in the 1990s in response to depressed market conditions in South Africa.

The external trade of South Africa had responded vigorously to the stimulus

214   *The decline of the South African economy*

of the higher gold price in the 1970s, but market forces were increasingly affected by political developments. When the gold price began its long decline, market forces in an increasingly monopoly-dominated economy were unable to reverse it. Declining real per capita incomes inevitably held down the growth of imports, as a relatively stagnant home economy reduced the opportunities for investment and the import of producer goods, while exports remained heavily tied to minerals and precious metals. Private enterprise in the secondary sector, along the lines of developments in Taiwan, was prevented by a long protectionist tradition, by the presence of relatively few monopoly corporations and, in the 1990s, by unrealistic trade unions and labour legislation that was singularly unsuited to South African conditions. External trade mirrored these realities.

REFERENCES

Botha, D.J.J. (1973), 'On tariff policy: the formative years', *South African Journal of Economics*, **43**, pp. 321–55.
Foreign Trade Statistics, Department of Customs and Excise, various years.
Monthly Abstract of Trade Statistics, Department of Customs and Excise, various years.
Reynders, H.J.J. (1975), 'Status and strategy', *South African Journal of Economics*, **45**, pp. 123–31.
Zarenda, H. (1975), 'Export promotion versus import replacement', *South African Journal of Economics*, **45**, pp. 111–22.

10. Balance of payments, 1970-1999

Philip Mohr

10.1 INTRODUCTION

The 1950s and, in particular, the 1960s were decades of stable economic growth in South Africa, despite periodic political turbulence. Average annual economic growth rates of 4.7 per cent (1950s) and 5.5 per cent (1960s) were recorded, along with average annual inflation rates of 3.7 per cent (1950s) and 2.4 per cent (1960s). Exchange rates were stable, gold output increased and the gold price was fixed. During the last three decades of the twentieth century all this changed. Average annual economic growth fell to 3.3% in the 1970s, 2.2 per cent in the 1980s and 1 per cent in the 1990s. Average annual inflation rose to 9.7 per cent in the 1970s and 14.6 per cent in the 1980s before declining to 9.8 per cent in the 1990s. Exchange rates were volatile, gold output fell and the gold price became an important source of instability. Above all, the balance of payments became a major determinant of the pace of economic activity and the direction of economic policy in South Africa.

This chapter reviews some of the important developments in the South African balance of payments from 1970 to 1999. Section 10.2 provides an overview of the current and capital account balances during this period and identifies some of the main subperiods during the three decades in question. Section 10.3 deals briefly with the openness of the South African economy. Sections 10.4 and 10.5 focus on the current account and capital account, respectively. Section 10.6 concludes with some summary remarks on international trade and financial policy during the period under review.

10.2 CURRENT AND CAPITAL ACCOUNT BALANCES

Table 10.1 summarizes the balances on the current and capital account of the South African balance of payments from 1970 to 1999. Since balance of payments data are only available in nominal terms, all the balances are expressed as percentages of gross domestic product (GDP). In June 1999, the South African Reserve Bank changed the format of the balance of payments to comply with the latest *Balance of Payments Manual* issued by the

Table 10.1 Annual current and capital account balances as percentages of GDP, 1970–1999

Year	Current account	Capital account	Year	Current account	Capital account	Year	Current account	Capital account
1970	-7.2	4.8	1980	4.1	3.1	1990	1.8	-0.6
1971	-7.5	5.0	1981	-5.7	1.0	1991	1.9	-0.6
1972	-0.9	3.3	1982	-4.3	5.6	1992	1.5	-1.3
1973	-0.9	0.5	1983	-0.5	0.1	1993	1.1	-3.2
1974	-4.0	3.1	1984	-2.3	1.0	1994	0.1	0.5
1975	-6.5	5.1	1985	4.1	-6.6	1995	-1.8	3.0
1976	-5.4	1.5	1986	4.2	-3.5	1996	-1.3	0.5
1977	0.6	-1.0	1987	3.8	-2.0	1997	-1.5	3.1
1978	2.4	-1.1	1988	1.6	-3.3	1998	-1.6	1.0
1979	5.3	-4.4	1999	1.4	-1.9	1999	-0.4	3.4

Source: South African Reserve Bank, *Quarterly Bulletin*, various issues.

216

International Monetary Fund (Walters 1999). However, since the data were only revised for a limited number of years, Table 10.1 is still constructed using the distinction between the current account and the capital account, instead of the new distinction between the current account and the financial account.

As a developing country that imports mainly capital and intermediate goods, South Africa traditionally experiences a deficit on the current account of the balance of payments. Except for the period from 1959 to 1963, following major political upheavals in the rest of Africa and in South Africa, current account deficits were recorded in each year from 1946 to 1969. This trend continued during the first half of the 1970s, when a rapid expansion of domestic demand resulted in sharp increases in the imports of goods and services. These deficits were largely financed through net inflows of foreign capital. However, following the domestic political and social unrest in 1976 and the problems in Mozambique and Angola which began the year before, large outflows of short-term capital were experienced and from 1977 onwards net outflows of foreign capital were recorded.

The worsening situation on the capital account necessitated contractionary monetary and fiscal policies to dampen domestic demand and, hence, the imports of goods and services. The result was the longest and most severe recession since the Second World War. Towards the end of the 1970s, however, an international commodity boom catapulted the South African economy into a sharp, albeit short-lived, boom. Strong growth in South Africa, coupled with problems in other developing countries, gave South Africa access to the international capital markets, which were highly liquid as a result of the surpluses generated by the oil-producing countries following the 1979–80 oil boom. South Africa could therefore once again afford to run current account deficits. However, in 1985 South Africa experienced its own foreign debt crisis (discussed in Section 10.5) and was forced to repay much of its foreign debt. Moreover, the country was ostracized by the international capital markets. The authorities thus had to ensure current account surpluses to provide the foreign exchange for the country's debt commitments. This situation continued until the new political dispensation in 1994. Shortly before the 1994 elections, South Africa regained access to the international financial markets and after the elections large inflows of portfolio capital were experienced. Current account deficits could be financed again and significant deficits were recorded from 1995 onwards.

Regarding the data in Table 10.1, the period from 1970 to 1999 can be divided into five subperiods:

- The 1970–76 period, which was characterized by large current account deficits (proportionally the largest during the period under review) and substantial capital account surpluses.

- The 1977–80 period, which was characterized by current account surpluses and, except for the 1980 boom, capital account deficits.
- The 1981–84 period, which was characterized by current account deficits and capital account surpluses.
- The 1985–94 period, characterized by an unprecedented ten consecutive years of current account surpluses necessary to finance the capital account deficits resulting from the 1985 debt crisis.
- The 1995–99 period,, during which net inflows of foreign capital again allowed the country to run current account deficits.

The salient features of these subperiods are discussed further in the sections on the current account and the capital account.

10.3   THE OPENNESS OF THE SOUTH AFRICAN ECONOMY

The South African economy is an open economy but not as open as some East Asian and European economies (Mohr 2000: 143–5). The degree of openness can be obtained by expresing exports as a percentage of GDP, imports as a percentage of gross domestic expenditure (GDE), or the average of the two. Table 10.2 contains some data for South Africa for selected years between 1970 and 1998. Note that the ratio can be affected by the size of the denominator. For exarnple, in 1985 the domestic economy was severely depressed and this in itself tended to increase the ratios. Moreover, South African firms traditionally exported much more when domestic demand was depressed than during cyclical upturns, thus increasing the ratio even further during years of low or negative domestic economic growth.

No clear trend seems to emerge from the table. Bear in mind, however, that 1980 (boom), 1985 (recession) and, to a lesser extent, 1975 (recession) were all abnormal years. Perhaps the most significant trend is the increase from 1990 onwards, which is confirmed when each individual year's ratio is calculated.

As far as the direction of trade is concerned, South Africa's international trade is still dominated by the industrial countries. The bulk of South African exports are still destined for these countries, while most of the country's imports also emanate from the industrial countries. However, important changes have occurred during the period under review, particularly during the 1990s.

In 1974 (the earliest year for which data could be obtained) more than 85 per cent of identified South African merchandise exports were destined for the industrial countries, from which more than 90 per cent of identified

Table 10.2   Openness of the South African economy, selected years, 1970–1998

Year	(a) Exports of goods and non-factor services as percentage of GDP	(b) Imports of goods and non-factor services a percentage of GDE	(c) Average of (a) and (b)
1970	22.0	24.7	23.4
1975	28.1	29.8	29.0
1980	35.9	30.2	33.1
1985	32.2	25.5	28.9
1990	25.6	20.8	23.2
1995	25.1	25.0	25.1
1998	28.6	28.1	28.4

Note: These figures predate the reclassification of the balance of payments and the upward revision of GDP in June 1999. The percentages are thus significantly higher than those obtained nowadays by expressing exports and imports of goods and services as percentages of the revised GDP and GDE respectively.

Sources: South African Reserve Bank, *Quarterly Bulletin*, various issues (prior to June 1999).

merchandise imports originated. At that stage only 1.3 per cent of South African exports were to other African countries. The country's main trading partners (in declining order) were the United Kingdom, West Germany, the United States and Japan. In 1980, just over 80 per cent of the identified merchandise exports went to the industrial countries, while just over 88 per cent of the merchandise imports came from these countries, with the United States, the United Kingdom, West Germany and Japan (in that order) as South Africa's main trading partners. Africa's share in South African exports was still only about 1 per cent.

In 1990 the pattern was still much the same. Almost 77 per cent of identified merchandise exports went to the industrial countries, while more than 87 per cent of the imports came from these countries, with Germany, the United States, the United Kingdom and Japan (in that order) as South Africa's main trading partners. Exports to the rest of Africa still accounted for just over 1 per cent of identified merchandise exports. By 1999, however, the situation had changed quite significantly. Exports to the industrial countries were down to about 61 per cent of the total, while imports from these countries accounted for 71 per cent of total imports. The United States was South Africa's main trading partner, closely followed by Germany, with the United Kingdom and Japan in the third and fourth positions. The most significant feature, however, was the increase in the share of exports to the rest of Africa, which exceeded 15 per cent of total identified exports. Exports to Asia also exceeded the 15 per cent mark. South Africa had thus become a more open economy, not only in aggregate terms, but also as far as the geographical diversification of trade is concerned.

10.4   CURRENT ACCOUNT

10.4.1   Net Gold Exports

Gold continued to be an important factor in the South African economy during the period under review but there were some significant, sometimes even dramatic, changes compared to the situation during previous decades. Table 10.3 contains some data on gold and the South African balance of payments for selected years between 1970 and 1999. The first important feature is the persistent decline in the volume of gold production since 1970, when it reached a peak of just over 1 million kilograms. By 1999 the annual volume was down to 457 000 kilograms. The second important feature is the volatility of the gold price, particularly in US dollars. Between 1950 and 1970 the official price of gold had remained unchanged at US$35 per fine ounce, and the exchange rate between the rand and the dollar also remained unchanged. Towards the end of 1970 the free market price of gold started increasing. It reached $US195 per fine ounce on 30 December 1974 and subsequently fell to $US105 per first ounce on 26 August 1976. On 21 January 1980 the gold price reached an all-time high of US$850 per fine ounce. In 1999, however, the average price was significantly below US$300 per fine ounce. From the early 1970s, fluctuations in the dollar price of gold became a significant source of instability in the South African balance of payments and in the South African economy in general. The rand price of gold, however, increased fairly steadily as a result of depreciations in the value of the rand in terms of the US dollar and in 1999 the rand price was more than 65 times higher than in 1970. These increases helped to cushion the impact of the decline in the volume of gold production, but in the 1990s the contribution of gold exports to South Africa's total merchandise exports declined sharply. By the turn of the century it was matched and later overtaken by the contribution of the platinum group metals.

10.4.2   Merchandise Exports

South African merchandise exports are traditionally dominated by primary

Table 10.3   Gold and the balance of payments, 1970–1999 (selected years)

Year	Gold production (000 kg)	Gold price		Contribution of gold exports to total merchandise exports
		(US$)	(R)	(%)
1970	1 000	35	26	29.1
1975	713	157	118	32.9
1980	673	613	477	51.4
1985	673	317	711	43.9
1990	605	384	992	29.8
1995	523	384	1 393	20.7
1999	457	279	1 703	14.0

Note: Gold price is the average daily price on the London gold market in US dollars and rands.

Sources: South African Reserve Bank, *Quarterly Bulletin*, various issues; Minerals Bureau, *South Africa's Mineral Industry*, various issues.

and intermediate goods emanating from the mining and agricultural industries. This has two important implications. First, the value of South African exports is particularly vulnerable to developments in the flex-price international commodity markets where suppliers are price takers. Second, the impact of climatic conditions on agricultural production can be a significant cause of fluctuations in South African exports (and imports, when domestic shortages give rise to large agricultural imports). During the period under review, international commodity prices were highly unstable while periodic droughts and floods also left their mark. The situation was often worsened by unprecedented exchange rate instability, particularly after the move from a fixed exchange rate to a managed float in 1979.

Generally speaking, the most significant changes in South African merchandise exports since 1970 were sharp increases in non-gold mineral exports, particularly since the mid-1970s, and a most gratifying increase in manufactured exports since the mid-1980s. The result, already indicated in the previous section, was a sharp decline in the dependence on gold exports.

In the early 1970s the authorities were concerned about the large current account deficits and especially the weak performance of non-gold exports. This gave rise (in August 1971) to the appointment of a commission of inquiry into export promotion (the Reynders Commission) which reported in 1972. The Commission's report coincided with a commodity boom which saw a remarkable improvement in merchandise exports in 1972. The volume of non-gold exports increased by a massive 21.6 per cent and the prices of most categories of imports also increased significantly, the main contributors being diamonds, sugar, fruit, maize and basic metals. The volume of non-gold exports continued to rise during the rest of the decade, despite the depressed conditions in the industrial countries following the first oil shock. By 1980, the volume of non-gold exports were 92 per cent higher than in 1970. Among the factors contributing to this increase were: the spectacular increase in coal and iron ore exports from 1975 onwards, following the opening of new harbours at Richards Bay and Saldanha; the devaluations of the rand in June and September 1975; periodic favourable weather conditions; and the severe domestic recession from September 1974 to December 1977 during which domestic manufacturers were forced to exploit export opportunities in the growing world market. However, despite the export incentives introduced after the Reynders Commission, South African manufacturers still focused primarily on the domestic market and only resorted to exports when they experienced surpluses or excess capacity during domestic cyclical down-swings. This was largely because the South African manufacturing sector had developed as a result of import substitution in a protected environment. Despite often successful forays into the international market during domestic recessions, manufacturers tended to neglect export opportunities during the ensuing domestic cyclical upswings and tended to focus almost exclusively on the protected domestic market. As discussed below, this habit only started to change in the late 1980s. By the end of the century, experience and force of circumstance had instilled a new export mentality among South African business people.

Towards the end of the 1970s, South Africa experienced another commodity boom, led by a rapid increase in the gold price, and the balance of payments was particularly strong. The South African Reserve Bank allowed the rand to appreciate and subsequently defended the rand when the boom dissipated and the current account surplus changed to a large deficit. The result was an overvalued real effective exchange rate of the rand which contributed to a drop of almost 10 per cent in the volume of non-gold exports between 1980 and 1984. This is often cited as a typical example of the 'Dutch disease' where a sharp appreciation of the domestic currency, caused by a natural resource-related windfall, decreases the competitiveness and volume of manufactured exports.

However, from the middle of 1984 all this changed. Between June 1984 and December 1985 the effective exchange rate of the rand fell by about 53 per cent in nominal terms and 40 per cent in real terms. At the same time, the domestic economy went into its deepest postwar recession. The depreciation and the recession, combined with strong economic expansion in the industrial countries and improved agricultural conditions in South Africa following the severe drought of 1983/84, led to a 43 per cent increase in the volume of non-gold exports between 1984 and 1989. Particularly gratifying was the strong expansion in the exports of manufactured goods, including metal products, machinery, electrical machinery, motor vehicles and transport equipment. This was achieved despite the introduction of trade sanctions against South Africa. The consensus view is that the trade sanctions did not have a significant impact on the total volume or value of South African exports, although individual exporters and subsectors were undoubtedly affected (Botes 1992; Louw 1994). What it did achieve, however, was to make South African manufacturers more astute and more determined to succeed in world markets. The sanctions and the weak state of the domestic economy combined to change the inward-looking orientation of South African manufacturers which had hitherto characterized their approach to international trade.

The growth in non-gold merchandise exports was maintained during much of the 1990s and in 1999 the volume of these exports was more than 73 per cent greater than in 1989. The reasons for this continued growth included: the generally strong world economy and the accompanying growth in world trade; the relatively weak, even depressed domestic economy, particularly during the early 1990s; the changed attitude of South African manufacturers to exports referred to above; the opening up of new, non-traditional markets as sanctions and trade embargoes were lifted and South Africa rejoined the international economic community; the rapid growth in some of these new markets; the wide range of trade agreements entered into after the adoption of the new constitution; the decline in the nominal (and sometimes even the real) effective exchange rate of the rand; assistance to exporters under the General Export Incentive Scheme from 1990 to 1997 and the development of new manufacturing enterprises (such as Columbus Steel and Alusaf's aluminium smelter) specifically for the export market.

10.4.3 Merchandise Imports

South African imports consist mainly of capital and intermediate goods, with each category contributing approximately 40 per cent of merchandise imports. The volume of these imports is closely related to the level of domestic demand at constant prices. When real GDE increases, merchandise imports follow suit, resulting in a strong cyclical pattern in the country's import bill. This positive correlation between domestic demand and merchandise imports is one of the strongest relationships in the South African economy and explains why restrictive policies are usually applied when the overall balance of payments is in deficit.

During the early 1970s, the volume of merchandise imports rose sharply due to high capital spending by the public sector, mainly the public corporations and public enterprises. The first oil shock in 1973 also caused a sharp increase in the value of imports but this was largely offset by the increases in the price of gold and other commodity exports. During the subsequent cyclical downturn in the South African economy, imports tended to remain high, mainly because of government spending on defence equipment and the stockpiling of oil and other strategic goods, continued high levels of capital spending by public enterprises and public corporations, the introduction of television, and stockpiling and advanced purchases in anticipation of possible devaluations of the rand or intensified import controls. In these circumstances, the authorities were forced to apply restrictive monetary and fiscal policies in 1976 and 1977, coupled with tighter import controls and a temporary import deposit scheme. The position improved quickly and remained favourable until the next oil crisis which was again fortunately offset by a rising gold price.

South Africa's merchandise imports continued their typical pro-cyclical tendency during the 1980s. The volume of imports was at approximately the same level in 1989 as in 1980 but it varied considerably by up to 20 per cent from one year to the next, depending on the state of the domestic economy.

During the early 1990s, merchandise imports remained at extraordinarily high levels, given the depressed domestic economy. The reasons advanced for this fairly unusual state of affairs include: large imports of capital equipment in reaction to the increasingly problematic labour market situation; a decline in the relative prices of imported goods; the completion of previously postponed aircraft purchases by South African Airways; increases in agricultural imports as a result of serious drought conditions; and periodic pre-emptive buying in anticipation of a depreciation of the rand against the major currencies.

With the recovery in domestic demand from 1994 onwards, merchandise imports rose sharply. This was partly the result of significant trade liberalization, particularly the lowering of import tariffs, implemented during the decade. Towards the end of the decade, however, import volumes declined significantly in response to the decline in domestic demand, in particular the sharply lower fixed investment spending by the public corporations and private sector.

10.4.4 Services

South Africa has always had a significant deficit on the services account. During the period under review, this deficit ranged from a low of 2.9 per cent (1997, 1998) and a high of 5.4 per cent (1985). The most important categories of payments for services are dividend payments (which are related to the level of foreign investment), interest payments on foreign loans (which depend on the level of foreign borrowing and the level of interest rates), payments for international freight, insurance and transportation (which are related to the volume and value of international trade), tourist traffic and the remuneration of migrant workers. Service receipts consist of (smaller) similar flows in the opposite direction. The services deficit tended to narrow during the 1990s, mainly as a result of sharp increases in spending by foreign travellers in South Africa, a fall in interest payments following the repayment of large amounts of foreign debt and a rise in dividend and interest receipts following the relaxation of exchange control on residents during the second half of the decade.

10.5 CAPITAL ACCOUNT

Prior to 1970, South Africa experienced a relatively stable net inflow of foreign capital, interrupted only during the late 1950s and early 1960s by the political developments in South Africa and the rest of Africa. After 1970, however, the pattern became much more erratic, culminating in the 1985 debt crisis and international financial sanctions against South Africa. After the 1994 elections, the country re-entered the international financial markets but also became vulnerable to speculative international flows of portfolio investment.

During the early 1970s, there were still significant net inflows of foreign capital into South Africa (see Table 10.1) but these inflows were mainly the result of substantial borrowing by public corporations, public enterprises and local authorities to finance their high levels of capital spending. From 1975, however, the country experienced large outflows of short-term capital in response to the rapidly deteriorating political situation in Angola and Mozambique, increased economic uncertainty due to the deepening recession in the domestic economy, increased domestic political unrest and uncertainty (particularly after the Soweto riots in June 1976) and periodic expectations of a devaluation of the rand (which resulted in unfavourable leads and lags in the foreign exchange market). In January 1976, the South African government obtained its first loan from the International Monetary Fund (IMF). The first annual capital account deficit during the period under review (and the first since 1963) was recorded in 1977. The South African Reserve Bank was forced to borrow from the IMF again and the capital account remained in deficit until 1980, an extraordinary year in which significant surpluses were recorded on both the current and the capital account.[1]

During the first few years of the 1980s there were some large net capital inflows. The international capital markets were still highly liquid following the second oil crisis and the deep recession in the industrialized countries.

When other developing countries failed to meet their foreign debt commitments from 1982 onwards, South Africa, with its impeccable debt service record, became a sought-after borrower internationally (Bell 1993: 93). Moreover, the South African authorities also encouraged foreign borrowing from time to time, for example by providing forward cover at attractive rates (Smit 1984: 214). This intensified some of the important changes which had occurred in the composition of capital inflows since 1970.

Broadly speaking, there had been a shift from long-term direct investment in the non-monetary private sector to shorter-term borrowing by the public sector and the banking sector (Van der Merwe and Bester 1983). At the time, Smit (1984: 314) also drew attention to 'the relatively large uncovered interest rate differentials ... coupled with the lack of experience of many domestic enterprises regarding the magnitude of the potential losses involved in uncovered forward borrowing'. These were prophetic words. Many South African borrowers suffered severe losses due to the massive depreciation of the rand against the major currencies in 1984 and 1985.

All the above-mentioned developments contributed to the South African debt crisis of 1985. This crisis is often ascribed solely to domestic political events such as the intensification of political unrest, the declaration of a partial state of emergency (20 July 1985) and President P.W. Botha's infamous Rubicon speech (see, for example, Bethlehem 1988: ch. 4; De Kock 1989: 1-2). The source of the crisis, however, can be traced to various international and domestic economic and political developments since the early 1970s (Mohr 1991: 55). Bell (1993: 93) also emphasized the collapse of the gold price, the sharp decline in exports generally, the unprecedented sharp depreciation of the rand, prior short-term borrowings and developments in international capital markets and concluded that there 'were thus business reasons enough for a debt crisis' (see also Krogh 1990: 15-17).

The foreign debt moratorium of August 1985, the subsequent repayment agreements and the introduction of financial sanctions forced South Africa to become a capital-exporting country. South Africa also experienced capital flight, although the extent of it remains unclear (Smit and Mocke 1991). From 1985 to 1993 there was a cumulative net outflow of capital of almost R58 billion and throughout this period the authorities were forced to ensure the maintenance of a current account surplus to help finance this outflow.

From the middle of 1994, once it became evident that South Africa's political transition would proceed relatively smoothly, the net outflow changed into a net inflow and between July 1994 and December 1999 the country experienced a net inflow of capital of more than R84 billion. These inflows were erratic, however, and most of it consisted of speculative portfolio investment in South African bonds and equities, rather than the more sought-after direct investment which had characterized capital inflows prior to 1970.

Thus, while the surpluses on the capital account allowed the country to run current account deficits and to achieve positive (albeit low) growth, the economy became vulnerable to short-term changes in investor confidence, as illustrated in 1996 and 1998.

From the middle of February 1996, for example, there was a large net outflow of foreign capital. Massive speculative outflows occurred and flows across the Johannesburg Stock Exchange were particularly volatile. This foreign exchange crisis was triggered by a number of factors, including fears that sound macroeconomic management would be compromised by the appointment of Trevor Manuel as the first African National Congress (ANC) Minister of Finance, rumours about President Mandela's health, concerns about the removal of the remaining exchange control on residents, and fears that the growing political consensus that had developed since 1994 might disintegrate. The turmoil on the foreign exchange market continued until the announcement of the government's Growth, Employment and Redistribution (GEAR) strategy in June 1996 and the confirmation of South Africa's relatively favourable credit ratings by the prominent international credit-rating agencies.

Matters improved significantly in the second half of 1996 and the first half of 1997 but during the second half of 1997 the financial crisis in a number of Southeast Asian countries triggered a confidence crisis in emerging market countries, including South Africa. When it appeared initially that the crisis would be restricted to Asia, the net inflow of capital into South Africa resumed in the first quarter of 1998, only to reverse again later in the year when the fragility of the Japanese economy became obvious. Investor sentiment was further affected by a crisis in Russia and the announcement that Tito Mboweni, an ANC politician, was to succeed Dr Chris Stals as Governor of the South African Reserve Bank in 1999. The gradual relaxation of exchange control on residents from 1995 onwards (see Section 10.6) and sharp depreciations of the rand against the major currencies further increased the vulnerability of the capital account of the South African balance of payments to changes in investor sentiment. The upshot of all this was an unprecedented volatility in international capital flows.

10.6 POLICY MEASURES RELATING TO THE BALANCE OF PAYMENTS

Economic policy during the 1970s was characterized by a significant degree of intervention and direct control. Quantitative controls on imports were often applied, extensive exchange controls applied to residents and non-residents and until January 1979 the rand was not allowed to float against all currencies. After the breakdown of the Bretton Woods system of fixed exchange rates, the South African monetary authorities experimented with a number of exchange rate regimes. From 27 June 1975 to 23 January 1979 the rand floated with the US dollar. The most significant event during this period was the 17.9 per cent devaluation of the rand against the dollar on 22 September 1975.

Exchange control on non-residents had been in existence since June 1961 when the blocked rand was introduced to block the repatriation of South African assets by non-residents. The blocked rand system remained in force until 2 February 1976 when it was replaced by the securities rand. With the introduction of an independent managed float on 24 January 1979, the securities rand was replaced by the financial rand. The dual exchange rate system remained in force until 5 February 1983 when this form of exchange control on non-residents was removed. However, it was soon reinstated (on 1 September 1985) following the country's debt crisis and was only removed again on 13 March 1995.

The liberalization of South Africa's international trade and financial relations commenced during the 1980s (Bell 1997: 71–4) and was pursued more vigorously in the 1990s. By the end of the decade, most of the controls which had characterized South African international trade and financial policy in earlier decades had been either abolished or modified significantly. On 15 April 1994 South Africa signed the Marrakesh Agreement, following the Uruguay round of multilateral trade negotiations, thereby agreeing to lower import tariffs and eliminate non-tariff barriers to trade. By the end of the review period, South Africa had more than fulfilled its obligations under this agreement.

As far as the capital account is concerned, exchange control on non-residents was abolished with the reestablishment of a unitary exchange rate system on 13 March 1995. In July, the authorities started to gradually relax exchange control applicable to residents. Initially, insurance companies, pension funds and unit trusts were allowed to undertake foreign investments through swap arrangements with foreign investors. This dispensation was extended on 23 January 1996 and again on 14 June 1996 and 14 March 1997. A significant step was taken on 1 July 1997 when private individuals who were taxpayers in good standing with the tax authorities were permitted to invest up to R200 000 abroad, or to maintain foreign currency deposits to the same amount with authorized foreign exchange dealers. This limit was raised to R400 000 on 11 March 1998 and to R750 000 in 2000. Various further exchange control liberalization measures were also applied.

At the start of the twenty-first century South Africa's international trade and finance were thus subject to few remaining controls and indications were that these would also be abolished as soon as circumstances permitted.

NOTE

1. The only other year in which this was achieved was 1994, but then the surpluses were very small (see Table 10.1).

REFERENCES

Bell, T. (1993), 'Should South Africa further liberalise its foreign trade?', in M. Lipton and C. Simkins (eds), *State and Market in Post Apartheid South Africa*, Johannesburg: Witwatersrand University Press.

Bell, T. (1997), 'Trade policy', in J. Michie and V. Padayachee (eds), *The Political Economy of South Africa's Transition*, London: Dryden Press.

Bethlehem, R.W. (1988), *Economics in a Revolutionary Society*, Craighall: AD Donker.

Botes, E. (1992), 'Die invloed van buitelandse sanksies op die Suid-Afrikaanse ekonomie' (The impact of foreign sanctions on the South African economy), Unpublished MCom dissertation, Pretoria: University of South Africa.

De Kock, G.P.C. (1989), *Growth-oriented Economic Policy: South Africa - A Case Study*, Pretoria: South African Reserve Bank.

Krogh, D.C. (1990), 'Economic stabilisation and structural change', Inaugural address as Professor Extraordinarius, University of South Africa, Pretoria, 25 June.

Louw, M.H.S. (1994), 'Economic sanctions against South Africa during the eighties', Unpublished DCom thesis, Pretoria: University of South Africa.

Mohr, P. (1991), 'Notes on the balance of payments and economic activity and policy in South Africa', *South African Journal of Economic and Management Sciences*, **6**, November.

Mohr, P. (2000), *Economic Indicators* (revised edn), Pretoria: Unisa Press.

Smit, B.W. (1984), 'An investigation of the determinants of international short-term capital movements with special reference to the position of South Africa (1973–1983)', Unpublished DCom thesis, University of Stellenbosch.

Smit, B.W. and Mocke, B.A. (1991), Capital flight from South Africa: magnitude and causes', *South African Journal of Economics*, **59** (2), June.

Van der Merwe, E.J. and Bester, M.C. (1983), 'South Africa's foreign liabilities and assets, 1956 to 1981', *South African Reserve Bank Quarterly Bulletin*, June, pp. 23–35.

Walters, S.S. (1999), 'A note on the revision of the balance of payments accounting framework', *South African Reserve Bank Quarterly Bulletin*, June, pp. 54–7.

11. The situation in 2000

Stuart Jones

At the end of the twentieth century the long decline of the South African economy may have finally come to an end. Much depends on the policies adopted and implemented by the African National Congress/Communist Party government. The signals coming out of Pretoria are confusing. At one moment, when addressing Western bankers, the right noises are made but then almost immediately contradicted by hardliners in the government. After seven and a half years in power very little has been accomplished in the area of privatization and in increasing the efficiency of government. Indeed, aggressive affirmative action policies have led to growing inefficiency across a broad range of services but most noticeably in the education, public health and crime prevention.

Agriculture, as Nick Vink and Stefan Schirmer have shown, has seen the fresh breeze of market forces lead to the dismantling of the producer-dominated control structures across a wide range of commodities and an attempt to bring about more efficient land usage, but the thorny problem of land ownership has not been resolved, and this has led to a fall in farm values. Talk of creating small farms for grain growing at a time when large grain growing enterprises are the norm, seems a little unreal and, in the light of the destruction of much of the commercial farming in neighbouring Zimbabwe, the future of agriculture would appear to be at a crossroads.

The situation in mining is clearer. The long-term decline in the gold mines is well under way and has been counterbalanced, to a great extent, by the rise of the platinum group of metals in the 1990s and the continued expansion of coal mining and other industrial minerals such as iron ore and manganese. Mining's importance as an earner of foreign exchange remains vital to the economy, as does its contribution to the total employment picture.

Indeed, mining's importance to the South African economy has been emphasized by the relative failure of manufacturing to lead the country into sustained economic growth. Without a doubt the failure of South Africa to develop an internationally competitive manufacturing sector has been the dominant feature of the economy in the last third of the twentieth century. Import-substitution policies led to lower-value-added manufacturing sectors receiving attention at the expense of the more valuable raw material processing industries. This problem has deep roots that stretch back to the 1960s. In the 1990s the ill-disciplined trade union introduced a new dimension into manufacturing, at a time when new labour laws added significantly to total costs. With Asia's low-cost producers just across the Indian Ocean, the future for manufactured exports other than the beneficiation of minerals is at best problematic.

Transport services, as Trevor Jones has argued, may have been the victim of incorrect pricing on the part of the government; but they have improved enormously in this period. Putting aside the question of whether capital has been spent wisely, there can be no doubt that motorways and containers have 'revolutionized', the speed with which goods can be transported across the length and breadth of the country, even if remote rural areas have been neglected. Railway services, with the exception of the lines carrying coal and iron ore for export, have deteriorated. Long-distance passenger services cannot compete with cars and buses on land or planes in the air. There is simply not the density of population to make a high-speed railway link between Johannesburg and Durban economically viable.

It is in the financial services areas that South Africa has always enjoyed a lead over other African countries and this was still true in 2000. Banking perhaps experienced the greatest changes with its range of functions expanding enormously. In its sophisticated money market operations and merchant and industrial banking activities, the financial sector could compare favourably with other Commonwealth countries. Its stock exchange was transformed by the ending of the isolationist environment in 1994 and experienced an explosion in turnover. Hitherto the Johannesburg Stock Exchange had, by international standards, been noted for its high capitalization but low turnover. This is changing, but the perceived high-risk environment has precipitated a flight of some of the country's major firms out of South Africa in order to secure bases in countries with stable currencies and the absence of damaging exchange controls.

Under the post-1994 ANC Communist Party governments the domestic budget has been brought under control, but the balance of payments has fluctuated. Before 1994 the country needed to maintain a large current account surplus to meet its debt payments. This restriction fell away in 1994 and since then the current account has deteriorated and the country has relied upon inflows of funds to sustain its currency. These have not been flows of direct investment, but short-term inflows into banks or the stock exchange, which have exerted a destabilizing effect upon the domestic economy.

In 2000 South Africa remains a very open economy in terms of the weighting allocated to foreign trade in its GDP, but the country's importance to the international economy has declined with the demonetarization of gold. It has also declined as a destination for foreign investment, before the more attractive destinations of Europe, America and Oceania. Race relations may be an obsession of the government, but it is likely that it will be the country's mineral base that will keep it in the public eye and enable South Africa to play an important role in the international economy. It remains unlikely that South African manufacturers will be able to emulate the East Asian tigers and become large-scale exporters of consumer goods, which leaves a large question mark over how, in the future, real per capita incomes are to be raised and poverty reduced.

Capitalist enterprise was the main driving force behind the growth of the South African economy in the last three decades of the twentieth century. That it did not achieve a higher growth rate than that of the population was the result of interference by socialist and nationalist-minded politicians and the inefficient allocation of resources that accompanied this interference. Yet bureaucratic control over prices in agriculture, coal mining and transport have been reduced. Unfortunately the beneficial consequences of such policies have frequently been nullified by import-substitution policies, direct control over petrol prices and, in the later 1990s, by a deluge of racial quotas and affirmative action policies that have reduced efficiency and competitiveness across a wide range of activities in both the public and private sectors.

Tight central control was a feature of National Party government. It remains a feature of the ANC/Communist Party government. In this respect little has changed. It is difficult for market forces to speed up economic growth, while exchange controls continue to exert their baleful influence upon the economy. Twenty years ago Milton Friedman, on a visit to South Africa, pointed out the damage they were doing. His advice was ignored then and it is still ignored today. As with privatization, lip-service is paid to the idea of the government's withdrawal from direct control over productive sectors of the economy, either by excessive interventionist legislation, ownership of telephones, airlines, pipelines and electricity production, or by its control of currency transactions, but little action has followed to allow the market to determine the allocation of scarce resources and the real value of the currency. Capitalist enterprise still operates with one hand tied behind its back. Restrictions on capitalist enterprise are the principal reason why the economy went into decline in the last quarter of the twentieth century.

Index